SCANDALS
IN HISTORY

SCANDALS
IN HISTORY

ED RAYNER AND RON STAPLEY

The
History
Press

First published 2008

The History Press Ltd
The Mill, Brimscombe Port
Stroud, Gloucestershire, GL5 2QG
www.thehistorypress.co.uk

British Library Cataloguing in Publication Data.
A catalogue record for this book is available from the British Library.

ISBN 978 0 7509 4873 9

Typesetting and origination by The History Press Ltd.
Printed in Great Britain

Cover images courtesy of EMPICS, Mary Evans Picture Library and Topfoto

Contents

Contents

Preface

Notions of what is scandalous vary from age to age. What would seem quite shocking to the modern mind would conspicuously fail to shock someone living in the seventeenth century. In that century, matters of religious faith, much of it close to superstition and magic, were much more in evidence than they are in our own age. That age's sensitivity, on the other hand, to violence, poverty, pain and to sudden death, was much less. In much the same way, the strictness of the Victorian code of morals is markedly in contrast with the lax standards of our own 'permissive age'. For example, the Victorians have the reputation of being reticent and prudish about sex. They did not, however, swear off sex simply because they were building an empire: indeed, the merest glance at the population statistics will show that they did not swear off sex at all. Likewise, even a glance at Victorian pornography will reveal it to be of the most explicit and carnal variety, and quite repulsive to the modern reader.

It is not that the Victorians were *more strict,* or the Tudors *less strict,* than us. It is rather that in both cases the strictness was *about different things.* Today we tend to reserve our strictness for matters to do with political and economic equality, the humane treatment of the handicapped and the disadvantaged, consideration and equality for women, and — that bugbear of modern social manners — political correctness, whilst they aimed at different targets. All the same, people of every generation know a scandal when they see one, and get their teeth into it with a fair relish.

The scandals dealt with in this book are divided into eight broad categories:

1. *Scandals relating to sex*. These perhaps come first in many people's minds when they are considering scandals.
2. *Scandals involving murder or similar violence*. These, because they are gruesome, run sexual scandals a close second.
3. *Financial and associated scandals*. A popular third, since wealth is almost as fascinating as death. They are not confined, however, to run-of-the-mill dishonesty over financial matters.
4. *Political scandals*. Because there are public figures involved in them, these seem to have a perpetual fascination for ordinary people.
5. *Royal scandals*. Likewise, even when less than salacious, these have a lively and never-ending appeal.
6. *Religious scandals*. Like sex, religion seems all the more interesting when it is on the smutty side.
7. *War scandals*. There have always been cover-ups relating to wars, and here are some of them.
8. *Scientific scandals*. Even technical and scientific matters have not always been exempt from popular rumour and sleaze.

The authors apologise for any omissions of what you may consider equally obvious scandalous examples, but considerations of the space available have required us to limit the number of entries this book contains.

Ed Rayner
Ron Stapley

SEX SCANDALS

Was W.E. Gladstone a whited sepulchre?

The curious story of the frequent encounters between one of the greatest of Britain's elder statesmen of the nineteenth century, William Ewart Gladstone, and the common prostitutes of London in the middle years of the nineteenth century, though successfully hushed up then and afterwards, was one of the strangest scandals of Victorian and of modern times. Or perhaps 'non-scandal' would be a better term for it, since the greatest of his admirers Mr (later Viscount) John Morley in his multi-volume biography of the great man, completely ignored it, and later biographers, such as Philip Magnus and Roy Jenkins, presented it in such a sanitized version that not even the tenderest of susceptibilities could be disturbed. Yet Gladstone's own diaries, fourteen vast volumes each dealing with a few years or less of his long and eventful career, contain ruthlessly honest (if not entirely explicit) details of the whole scandal. There the facts of his dealings with these street-women, if not his motives, are set out in full, and his own guilty feelings amply illustrated, not only in the tone of self-reproach in which repeated episodes are described, but by his frequent use of a symbol in the margin (ζ) bearing a striking resemblance to a whip, which has suggested to many that the great man practised self-flagellation to control his carnal urges. Do these facts reveal a new and entirely unexpected side to the statesman's character?

There is no doubt that Gladstone was a highly intelligent man, of wide and cultivated interests, deeply committed not only to politics and religious affairs, but to philosophical and artistic matters as well. He took a brilliant double first at Oxford. When he entered politics, he worked sometimes sixteen hours a day, doing twice as much as any other man, keeping extensive written records of his progress and achievements, as well as writing innumerable letters in his own hand. He read voraciously everything he could get hold of, reading upwards of a dozen books at the same time. He never wasted a moment, but filled in his time writing even during his lengthy train journeys. Like many gifted people he had a tremendous energy, and this perhaps helps to explain his sexual as well as his intellectual drive.

At the same time he was often uncomfortable in the company of women, though there is no suggestion that he was anything other than undeviatingly faithful to his wife Catherine, whom he married in 1839. The pair of them were high-principled, religious and rather uncommunicative people who baulked at close intimacy. At the same time he believed he had powerful sexual urges, and suffered severe pangs of moral guilt as the result of them. Before his marriage he had already undertaken a number of liaisons with possible spouses: one of them a pleasant and well-connected young lady called Caroline Farquhar, whose family did not consider him enough of a gentleman (her mother also, strangely, objected to the way 'he carried his bag' – though whether it was because of the way he carried it, or whether because he carried it at all, she never made clear); another was with Lady Frances Morton, the pretty eighteen-year-old daughter of the Earl of Morton, who remained friendly with Gladstone for the rest of her life, though her family did not think enough of him to agree to the match. At the same time, Gladstone remained rather stuffy and off-hand with the wives chosen by two of his brothers (one of them on the grounds that she was a Unitarian). It appeared to the rest of the world as if Gladstone was over-choosy and difficult to please, yet he always reproached himself for having what he thought were lustful and improper longings after females, and passed through a phase at about the same period in which he considered himself deserving of punishment because of his unhealthy interest in printed pornography – in one case French and English verse which to any normal observer was not even marginally salacious. It seems likely from his sensitivity to such matters that his highly developed religious sentiments had created what was not unusual in a man of his time and class – feelings of moral guilt.

At the same time he showed another and even more remarkable tendency: that of showing concern for what were known at the time as 'fallen women'. He first evinced this when at Oxford in 1827, and developed it in 1846 when he took an interest in the society that dealt with these unfortunates operating from the Margaret Street Chapel north of Oxford Circus, later beautifully rebuilt by William Butterfield as All Saints, Margaret Street. After 1849 Gladstone took to the practice of seeking these women out in the course of the late-night walks which he maintained were so beneficial to his health, engaging them in conversation and even taking them back to their rooms for a sustaining cup of cocoa. He made no attempt to keep these meetings secret, though the practice did raise eyebrows among those who knew about it, and led to ribald speculation about whether his motives were as moral as he pretended, or whether perhaps he simply 'liked his bit of rough'.

Some of these women he sought out many times, developing close relations with them, though what their opinions were of the unusual civility he bestowed on them history does not relate. Some remain anonymous and appear in the diaries only fleetingly. Others appear over a period stretching into months. One such was Elizabeth Collins, regarded by Gladstone not as a mere whore, but astonishingly as 'a most lovely statue, beautiful beyond measure' (a judgment he chose to couch in Italian). Another was a woman called Emma Clifton, about whom he wrote rather cryptically: 'I made I hope some way – but, alas, my unworthiness!' A third was a young woman called Lightfoot (his diaries call her P. Lightfoot, but Gladstone never tells us her first name). Of her he observes that she 'did him more harm than good' and that 'my trysts are carnal, otherwise the withdrawing of them would not leave such a void'. All these episodes were in the period from 1849–52, but others continued later – with a Marion Summerhays in 1859, and at least one other young woman whilst he was holidaying in Naples. In the 1870s, too, he became acquainted with the famous Victorian adventuress Catherine Walters[1] with whom he corresponded regularly and to whom he gave occasional presents. None of this involved even the slightest effort at secrecy or concealment; indeed, one of his regular 'beats' was outside the Argyll Rooms in great Windmill Street, off Piccadilly Circus – a place which even more in Victorian times was synonymous with being thronged with people (he was a public figure, and could have been easily recognized). His political friends seem to have been perfectly aware of his odd habits, though practically all of them knew him well enough to avoid putting any lewd construction on his behaviour.

1 See also the entry on *What was the truth about Skittles, the last Victorian courtesan?*

But they also knew that this behaviour could be interpreted less generously, and from time to time tried to persuade him to desist. Indeed, in 1882, when they were his cabinet colleagues in his second ministry, Lord Rosebery and Lord Granville tossed a coin to decide which was to tackle him about his unacceptable conduct: Rosebery lost, and bearded the Grand Old Man with his complaint. Gladstone was quite obdurate. He had a clear conscience, he said, and could not accept that anyone should think he had done anything to be ashamed of; he insisted (in the face of prevailing medical opinion) that night walks were good for him; he had taken them for many years and was not going to change his habits now. So Rosebery was sent off with a flea in his ear, and Gladstone's 'rescue work' went on.

His critics' only effort to dish the dirt on Gladstone came only after his death, when one Captain Peter Wright, in 1927, published a book containing scurrilous insinuations against him over his dealings with London prostitutes. Gladstone's two sons, Henry and Herbert, reacted with predictable ferocity in defence of their father's monumental reputation: Henry got Wright drummed out of his club. He took recourse to the law to get himself reinstated (he was successful, and was awarded £125 damages for the inconvenience). Later he sued Herbert for damages. This second suit failed, and, after a savagely hostile summing-up from Mr Justice Avory, Wright's case was dismissed and the Gladstone brothers were cheered on their emergence from the Law Courts for the work they had done in maintaining 'the high moral character of the late Mr Gladstone'. This was unusual, if not unique, as an occasion when the law courts were used to preserve the reputation of a man who had been dead for twenty-nine years.

Why were Victorian music-halls the battleground between prudes and prostitutes?

The years at the end of the nineteenth century witnessed one of the most heated controversies of the 'Naughty Nineties' over the use of music-hall 'promenades' as places of assignation between the sexes, and, in straight-laced Victorian England, as places where gentlemen about town could arrange a discreet meeting with the ladies of the night.

These promenades, like that of the Empire Theatre, were sometimes very large and luxurious, and there it was possible for sweetly-smelling, over-dressed young women to organize the emptying of the pocket books of the raffish male clientele. The 'ladies' were bought fizzy light wine masquerading as champagne, and given boxes of chocolates which many of them subsequently sold back to the barmen behind the counter. R.C.K. Ensor, in his book of the period, *England, 1870–1914*, solemnly declared:

> Immorality paraded itself as never before during the Queen's reign, especially in the music-halls. At their head figured the Empire Theatre, whose promenade, then a very large one was, from 1889–1894, regarded universally and quite openly as the regular market for the more expensive class of loose women.

It was a time of curiously double standards, perhaps best characterized by the conventional gentleman who, discovering that the young lady of his dalliance had never received church confirmation, arranged to have that omission rectified before continuing his affair with her. Prostitution was generally regarded as a means of canalizing vice away from healthy homes. Yet, while efforts were still being made to regulate this vice, the campaign by Josephine Butler, the Victorian campaigner for female rights, to repeal the *Contagious Diseases Act* (which required the licensing of brothels and the periodic medical testing of the women who worked there) had just been successful in 1886. The age of consent for females was no more than thirteen, and the publisher W.T. Stead had just shocked London by revealing that he had been able to buy a girl of that age, virtually as a slave, for just a few pounds. There were many people who were scandalized by the 'promenades', and who saw no real difference between the elegantly-dressed prostitutes paying their five-shilling entrance fees to these 'lounges' and their more bedraggled sisters swarming gratuitously in the streets of theatreland. Such critics regarded the *Empire* as a den of vice, since, after having been opened in 1884, it steadily slid downhill afterwards from opera to comic opera and then to burlesque before it found itself a music-hall, presenting lascivious displays of 'can-can' dancing and even suggestive of living 'tableaux' (which were perfectly all right as long as they didn't move). The theatre owners riposted that their 'lounges' were perfectly orderly; they were even, indeed, a sort of 'club' known to Englishmen all over the world as one of the decent comforts of home.

The leader of the campaign against the 'promenades' was a Mrs Laura Ormiston Chant, a kind of Victorian Mary Whitehouse who took it upon herself to speak up for decency and clean living. She visited the *Empire* herself and found that she was stared at. She noted grimly that the dancing was suggestive, the garments of the visiting ladies flashy and vulgar, their language coarse, and that there was too much 'pulling and jostling' between them and the men. When her protests to the theatre manager, George Edwardes, were unavailing, she took it upon herself to oppose the renewal of the theatre's licence before the LCC Watch Committee. At the committee hearing she easily outshone the barrister representing the *Empire*. It was her view that the theatre promenade was the 'habitual resort of prostitutes in pursuit of their traffic', and, in succession, her battery of equally determined witnesses also testified that it was a 'place of procurement'; it was a place of dancing, 'calculated to incite impure thought and passion'; it was a place where the 'moral character of the women there could be inferred from their dress'; it was a place where 'accosting' was common; and that it was 'the worst place in Europe'. Here English hypocrisy was on display at its most rampant, and in spite of a stout defence by the applicants offering healthy common-sense as the remedy for all this prurient concern, the committee refused the renewal on the grounds that the place was used 'for purposes such as the Council could not properly recognize by its licence'.

Immediately a furious counter-attack was launched by the *habitués* of the music-halls against the intolerable female busybodies who had deprived them of their social life and of their entertainment. Both the *Morning Post* and the *Daily Telegraph* produced columns of letters (sometimes six or seven columns daily) protesting at their intolerance and working up a fine lather of indignation against what one writer called 'Prudes on the Prowl', a fine phrase which soon became the title of a popular song. One of the letters, signed by 'Puritan' with his tongue in his cheek, complained bitterly about disgusting dress, and said he had counted no fewer than twelve so-called ladies at the *Empire,* where *not one was wearing gloves.*

Mrs Chant, nevertheless, had what could only be called a field day. She wrote and spoke repeatedly on the subject; she wrote pamphlets, the most famous rather unpatriotically entitled *Why We Attacked the Empire,* in which she made mincemeat of her detractors. She was constantly being interviewed by the press, and had there been any television programmes she would certainly have figured largely in them. To the *Pall Mall Gazette* she confided that she was not hostile to the music halls 'as such'; that she was 'passionately fond' of dancing; that her French friends, though accustomed to the performances at the *Moulin Rouge,* nevertheless walked out of the *Empire* with the comment 'C'est trop fort!' She called the *Empire* 'the moral dustbin of the Metropolis'. Her contention that she knew theatre girls who regularly made £20 or £30 a week from prostitution drew the thoughtful reply from G.B. Shaw that 'the problem for Mrs Chant is to make it better worth an attractive girl's while to be a respectable worker than to be a prostitute'. A certain Alderman Routledge suggested that Mrs Chant would better have employed her time working on behalf of the prostitutes on the streets, or even, astonishingly, 'investigating what went on in the galleries of some churches on Sunday nights'. Even *Punch* joined in the attacks on her, and produced a full-page cartoon depicting 'Mrs Prowlina Pry' surveying the *Empire* theatre, placarded with '3,000 Employees Will Be Thrown Out of Work'.

Meanwhile, the *Prince of Wales* theatre was the venue of a large indignation meeting arranged by the Theatrical and Music Hall Operatives and by other associated trade unions even including the Amalgamated Society of Railway Servants, and George Edwardes was pursuing legal opponents, real and imagined, through the courts. Nevertheless, in the autumn of 1894 the LCC confirmed the earlier decision and the *Empire* was forced to close for alterations to its notorious promenade. Popular indignation raged against the 'Establishment': even the Stock Exchange hooted out one of its members, and members of the LCC were booed in the streets. The manager of Toole's Theatre offered his premises for benefit performances for former *Empire* employees, and they were put on half pay for a week.

In fact, however, the alterations took only a few days and the theatre returned to business in November with a modified licence after a slight reduction of the promenade area and the erection of canvas screens to separate the auditorium from the bars. A young Sandhurst cadet called W.S. Churchill, who had never seen anything objectionable at the *Empire,* spent some time polishing a speech which he intended to give to the executive committee of the recently established Entertainments Protection Committee, but found he was the only member of the public present – so he gave up his quest and went to the theatre instead. He, and other young gentlemen like him, soon found that the canvas screens were as flimsy as they looked, and made short work of them with their walking sticks on Saturday night, crying 'Long live Edwardes!' while simultaneously wrecking his theatre. Edwardes magnanimously forgave them for the high spirits of their youth and in 1895 resumed his activities with an unconditional licence. The *Palace* and the *Alhambra* speedily followed suit and established promenades of their own. Thus the scandal of the music-hall promenades became one of the main features of Edwardian England, and continued during the First World War, when General Smith-Dorrien complained that his young officers, visiting them on leave from the trenches, were deprived both of their money and their clean bill of health. The Bishop of London agreed with him, calling what happened on the promenades 'licensed prostitution'.

In 1916 Alfred Butt announced his intention to do voluntarily what the LCC had failed to make him do; he was closing his promenade in response to the change in public feeling. He was followed by Sir Oswald Stoll, who had newly acquired control of the *Alhambra*. It did not sound the death-knell of the music-hall, as many had predicted; this was brought about by the coming of the talking pictures in the 1920s.

What was the truth about Skittles, the last Victorian courtesan?

Skittles was the last great courtesan, her name synonymous with scandal. By profession she was a prostitute; the Victorians, broad-mindedly raffish as many of them were, would have called her a 'whore', while the effete twentieth century would have applied to her the much paler and more euphemistic term 'call-girl'. Whatever the name by which she went, she led a colourful and glamorous life in London and Paris which lasted through the whole of the Second Empire in France and for most of the later Victorian and Edwardian periods in England. She was in France at first the protégée of the elderly Achille Fould, finance minister of Emperor Napoleon III, while in England she counted among her many acquaintances the Marquis of Hartington and numerous other members of the Cavendish family, and Edward VII himself (whom she referred to rather disrespectfully as 'Tum-tum'). She was honest and directly spoken, remaining fresh-faced and curiously unsophisticated in a florid and over-dressed age. Parisians loved, and even cultivated, her English accent, Englishmen loved her northern dialect with its hint of Liverpudlian, a local touch she was proud to maintain. She remained for most of her life a celebrated, and sometimes notorious, figure in both countries.

She was born Catherine Walters in 1839 in the back streets of Toxteth, Liverpool, close to the docks. Her father, Edward Walters, a retired sailor, was by trade a 'tide-waiter', i.e. he was one of the many casual labourers who waited for ships to come up the Mersey on the high tide and then helped to unload them; in more modern times he would have been called a stevedore. He and his numerous family later moved to the Wirral when Catherine was only eleven, and with the help of a small pension from his seafaring work set himself up as an ale-house keeper. The sailors she met with there were rough and hard-swearing with money in their pockets from their last voyage and willing to spend it on anything female that crossed their paths. Catherine knew very early on about the effects of drunkenness and coarse and violent language, and, as a slum–child, knew all about shared bedrooms, shared beds and communal lavatories; her father beat her regularly and her step-mother (her real mother had died and been buried in Toxteth) was cowed and bullied just as she was herself. But she remained independent and self-reliant, and in spite of the dirt and poverty with which she was surrounded, retained her intelligence and her pert elfin charm. By the time she was a teenager she left home and went to live with her grandmother back in Toxteth, where she got herself a job in the Black Jack Tavern close to the docks, working in the skittle alley and earning herself the nickname that was to accompany her for the rest of her life. Her vivacity, allure and quickness in repartee made her name locally, and she was soon working successfully as a prostitute much sought after by the inn's clientele. The age of consent for females at that time was 13, but Catherine had probably lost her virginity whilst she was still a child. The family moved again, this time to the Cheshire Hunt area near Tarporley, where she learned to ride. She already had acquired the rudiments of riding, either because she had access to livery stables, or else because as a child she had been fond of going to the circus; now she became a very accomplished horsewoman and was allowed to ride with the country folk. When she was twenty, however, she decided to seek her fortune in London, perhaps as the companion of a young man of means who had persuaded her to run away with him.

In London Catherine soon became an habituée of the fashionable West End. She came to patronize Kate Hamilton's brothel in Prince's Street, off Leicester Square, where she used her visits (though she was never regularly employed there) to meet well-connected young army officers and other gentlemen-about-town. She made the acquaintance of the proprietor of a successful livery stables in Bruton Mews, adjacent to Berkeley Square, who employed her to advertise his services by riding one of his handsomest horses on Rotten Row in Hyde Park or along 'Ladies' Mile' on the north side of the Serpentine. She was soon attracting crowds of admirers in the Park, and was even painted by Sir Edwin Landseer as *The Pretty Horsebreaker*. She made the acquaintance first of William Frederick Windham (known from his days at Eton as 'Mad' Windham on account of his madcap behaviour), the dissolute and irresponsible son of General Windham of Felbrigg Hall in Norfolk, and later, in 1862, of Spencer Compton Cavendish, Lord Hartington, eldest son and heir to the seventh Duke of Devonshire.

With Hartington she had a protracted and torrid affair (insofar as it was possible to be torrid with one so lumpish), driving him from the side of the beautiful Louise ('Lottie'), Duchess of Manchester, until family pressure forced him to take panicky refuge in the USA, while Skittles emigrated in the opposite direction to the spa town of Ems in the Rhineland. Here she found herself pursued by another lover, Aubrey de Vere Beauclerk, a rather lurid young nobleman from Northern Ireland who was already married. He insisted in leaving his long-suffering young wife and fleeing with Skittles to New York, where she found herself in the middle of the American civil war with two discarded lovers, both temperamentally totally opposed to each other. Beauclerk eventually returned to his wife with his tail between his legs, whilst Hartington came back to patch things up with his family and with the glamorous Lottie.

Catherine spent the rest of the 'Gay Sixties' in Paris. At the time the city, elaborately improved by the Imperial minister Haussmann, attracted the attention of much of fashionable Europe, its dazzling and gilded surroundings providing the setting for a social life profligate to the point of degeneracy. Since she knew little French, Catherine gravitated towards the English colony there, one of whose fashionable *cocottes* (known disrespectfully to Parisians as *'les horizontales'*), Cora Pearl, once tried to shock by having herself served to her dinner-guests out of a silver platter wearing nothing but a string of pearls and a few sprigs of parsley, and then doing a few high kicks on top of the table. Another of the *demi-mondaines,* known as La Barucci, renowned for her habitual lateness and reproached for it by the Duc de Grammont-Caderousse when she appeared before him in a daringly low-cut gown, turned her back on him, flipped up her voluminous skirts and presented him with her white-clad buttocks. It was in Paris that Catherine accepted the protection of Achille Fould, Napoleon's bearded and elderly minister of finance. He installed her in a sumptuous apartment in the Avenue des Champs Elysées and allowed her to make her daily excursions to the Bois de Boulogne, where she outshone on horseback many other fashionable *équestriennes.* She even made the acquaintance of the Emperor himself, when she was introduced to him at dinner. He said he had never heard of the game of skittles, but sportingly agreed to a competition in an adjacent room, where footmen set up nine champagne bottles to be used for the purpose: he bowled at them and knocked over two to sycophantic applause, while Catherine, who had not lost her skills, knocked over the remaining seven with a single shot.

Fould, shrewd and kindly, lavished much time and money on Catherine, improving her halting French and taking her to concerts and galleries, whilst asking for little in return. He introduced her to the fashionable balls at the British Embassy, where she met Lord Hubert de Burgh (later Earl of Clanricard) and met also a young man, very junior in the Embassy and slightly younger than herself, called Wilfrid Blunt. He was a writer of sentimental poetry and fell madly in love with her, inveigling her to spend three days and nights of passion with him in the Rue Jacob, where she – unusually for one so level-headed – also fell in love with him. Both agreed, however, that a marriage between them was impracticable, and though they remained thereafter in each other's thoughts, they met only briefly and occasionally thereafter. Blunt was posted to Lisbon, to Frankfurt and finally to Buenos Aires (he eventually returned to England and married Lady Anne King-Noel, grand-daughter of Lord Byron), whilst Catherine remained in Paris. But she was growing bored with her life there, and was spending an increasing amount of time in England, where every season she indulged her passion for fox hunting, chiefly in Leicestershire with the Quorn or the Billesdon ('South Quorn') hunts. After the death of Fould in 1867 and the fall of Paris in 1871 during the Franco-Prussian War, she never lived in France again.

She had met Edward, Prince of Wales, before, whilst she was still in Paris, and now took up with him once more. Like him, Catherine had the common touch, sharing also his enthusiasm for fox hunting. Finally she became his lover. She also got to know Squire Tailby, Sir Arthur Hazelrigg and Harry, the young Marquis of Hastings, together with the whole group of other great Leicestershire hunting figures. At this time she incurred the lasting enmity of Lady Stamford, the wife of the Master of the Quorn, who never rode to hounds again after a quarrel with her husband in which she presented him with the choice of herself or Catherine in the hunt (unfortunately he chose wrongly).

Catherine also spent a good deal of time in London, taking a house in Chesterfield Street. Here for the first time she was introduced to W.E. Gladstone, the Leader of the House of Commons (known to other members of Catherine's profession as 'Old Glad-eye' because of his reputed fondness for trawling the city streets to save fallen women and then taking them home with him for a cup of cocoa).[1] Gladstone talked to Catherine in a courtly fashion and brought her a pound of tea as a present. Oddly, they found they had a lot in common. Their background circumstances were quite different, but both were born in Liverpool and remained fond of it; thereafter Catherine always had a letter from him on her birthday. In 1872 she moved to South Street, which was closer to the Park and to Piccadilly.

By the end of the 1860s Gladstone was Prime Minister, and Bertie, Victoria's son, whose style of life he hated, often entertained Catherine at Marlborough House. Gladstone thoroughly disapproved, writing to the Foreign Secretary: 'To speak in general terms, the Queen is invisible and the Prince of Wales is not respected.' The seventies came and Catherine, sadly, was beginning to feel the onset of middle age. She was outshone by the youthful empress Elizabeth, wife of the Austrian Franz Josef, who spent a good deal of time in England and often appeared on the hunting field. Nevertheless, Catherine took up the new craze of roller-skating enthusiastically until 1876, though she was not as good at it as she would have wished. She soon began to suffer from incipient arthritis in the joints, and so found walking increasingly difficult. Bertie, meanwhile, had taken up with Lillie Langtry, and was as devoted to her as his inconstant soul would permit. Catherine shortly after met her last amour, the Hon. Gerald Le Marchant de Saumerez, who attached himself to her when he was scarcely out of Eton, and was as young and unsophisticated as the youthful Blunt had been, but in his case never as much interested in her as he was in his career. A keen soldier, he served in the Ashanti wars with the Lancers, and distinguished himself in the Boer War with the Rifles. Though over the age of military service at the time of the First World War, he dyed his hair black and saw active service in France as a gravedigger on the western front.

By the beginning of the new century Catherine Walters was an old lady. In 1901 the Queen died, and in 1910 Edward VII in his turn. All her friends were dying around her: Hartington, now eighth Duke of Devonshire, in 1908, and his wife Lottie shortly after. Most of Catherine's

1 See also the entry on *Was W.E. Gladstone a whited sepulchre?*

Parisian friends and rivals had now also died. About this time she began to be known as Mrs Baillie, though whether she had actually married Alec Baillie (brother of Col. Jim Baillie in the Fernie country at Illston Grange, close to Illston-on-the-Hill, Leicestershire), as Edward had asked him to do, or whether this was a title of convenience is not precisely known. Like many others, she was deeply shocked at the outbreak of the Great War. She knew the Kaiser and thought him such a charming young man when she met him. She had received several letters from him, which she later sold, giving the money to help the wounded soldiers. During the war, she continued to live in South Street, and from time to time met her old flame, Wilfrid Blunt, whose own wife was now dead. She also kept in touch with Gerald de Saumarez, but at the age of eighty she was in a wheelchair, half-blind and very frail. She died in 1920. On her death certificate she was described as a 'Spinster of no occupation'.

Oscar Wilde: victim or villain?

Oscar Wilde was one of the outstanding writers of his generation, bursting into the late Victorian world of letters with almost as much disreputability as brilliance, and even seeming to court notoriety; but whether he deserves more pity than blame for the outcome of his career remains an open question. He said of himself in one of his essays: 'There is only one thing in the world worse than being talked about, and that is not being talked about', and one is left with the impression that perhaps he courted his ill-repute quite deliberately. All the same, his treatment at the hands of strait-laced Victorian society excites sympathy as well as blame.

Oscar Finghal O'Flaherty Wills Wilde was the second son of Jane Francesca Wilde, journalist and poet, and Dr (later Sir) William Wilde, a surgeon and oculist, and was born in 1854. Wilde went first to Trinity College, Dublin, where he read Classics, and then to Magdalen College, Oxford. In spite of his long hair, epigrammatic conversational style, effete behaviour and his parade of aestheticism (he was known to his Oxford contemporaries as 'O'Flighty') he was nevertheless quite brilliant as a student, strongly influenced by two of the great scholars he encountered there, Walter Pater and John Ruskin. Whilst at Oxford he won the Newdigate Prize for poetry. In 1884 he married Constance Lloyd and moved into a house in Chelsea, where his sons Cyril and Vyvian were born. He became Editor of *Lady's World* in 1887, and though sacked in 1889, continued to work as a journalist and writer. In 1881 he visited America on the occasion of the New York presentation of Gilbert and Sullivan's new operetta *Patience,* and his velvet and fur, his embroidered Byronic shirts and his knee breeches took the whole country by storm. His first book, *The Picture of Dorian Gray,* was published in 1890, telling the story of a young man who succeeds in retaining his youthful good looks at the same time as his painted portrait becomes steadily more vile and corrupt, and this book brought him notoriety on account of its supposed decadence. Despairing of Victorian moral and artistic standards, he spent some time in Paris, where he wrote a play, also alleged to be scandalous, *Salomé*. When he returned to London in 1892, he produced a number of brilliantly successful comedies, including *Lady Windermere's Fan, A Woman of No Importance, An Ideal Husband,* and in 1895 perhaps the greatest, *The Importance of Being Earnest*. All these consolidated the grip which Wilde had on the intellectual and artistic world in Britain.

Nevertheless there was a seamy underside to his career. He had ceased his attentions towards his wife soon after the birth of his younger son in 1886, and had entered upon a series of stormy homosexual relationships with a string of young men. The most important of these relationships, which was to stay with him for the rest of his life, was contracted in 1892 with Lord Alfred Douglas, affectionately nicknamed 'Bosie', the son of the Marquis of Queensberry. He furiously denounced the affair, leaving his card at Wilde's London club on which he accused Wilde of 'posing as a *somdomite* [sic]'. Wilde, encouraged by his young lover, issued a writ for libel against Queensberry, and the case came to trial in 1895. The legal defence was led by Edward Carson, who produced a string of 'rent boys' to prove the Marquis's allegations. Wilde lost the case and shortly afterwards was arrested by the police on charges of gross indecency, homosexual practices being at this time against the law. In spite of a spirited defence, Wilde was convicted and was sentenced to the maximum term prescribed by the law of two years' imprisonment. He served out his sentence in Reading Gaol, abused and reviled, and here he wrote perhaps the most moving of his poems, *The Ballad of Reading Gaol*.

On his release in 1899 he wrote to and was reconciled with 'his darling boy', and, calling himself Sebastian Melmoth, led a semi-fugitive life travelling round Europe with him until his death in Paris at the early age of forty-six, in a small Left Bank hotel in 1900.

Recent research has shown a deeper and even more sinister feature of Wilde's case. According to a book published in 2003 and based partly on witness statements and partly on an unpublished diary (presently in the Bodleian Library) by Edmund Trelawny Backhouse, a homosexual associate of the principals in the case, there was a further reason for the public clamour and notoriety attendant on Wilde's arrest and conviction.

Backhouse suggests that the affair was a plot by the Victorian upper-class establishment to divert public attention from a two-year homosexual affair occurring at much the same time between the young and accomplished Liberal Prime Minister, the Earl of Rosebery, Gladstone's successor in 1893, and Viscount Drumlanrig, the elder brother of Douglas, Wilde's own lover. The furious Queensberry had threatened to expose Rosebery's affair with his elder son, and Rosebery's government, anxious to avoid public scandal touching upon so eminent a figure as the Prime Minister, pushed forward Wilde's prosecution for his affair with Bosie in 1895, partly with a view to soothing the angry father's feelings of outrage. Rosebery had first met Drumlanrig, then a twenty-four-year-old Coldstream Guard, at an intimate party in London in 1892, and shortly afterwards appointed him his private secretary, even arranging for him to be elevated to the Lords so that he could become a junior minister in Rosebery's government. Queensberry was outraged to have two homosexual sons and particularly detested Rosebery whom he contemptuously referred to as 'a Jewish nancy boy'. Drumlanrig died soon afterwards in mysterious circumstances in a shooting accident in a field in Somerset, a number of his friends suggesting he committed suicide by shooting himself in the mouth, and not as the coroner more charitably suggested by tripping over a stile whilst carrying a loaded gun.

If he had lived in a later generation, Wilde might have avoided the censure that at the end of the Victorian era was tantamount to a death warrant. But, as it was, his condemnation revealed the horror with which homosexuality was regarded at the time, the dread of the discovery of homosexual secrets by the public and the lengths to which respectable people would go to cover up their shameful activities. This was all part of the narrowness and the rigidity of contemporary morality and the violence with which respectable Victorian society reacted against anyone who rejected its standards and refused to conform to them. The judge who condemned him to prison for his crimes was almost apoplectic in his fury, denouncing his case as quite the worst he had ever encountered. But it was not simply that Wilde was homosexual, or that he defied convention and paraded his non-conformity before scandalised contemporary eyes; he was genuinely contemptuous of the life and manners of his entire generation. He objected to their hypocrisy, their materialism, their meanness, their lack of imagination. He inveighed against pretentiousness, which was distinctly odd, considering that he was himself a dreadful *poseur*. He ridiculed especially the dual standards, the braying superiority and the bone-headed stupidity of the upper classes (of whom he should perhaps have again considered himself one), famously condemning their fox hunting habits as 'the unspeakable in full pursuit of the uneatable.' He always conveyed his critical attitudes with a mordant wit, ridiculing the objects of his criticism, and sparing the feelings of nobody he condemned. All this made him quite insufferable to the Victorians, who prized above all social discipline and modest and uncritical acceptance of all their generation stood for. Nevertheless, though intolerant of stifling morality, he remained at heart artistically an idealist, and this gave a tragic dimension to his heartfelt observation in *The Picture of Dorian Gray* that 'we are all in the gutter, but some of us are looking at the stars.'

The Reverend Harold Davidson: innocent or sex maniac?

The Reverend Harold Davidson, Rector of Stiffkey (pronounced Stewkey) in Norfolk, who was tried in a blaze of publicity in a consistory court and subsequently formally defrocked in Norwich Cathedral, was either a misunderstood loony or a compulsive womanizer. Either way, he was responsible for one of the most notorious and spectacular sex scandals of the years between the two World Wars.

Davidson was born in 1875, and began his working life as an actor. However, soon after 1900 he decided to enter the church, enrolled in theological college and was ordained. He became Rector of Stiffkey, close to Wells-next-the-Sea near the north coast of Norfolk, in 1906. It was in this benefice that he spent most of his adult years, except for a short time during the First World War when he enrolled as a naval chaplain. During this time, whilst his ship was docked in Egypt, he got himself arrested during a police raid on a brothel in Cairo. His explanation was that he was there for entirely innocent purposes, endeavouring to give help to the unfortunates who were working there; and the aftermath of this episode set the tone of much of his later career – caught in flagrantly compromising circumstances, but surprised and somewhat indignant that anyone should question his motives.

Returning from naval service to England in 1920 he took to the habit of spending a good deal of time with fallen women, chiefly in London, ostensibly for the purpose of rehabilitating them. Though his clerical duties related solely to Norfolk, he would catch an early train to Liverpool Street on Monday morning, and often would not return home until the last train on Friday evening. His parishioners for the most part indulged him. They found it mildly amusing that their rector should call himself the 'prostitutes' padre' and spend most of his time chasing girls in the West End; that was just the way, they imagined, in which the dottier members of the clergy behaved, and it was not for them to doubt his declarations from his pulpit that in consorting with the unfortunate he was doing the work of God.

Reverend Davidson hunted only for pretty young girls. He said he thought that ugly ones were not in so much danger or temptation. At the same time he presumably thought that older women, having already embarked upon their chosen careers, were unlikely to wish for the redemption he offered them. So he would pick up some solitary lass, preferably pretty and between the ages of fifteen and twenty-one, tell her how much she resembled this film star or that, put his arm round her and assure her of his affection and his good intentions. He would talk to such girls endlessly, giving them worthy advice, and if they were lucky would provide them with money and lodging. If they were *very* lucky they might even get a pleasant weekend in Paris in his company – not that it was ever clear whether this excursion would reinforce his moral message or have the contrary effect. He soon had strings of girls being looked after, sometimes several at once. He gave them pet names, and encouraged them to call him 'Uncle Harold'. Davidson was very tactile: he would kiss them, caress them and pat them affectionately on the bottom. He was even known to have pulled down their lower lips, as if they were horses, to examine the state of their teeth. He was frequently seen in Piccadilly, Marble Arch and Trafalgar Square. Some of the girls thought he was a 'toucher' or just a harmless 'talker' i.e. a client who wanted nothing further in way of personal service than contact or conversation; others, seeing the approach of his grey-headed, gnome-like figure in clerical garb (he was only 5′ 3″ tall), dodged aside into a doorway to avoid him, and tried to escape his inevitable invitation into a café for tea. Some public nuisances are banned from public houses or clubs; Reverend Davidson was unusual in being banned from Oxford Street tearooms, where he was supposed to have made obscene suggestions to various waitresses.

Eventually, in 1931, one of his parishioners, an elderly military gentleman, Major Philip Hammond, who had served in the Boer War, grew very wrathful over the suspicious traipsing of various young females down to the Rectory in Stiffkey and the continual neglect of Davidson's clerical duties in his parish. Finally it was the Rector's failure to turn up for an armistice day service that November which eventually persuaded the Major to write a letter of complaint to the Bishop of Norwich, citing the Clergy Discipline Act of 1892, and asking him to take immediate corrective action.

Davidson proved, however, to be a difficult man to find. He was so busy with his extracurricular activities in London and elsewhere that the Bishop could not contact him, and was eventually compelled to employ the services of a private detective and later the police in his enquiries. One of the girls, a certain Rose Ellis, was cajoled into making a statement to a policeman in which she gave details of her relations with Davidson. Subsequently rather regretting the breach of confidence, she confessed what she had done to her mentor, who not only bitterly reproached her for her betrayal and for accepting £40 as a reward for giving her testimony ('Ten up on Judas,' he said. 'He only got thirty'), but wrote a lengthy and vituperative letter to the Bishop of Norwich protesting his innocence of any wrongdoing, alleging that the police had used improper methods to extract their information and had secured Rose Ellis's testimony only by 'bribing her with money and drugging her with alcohol.' His increasingly eccentric behaviour was shown also by the fact that at the time he wrote (in purple ink) to the Duchess of Devonshire, stressing that his wife and family were in want and suffering, and suggesting that any contribution of from £300–£500 would be of help.

Nonetheless in March 1932 Davidson was indicted before a consistory court, not in Norfolk, where a court of the Diocese of Norwich would normally be convened, but in Church House, Westminster, to which witnesses could more readily be summoned. Davidson threatened to summon upwards of 400 witnesses to his character and good behaviour, though happily he did not carry out this threat. He did, however, take the precaution of selling his story to the press for £750, only to find that the Bishop brought an action against the offending paper after only two episodes and had it suppressed.

Lurid tales were told at the trial detailing the Rector's behaviour with a whole crowd of females – allegations that were graphically detailed in the popular press – whilst he strenuously protested his innocence of everything. One witness, a formidable lady by the name of Osborne who continued to pursue Davidson in the courts long after the trial for £43 which she said he owed her in unpaid rent for rooms let out to him, produced a photograph of a family group taken at Stiffkey and which was said to include Mrs Davidson, though she was holding a bunch of leaves in front of her face and was so gawky and angular that she was taken by the presiding Chancellor to be a boy. The Rector, however, made no effort to use his odd wife as a justification for his even odder behaviour. He spent most of his time in court in vigorous protest, claiming to be 'a great authority on brothels' and even illustrated his testimony at one point by providing a brief burst of tap-dancing. Another photograph produced in evidence showed Davidson this time with his arms round a girl photographed from behind who, apart from a voluminous shawl about her shoulders, was showing her bottom and was obviously naked. Davidson, calling himself 'a poor fool of a parson', said he had been duped, and that the girl in question had told him she was aiming at a photographic career modelling swimsuits. But the outcome of the trial was a foregone conclusion: after six weeks Davidson was found guilty on all counts and was sentenced to be defrocked.

The following Sunday he preached to a fascinated and overflowing congregation in Stiffkey, refuting the court's decision and reminding his hearers that Christ too had been persecuted for his beliefs. He appealed to the Privy Council twice against the verdict, but all in vain. He was summoned to Norwich Cathedral in October to be ceremonially defrocked. He arrived late, constantly interrupted the proceedings, embarked on an apparently endless speech of self-justification, and finally fled from their presence hysterically into the main body of the church, where he flung himself on his knees to pray; finally, as they pronounced sentence, he shrieked out his intention to appeal to the Archbishop of Canterbury. By this time, his fellow clergy as well as most of the rest of England had come to the conclusion that the Reverend Davidson was guilty but hopelessly insane.

Later events proved the probable correctness of this opinion. Reverting to his showbiz persona – if he had ever left it – Davidson sat in a barrel for some time preparing his defence on Blackpool promenade, protesting his innocence in a sideshow from ten in the morning until midnight, with short breaks for meals. Thousands flocked to see him until the town council secured his conviction for obstruction in the Magistrates Court, and banned him from appearing. Later, for some years, he put on shows in music-halls and cinemas, though not at the Harrogate Nudist Club, where its owners prudishly banned him from appearing. Finally, in 1937, he appeared in a Skegness Amusement Park in a lion's den, 14″ by 8″, with a docile and rather elderly lion called Freddie, who one day unexpectedly took exception to his sharing his cage, attacked him and mauled him to death. Thus his end proved to be almost as unexpected and quite as spectacular as the rest of his strange career.

The Profumo scandal: the original 'Tory sleaze'?

The affair of John Profumo, Minister of War in the Macmillan government in the early 1960s, with the showgirl Christine Keeler, contributed to the disgrace of the Conservative government and its defeat in the general election of 1964 after thirteen years in power. Whilst illicit liaisons between public figures and women of easy virtue were not unheard of, the fall-out from the affair had the effect in the public mind of discrediting the Conservatives for many years, with rumours of political 'sleaze' which pursued them for the rest of the century.

The Sixties were a curiously ambivalent decade: staid and conventional on the one hand, and casual and permissive on the other. For those of the older generation with memories of the war, times were better than they had been, though some scepticism remained over the Premier's claim that the British nation had 'never had it so good'; but, on the other hand, the younger generation were much more brash and uninhibited than their elders, shamelessly experimenting with soft drugs, strip joints and trial marriages, and going along with the shameless suggestion in the new satirical magazine, *Private Eye,* that the nation had 'never had it so *often'.* With the popular press gloating pruriently over its details, the affair was meat and drink to satirical TV broadcasts and continued to scandalize the mass of the public for years.

John Profumo became Minister of War in the Macmillan cabinet in July 1960. Something of a 'toff', Profumo was balding, educated, well-spoken and extremely rich – the very epitome of Conservative respectability, his main claim to distinction being that he was married to the popular British film star Valerie Hobson. It was this very respectability that made his disgrace so shocking. In July 1961 Profumo and his wife were amongst about twenty other rich and influential people, including Ayub Khan, the new President of Pakistan, whom Lord Astor invited to a weekend party at Cliveden, his estate in Berkshire. At the same time, and unknown to them, another weekend party had been arranged by Dr Stephen Ward, a fashionable West End osteopath who had been offered by Lord 'Bill' Astor a house on his estate called 'Spring Cottage' on the Thames where, at a nominal rent, he spent most weekends. In addition to his flourishing practice, Ward was a talented artist earning good fees producing pencil sketches of leading figures for various magazines. He was also a name-dropper and something of a socialite who cultivated the acquaintance of a wide group of trendy friends, entertaining them almost weekly at his fashionable address at Cliveden, where he enlivened the evenings after dinner with sex games, wife-swapping and other fashionable Sixties-ish pursuits. To this end Ward had built up a clientele of nightclub hostesses and go-go dancers as young female 'escorts', including Mandy Rice-Davies and Christine Keeler, to provide his guests with the sort of services they required.

Christine Keeler was a twenty-year-old who had left home at sixteen after a self-induced abortion and had found work in London as a topless dancer in the West End, where she mingled with the customers between acts, providing them with over-priced drinks at their tables and occasionally supplementing her slender earnings by selling sexual services to them. She was young, dark-haired and attractive, and quite undeniably good-looking, but whether she was quite the manipulative whore the papers made her out to be was more open to question. Indeed, beneath her sophisticated veneer Christine was still at heart a teenager, having nightly to fortify herself with stiff glasses of whisky before her bare-breasted act at the club, and confessing further to feeling shocked the first time Ward's cut-glass guests unaccountably embarked on a group striptease, the ladies first gaily taking their own clothes off and then starting to disrobe the gentlemen. Her relations with Ward himself were close without being intimate; as Christine put it, he never 'took advantage' of her. In London, the pair of them shared his flat in Wimpole Mews; they may have had sex, but he was always a gentleman and always treated her with consideration. To her he was something of a father figure, her own father having walked out on the family whilst she was still very young. In testimony she later agreed that she gave Ward money, but said it was for rent – and that in any case he always gave her back far more than she ever gave him.

At his weekend party Ward had the permission of Lord Astor to add a little distinction to the occasion after dinner by using the swimming pool in the grounds of the estate. Unfortunately Christine had no swimming costume with her, and the one she borrowed was not a good fit, so she was encouraged by Ward to enter the pool without one. While she was in the water, Profumo and Lord Astor came upon her during their after-dinner stroll in the grounds, and having swum round aimlessly for some minutes in the safety of the pool, she eventually tried to scramble from the water to put on her costume. Unfortunately Ward got to it first and threw it into the bushes, and Christine was forced to resort to a quite inadequate towel to preserve her modesty. Profumo gave chase, and in the ensuing horseplay she lost the protection of her towel and was left completely nude. It was at this juncture that Mrs Profumo and the rest of the party arrived at the pool. Unexpectedly, the two sets of guests got on quite well, and instead of reproaching the minister for his behaviour, agreed to renew their contacts by meeting again at the pool the next evening.

The following evening, one of the guests was Eugene Ivanov, a young man about town serving as naval attaché in the Soviet Embassy, fluent in English, and one of Ward's carefully cultivated circle. Ivanov also happened to be a serving member of the KGB. In the course of the evening both Profumo and Ivanov asked for, and got, Christine's telephone number. However it was Ivanov who drove her home on that occasion. He cracked a bottle of vodka with her in Ward's flat, and ended the evening by having sex with her on the hearthrug. In the course of the next few days, Christine became mistress to both of them. It did not take Ivanov long to realize that he was holding a trump card with his new acquaintance, but Profumo remained oblivious of the security implications of his new conquest and behaved quite indiscreetly, taking Christine with him on visits quite publicly in his ministerial car and often alternating with Ivanov in meeting her at Ward's flat at Wimpole Mews – though the two never actually met there. Later he realized he could not go on making such regular visits to the flat, and suggested instead that she come to him in his house in Regents Park whilst his wife was away; he even suggested that he should get Christine a flat. She, however, was unwilling to abandon Ward's protection. Her liaison with a minister of the crown much interested

MI5, who warned Ward of a possible security risk and advised him not to associate with Ivanov. Ward was delighted to have become so readily the centre of attention, and tried to play both ends against the middle, telling MI5 what it knew already – that Ivanov was a Soviet agent – but suggesting that with a little effort he might be persuaded to defect and work for Britain; whilst at the same time he (Ward) jokingly asked Christine to find out in the course of her pillow talk with Profumo the location of US missile bases in Britain, information which he rightly judged would be of prime importance to the Soviet Union's espionage service. There is, however, no evidence that Christine ever asked for, or was ever given, any classified security information: to this day, she continues to insist that she would never do anything to betray her country. Nevertheless, tongues were already beginning to wag, and rumours of the affair soon surfaced in the gossip columns of the newspapers. When the matter of Profumo's indiscretion began to be mentioned in the corridors of Westminster he thought it safer to discontinue the association, so he wrote Christine a farewell letter, and after one final meeting (when they had sex on the back seat of his car) finished his affair with her. Christine subsequently claimed that she became pregnant as the result of this meeting and in order to prevent Profumo's involvement in any scandal arising from it had a further abortion.

Thereafter Christine resumed her modelling career, appearing in a number of commercial advertisements, and making various professional appearances in West Indian clubs in London. One of her new lovers was one 'Lucky' Gordon, a demanding and quick-tempered individual who held Christine prisoner at knifepoint on more than one occasion and repeatedly raped her. Escaping back to Ward's flat she bought herself a handgun for protection, and accepted the protection of Johnny Edgecombe, another West Indian who had intervened to protect her in a fight with Gordon. He had sided with her in a quarrel, and had been severely slashed in the face for his pains. He had taken possession of her gun and was now seeking to claim proprietary rights over her. Again she fled back to Ward, but Edgecombe came after her, and when she refused to admit him to the flat in Wimpole Mews, he tried to shoot the lock off the door and took a shot at his cowering victim whom he had glimpsed in an upstairs window. The police came and arrested him, and threatened to charge him with attempted murder. It was clear that the whole affair was about to blow: if Christine appeared in the witness box and was questioned in public about her contacts the whole sorry story of her involvement with Profumo might come to light. Ivanov therefore took a flight back to Moscow, and Ward decided to smuggle the frightened girl out of the country. Tracked down in Spain by reporters from the *Daily Express* she sold the 'full and frank' story of the entire affair to the papers for £800. But Lord Beaverbrook refused to publish it, on the grounds that if he did the paper might be sued for libel. So the white establishment closed ranks against the threat. Hence when Edgecombe came to trial at the Old Bailey, Christine did not appear in the box. Instead MI5 intervened to persuade the police to drop the attempted murder charge, thus protecting Profumo from any enquiry into his behaviour, and as a result Edgecombe was sentenced to seven years on the lesser charge of possessing an illegal firearm.

But by now the cat was really amongst the pigeons. The newspapers insinuated all they dared about Profumo's involvement with Christine, whilst in Parliament the inter-party conspiracy of silence was broken by veteran Labour MP George Wigg, who demanded assurances from the government that the rumours about Profumo were false and that there had been no breach of security in the minister's personal conduct. Profumo was not in the Chamber when the question was asked, but he later came to the dispatch box and sought to brazen it out by conclusively denying any impropriety in his relationship with Christine. She, still in Spain, was again approached by the newspapers and sold them the story – this time for £2000 – that the rumours were entirely false and that she was innocent of any wrongdoing. She then returned to a public hullabaloo in London.

For a time it looked as if Profumo would get away with his denial, but the security forces, puzzled by the ambiguities of Stephen Ward's behaviour and perhaps looking for a scapegoat, embarked on a detailed enquiry into the doctor's affairs. For a long time he stuck to his story that the rumours about Profumo were unfounded; but finally, harassed both by the police and by MI5, he confessed, in letters both to the Home Secretary and to George Wigg, that he knew all about the minister's affair with Christine and that his denials had been intended to shield him. Profumo, on holiday in Venice, realized the game was up, made a clean breast of it and resigned. His cabinet colleagues were furious with him – not so much for being involved in a sex scandal, but more for being caught out lying about it afterwards.

The police, meanwhile, interviewed 140 possible witnesses, and formulated charges under the Sexual Offences Act that Ward had been living on 'immoral earnings', even bringing pressure to bear on one unfortunate to testify that Ward had been her pimp. Mandy Rice-Davies spent a fortnight in Holloway on a trumped-up charge of possession of a forged driving licence in order to get her on to the witness stand, and Christine herself was afterwards sentenced to eighteen months for alleged perjury in 'Lucky' Gordon's case. Nevertheless she was able once more to sell her account of the scandal to the papers, this time for £23,000. She used the money to get a new home for her mother, now an invalid, who was distraught with the whole business. Ward sought to defend himself, but found himself in his hour of need deserted by all his former friends. They all denied coming to his cottage at Cliveden, or, if they had come, denied that anything out of the way had happened there. Bill Astor denied that he had ever had sex with Mandy Rice-Davies, providing her with her chance of producing her historic retort, 'Well, he would, wouldn't he?'. Ward was unable to bear the humiliation of his trial, or, worse still, the sense of betrayal he felt at his friends' desertion, and on the night before the jury reached its verdict, killed himself with an overdose of Nembutal. Before he died he left a letter addressed to the Home Secretary making a full statement of the circumstances of the affair. That letter has never been made public. A later enquiry aiming at improving the nation's security and conducted by Lord Justice Denning concerned itself chiefly with protecting leading politicians from the scandal, and for the most part occupied itself with the easier task of blackening Ward's and Christine Keeler's characters.

Profumo's career was ruined, though he managed to salvage his marriage; Macmillan was defeated by Harold Wilson at the election of September 1964, and thirteen years of Conservative government came to a discreditable end. Christine Keeler found it impossible to find employment afterwards on account of prejudice against her, and so was forced to live in straitened circumstances on social security; and Stephen Ward became the 'fall guy' who paid with his life for the entire affair. Mature judgment suggests that Christine Keeler was not by any means a wicked woman, but rather a lonely and unhappy chancer who found herself out of her depth in the 'swinging sixties'; that there was no real danger to Britain's security from Ivanov's role in it, but rather that, in the absurdly exaggerated postures struck during the Cold War, government security felt itself obliged to make a master spy out of a society playboy; and, finally, that the 'establishment' could always be relied on to do their best to stand together to hush things up, no matter what the cost in ordinary people's careers and lives.

SCANDALS INVOLVING MURDER AND VIOLENCE

The scandalous execution of Derek Bentley

In January 1953, Derek Bentley, a London youth, an epileptic with a mental age of eleven, was hanged for the shooting of a policeman in a botched attempt to break in through the roof of a confectionery warehouse in Croydon the previous November. This was a murder he did not commit. The gun was carried, and fired, by Christopher Craig, a friend of Bentley's, who had persuaded him to try to burgle the warehouse that night. Police evidence told very heavily against both youths: Craig for firing several shots, the most fatal of which struck PC Stanley Miles in the forehead and killed him; Bentley for shouting encouragement to shoot, even though he was under arrest at the time. In 1952, the sentence for murder was death, and was mandatory. Unsurprisingly, Craig was found guilty, and was sentenced; Bentley, furthermore, on the strength of the judge's recommendation that they should convict if they believed that he had 'encouraged' Craig, found him as an accomplice equally guilty for the deed. Christopher Craig, however, was only sixteen, and was too young for the death penalty; he was detained 'at Her Majesty's pleasure', and in fact served ten years before his release. Derek Bentley, on the other hand, was nineteen and not covered by the underage proviso, and so, in spite of the jury's recommendation for mercy, was sentenced to death. There were successive appeals, but these all failed, and Bentley was hanged. It was the only time in British criminal history that an accomplice was executed when the person directly responsible for the crime was allowed to live.

Derek Bentley was born in Blackfriars Road, Central London, in 1933. It was a difficult twin birth, and his younger twin died shortly afterwards. It was discovered that the elder twin was suffering from acute pneumonia, and in an age before antibiotics he was only saved by blood transfusions from his father. The family was working-class, and moved from one house to another in Central London, with the father working for a pharmacist as a pill-maker, then setting up his own little café nearby under the railway arches, and finally retraining as an electrician. Though poor and ignorant, they all considered themselves respectable and staunchly voted Conservative. Derek proved to be something of a mummy's boy, hated school and never learnt to read or write properly. From the age of five he began to have epileptic fits, often preceded by blinding headaches and vomiting. During the war he managed to avoid evacuation, and the family somehow struggled through the worst of the Blitz. After a brief spell 'in the country', as it seemed to them, that is in Edgware, in North London, in 1942, they went back to Hillingdon Street in Blackfriars during the V1 ('doodlebug') attacks and the attacks of the V2 rockets. During this renewal of the Blitz, the father worked in uniform full-time as an air raid warden in the ARP. They often slept on the platform at the Leicester Square tube station. At the end of the war, when Derek was twelve, the family went to live in Fairview Road, Norbury, midway between Streatham and Croydon and twelve miles from Central London.

Bentley got on little better at his secondary school, Norbury Manor, than he had at primary school, but his epileptic headaches got worse, and the phenobarbitone he took slowed him down and made him even dozier than he normally was. He became involved in two minor scrapes with the police, as the result of which he appeared at Croydon Magistrates' Court and was sent to Kingswood Approved School, near Bristol. The medical report[1] sent on to the school after him said rather severely that he was 'very backward intellectually and most of this is the result of congenital lack of intelligence.' All the same he was reasonably happy at Kingswood and was released a year early. He got work for himself in a menial capacity, but when he got his call-up papers for National Service at the beginning of 1952 he failed the intelligence test and was discharged from the forces.

At this time, Bentley fell in with a nicely-spoken middle-class boy, Norman Parsley, and with Christopher Craig. Craig was a Brylcreemed

---

1 He was examined at Guy's Hospital, which administered an electroencephalogram confirming his epilepsy, and later an intelligence test, which gave him an IQ of 66, a level rated as 'feeble-minded'.

youth of about fifteen or sixteen, who affected a bad American accent and fancied himself a gangster. He had a collection of upwards of forty handguns, some of which had been brought back from the war by dads and uncles, and a big collection of ammunition, much of which did not fit them. He used to swap guns with his mates, like cigarette cards. Not being very bright, Bentley was very easily led, and in November 1952 was persuaded by Craig to burgle the sweet warehouse in Croydon. It was in the course of this burglary that Craig used his gun to 'wing' one policeman and shoot another dead. The arrest and trial of the two, first in the Magistrates' Court and later in the Assizes before LCJ Goddard, led to their conviction and sentencing.

There was much that was unsatisfactory about the conduct of the trial. Some of these faults were perhaps not of critical importance, though they illustrated the attitudes of the police investigating the case. They claimed that Bentley was armed with a 'dagger-type' knife, though Bentley's parents claimed that this had been taken by police officers from their son's bedroom when they searched it. They also produced a suspiciously comprehensive statement signed several times by their son, though he could scarcely read and could not write at all. They also said he had made a number of verbal statements[2] which he always stoutly denied. When his parents saw him after he had been in the police cells, his face was bruised and swollen, but the warder stopped him from answering their question about his condition; later he said that he had been booted in the head when he bent to remove his shoelaces, and that had brought on another of his fits. In their report to the court, the police doctor denied that Bentley had fits, *or* that he was feeble-minded, *or* that he had been rejected for military service. In any case, the defence counsel was never shown the report.

But the most important failings in the prosecution relate to the way in which the case was conducted in court. LCJ Goddard, often called 'the hanging judge' by his numerous critics, was at his most meddlesome

2 These remarks were supposed to illustrate Bentley's complicity in the crime. He is said to have declared to police officers, 'He has a point 45 Colt and plenty of bloody ammunition, too', though normal people would have called it a 'Colt 45', and Bentley didn't know one gun from another; and, in the police car, 'I knew he had a gun but I *didn't think he'd use it.*' In fact, Bentley hardly ever spoke, especially to strangers, unless he was asked to do so.

and obstreperous; he constantly interrupted the defence counsel, making numerous uncalled for observations that detracted from his supposed judicial impartiality, and gave a grossly prejudiced summing-up before the jury retired.[3] He made much play with the remark that Bentley had addressed to Craig on the roof: 'Let him have it, Chris!' This, he maintained, was an incitement to him to fire the gun, not, as the defence made out, a request to hand over the weapon to the officers. The police said that the call was made *before* the shots were fired; Bentley said it was *afterwards* and that what he meant in any case was for Craig to surrender the gun before he did any further damage with it. He never called him 'Chris', he pointed out, but always, as Craig wished, 'Kid' or 'Kiddo'.

It was commonly believed that in the light of the jury's recommendation to mercy, Bentley would be reprieved on appeal, but he was not. The Court of Appeal turned him down; the Conservative Attorney-General, Sir Lionel Heald, refused the application to appeal to the House of Lords; and, in spite of two petitions containing about 150,000 signatures, the Home Secretary, Sir David Maxwell-Fyfe denied him a reprieve. The Speaker of the House of Commons refused to table a critical motion from Sydney Silverman dissenting from the Home Secretary's decision. Bentley's mother even wrote to the queen to appeal for her help, receiving only a polite acknowledgment in reply from Sandringham. Consequently on January 28th, Bentley was hanged.

Even posthumous justice was denied to Bentley. In 1990, after the deaths of both his mother and his father, a dossier of new evidence compiled by Bentley's sister was presented to the then Conservative Home Secretary, Kenneth Clarke, by the television producers of an ITV documentary on the case; and in 1991 another dossier, including the evidence of Christopher Craig himself. Both were rejected. It was only in 1993, when three judges in the high Court ruled that Clarke's rejection was 'flawed in law' that the new Home Secretary, Michael Howard, finally proffered a pardon. However, it was not a full pardon. It was merely an acknowledgment that Bentley should not have been hanged, an acknowledgment as hollow as the jury's recommendation to mercy in 1953.

---

3 In April 1947, when a Labour motion to abolish capital punishment had been passed in the Commons and sent up to the lords, Lord Goddard had used all his eloquence to retain both hanging and birching.

Was the 10 Rillington Place affair another official cover-up?

One of the most scandalous episodes in modern legal history took place in 1950, when a man, Timothy Evans, was unjustly convicted and hanged for murders committed by another, John Christie. The only creditable thing that can be said about this deplorable affair is that the heart-searching it generated contributed substantially towards the abolition of capital punishment in Britain in the late 1960s.

John Reginald Halliday Christie was born in 1898 and was brought up in Halifax. He was a clever boy at school, but terrified of his father, a harsh Victorian *paterfamilias,* and somewhat spoiled by his mother and his four sisters. Throughout his life he remained insecure with women he could not dominate, and submissive to men he thought were stronger than him. In 1916 he enlisted in the army, became a signaller in the 52nd Notts and Derby Regiment (the 'Sherwood Foresters') and was drafted to France in early 1918, where he suffered injury from an exploding mustard gas-shell which gave him gas-poisoning for a few weeks and shell shock thereafter, which took away his voice whenever he was stressed; disabilities which he exploited for the remainder of his life. Medically, however, his injuries were not serious, and his final war pension was only for 7/6d a week, and ceased altogether after eighteen months. He returned to civilian life in Halifax after his military discharge and married the daughter of a local family, Ethel Waddington, whom he alternately patronized and bullied. He served two short prison sentences before he left his wife with her relations in Sheffield in 1924 and moved to London to try his luck there. He had a variety of jobs and served two further short terms of imprisonment before asking her to rejoin him in the Notting Hill area. Here the couple eventually went to live in Rillington Place in 1938, in a rather poky three-storeyed end-of-terrace villa, adjoining what had been Bartlett's Iron Foundry. Ethel and he occupied the ground floor; there was a tenant on the first floor, but the top-floor flat was empty.

From 1939 until the New Year of 1944 Christie became a special constable, concealing his criminal record when he applied for the appointment, so getting back once more into uniform and gaining the status and authority he thought was due to him. The Jekyll and Hyde aspects of his character, however, became increasingly pronounced: on the one hand he was the precisely-spoken bourgeois model of respectability, but on the other he led another life in which he exercised his authority, circulating in seedy pubs and mixing with lower-class people. He also began to manifest unfortunate tendencies towards necrophilia. Taking advantage of one of Ethel's occasional visits to Sheffield, he took home a lonely Austrian student nurse called Ruth Fuerst, stripped and strangled her, had sex with her corpse, then buried her under the floorboards just in time before his wife returned home. Next day, when his wife went to work, he removed the body from the bedroom and put her in the washhouse while he dug a shallow grave in the back garden; then, when it got dark, he excused himself to his wife, saying he was going to the lavatory outside, and buried the body hastily close to the garden wall – too hastily, as it turned out, since he turned up her skull some months later while digging and had to dispose of it in a hurry. In early 1944 he decided to leave the police force and took up civilian employment in Acton, where he met Muriel Eady, a pleasant, rather plump dark-haired girl and a fellow employee in the factory. He saw her for several months, and in the autumn of 1944, again profiting from Ethel's absence in Sheffield, he invited her to his house on the pretext of helping her cure the catarrh she complained of by a special 'inhalation device' – in reality a rubber pipe connected to the gas supply – then gassed and strangled her, violated her corpse as he had Ruth Fuerst's and finally buried her in another grave alongside the first in the back garden. Though both girls were reported missing, the police do not seem to have been very assiduous in their search for them; this was, after all, a time when hundreds of persons disappeared because of flying bombs, and the civilian authorities had a lot of other important things to do.

All this occurred while a Mr Kitchener, an elderly gentleman who was somewhat deaf and had increasing trouble with his eyesight, occupied the first-floor rooms. The top-floor flat, a small bed-sitting room and an even smaller bedroom, was empty, until in 1948 a new couple of tenants moved in. They were Timothy Evans and his pregnant wife, Beryl.

Timothy John Evans was a Welshman, born in Merthyr in 1924, half-crippled with a tubercular leg occasioned by a childhood accident, and mentally very backward (he could hardly read or write and had an IQ of 68 in comparison with Christie's 126). In spite of what seemed to be an innate tendency to romance and exaggerate, Evans had a likeable personality. He and his wife, in spite of occasional quarrels, were genuinely fond of each other. In October 1948 Beryl had a baby daughter, Geraldine, and in the following autumn found herself pregnant again. She was dismayed at the prospect of the four of them living in two tiny rooms, and though her husband opposed the idea, began to think how she could obtain an abortion – at that time very much frowned upon – before her pregnancy became too advanced. It seemed natural to consult Christie on the subject, not least because he claimed some familiarity with medical procedures (indeed, he was known to some of his acquaintances as 'the Doc' and said he had once started training for a medical career). Christie felt his old necrophiliac urges begin to stir, and, profiting from Mr Kitchener's absence from the house for five weeks (he was in hospital for an eye operation), blithely volunteered to perform the abortion himself. Unfortunately this was the very time at which the local Council decided to heed Christie's frequent complaints and undertake repairs to the house, and sent round three men for the purpose in the first fortnight in November 1949. Though the three men they sent were in and out of the house regularly, renewing floorboards, plastering and mending the roof of the WC, their presence seems to have assisted rather than discouraged Christie in his real intention of forcing himself on the unfortunate Beryl to kill her and then rape her. This he duly did, although things did not go exactly according to plan. The gas was slow to work and Beryl panicked, so that there was a struggle and Christie hit her about the head before strangling her; then he had intercourse with her body and afterwards covered it with a quilt. When Evans returned home Christie told him that things had not gone according to plan and that Beryl had died during the abortion operation, and that he would 'dispose' of the body 'by putting it down the drains.' He had smeared blood round her pubic regions from her head wounds. Evans appeared not to notice these, any more than he noticed the ligature marks round her neck. He advised Evans to say nothing about it, since the police were bound to think that he had murdered his wife in the course of one of their quarrels. Instead he suggested that Evans say that Beryl had gone to stay with her father in Brighton. He promised to take little Geraldine to be looked after to a childless couple he knew in East Acton. Evans accepted Christie's instructions unquestioningly and did exactly as he was told. Ethel, meanwhile, showed little interest in what was going on, and repeated whatever her husband told her to say.

Christie later that day attempted to lug the dead body downstairs to Mr Kitchener's flat, but the corpse was heavy and unwieldy and he ricked his back, finally being forced to take the risk of asking Evans to give him a hand. There Beryl remained until after Evans had left Paddington *en route* for Wales, and the workmen had packed up and gone. Then Christie was able to hide the corpse in the outside washhouse behind some floorboards which the last of the men had given him when he quit the premises. About this time he disencumbered himself of little Geraldine by strangling her, too, and putting her body with her mother's.

At Merthyr Vale, where he was staying with his relatives, Evans continued to reproach himself for what had happened to Beryl, especially for taking off her wedding ring when she lay dead and selling it for a trifle of money. He was at first happy about Geraldine, since he thought she was being well looked after, but when it sank in that he had no real idea where she was he began to worry and even returned briefly to London to ask Christie about her, but was smartly brushed off and returned to Wales with no answers to his questions. After several weeks Beryl's friends and relatives in London became more insistent in their enquiries about her whereabouts, so in December, at the end of his tether, he went to the police in Merthyr and made a statement in which he confessed to 'disposing of' (Christie's phrase) his wife by putting her 'down the drains'. He tried to pretend that he had found his wife dead after she had taken abortion-inducing pills which a man he did not know had given to him in a transport café outside London. His knowledge of surgical procedures was clearly nil, and the rest of his story was received with some scepticism. All the same, the London police visited Rillington Place, where, when three of them had managed to lift the cast-iron manhole cover in front of the house, they found the drain quite empty. Evans now realized that Christie must have been lying to him and decided he was not going to try to shield him any further. He therefore made a second statement to the Merthyr police in which he told the true story of the attempted abortion and Christie's part in it. The London police interviewed Christie, who made a great play with being a former policeman himself. He denied everything, saying he was inclined to think that Evans was 'a bit mental' and that he had done away with his wife himself. By this time, the London police had searched No. 10 Rillington Place but found nothing. They did not look into the washhouse where the bodies were, nor did they notice that Christie was using Muriel Eady's thigh-bone to prop up his garden fence. It was only at the second search some days later that they discovered the bodies of Beryl and little Geraldine hidden in the washhouse behind a stack of old floorboards. Evans was brought back from Wales to Notting Hill police station and confronted with the double murder.

Evans was thunderstruck. This was the first he had heard that the little girl was dead. He went on to make two confessions: the first, very bold, within an hour of his return to London, and the second after a protracted session of questioning that lasted much of the same night, conducted by Inspector Black and Chief Inspector Jennings. Partly by bullying, partly by their power of suggestion, and partly because Evans was not very bright and seemed willing to agree to anything, they obtained from him a very detailed statement of the murders fitting in with their own version of events (but nevertheless inaccurate in a number of vital respects which were never referred to at Evans's trial – for example, the boards he said he hid the bodies behind in the washhouse were not there until several days *after* Evans had left for Wales, and the evidence of the workmen had afterwards to be doctored to show that they were). The defence team appointed for Evans's case seem to have been as gullible as the police were inefficient. Vital inconsistencies in the prosecution evidence were glossed over in the preliminary hearings in the Magistrates Court – it was only Christie's long familiarity with police procedures that enabled him to wriggle out of the question how it was that two dead bodies could have lain in his washhouse for nearly a month *without his noticing them*. Nevertheless in January 1950 he was indicted at the Old Bailey before Mr Justice Lewis, an experienced but critically ailing judge who died only days after the case was concluded.

Evans's case lasted several days. The prosecuting counsel, Christmas Humphreys, QC, was devastatingly logical and ruthless in pointing out the 'lies' which Evans had told (in spite of the fact that Evans's testimony – though he had not seen his earlier police statement and in any case could not read it – was remarkably consistent with the statement he had given at Notting Hill); while the defending counsel, Malcolm Morris, QC, floundered in the face of the conflicting evidence and was prevented from posing several key questions by obstruction from the bench. Evans, completely flummoxed by counsels' unfamiliar vocabulary, created a poor impression and frequently contradicted himself; Christie, on the other hand, created a good one, milking the story of his war and police service for all it was worth, and declaring that it was quite impossible for him to have carried Beryl downstairs as Evans alleged because of the acute fibrositis in his back (there was some truth in this – it was carrying the corpse downstairs that had *given* him a bad back!). Mr Justice Lewis was perhaps inattentive because of his illness, and consistently got hold of the wrong end of the stick. Clearly nobody in court was prepared to accept Evans's innocence, and the judge's final summing-up was extremely unfavourable to the defendant. The jury took forty minutes to find Evans guilty as charged, and Mr Justice Lewis donned the black cap and condemned him to hang.

Evans went meekly to the condemned cell at Pentonville, though he consistently continued thereafter to protest his innocence of either crime. Those in charge of his care marvelled at his equanimity and seemed disposed to believe his story that 'Christie done it'; his family certainly did – they always knew when he was telling the truth because then he looked them straight in the face, and always added the coded phrase, 'I bet you'. His appeal, however, failed, and this news and the news of Chuter Ede's failure to grant him a reprieve was received with resignation. Timothy Evans was hanged at the beginning of March 1950.

The conclusion of the case failed to bring any peace of mind to Christie, who was now showing signs of mental stress as well as complaining of diarrhoea, sleeplessness, fibrositis and catarrh. His condition was aggravated by his distaste for the number of black faces he saw around him; there were a large number of West Indian immigrants in Notting Hill, and one of them, a Jamaican, had even bought the house where Christie lived. For a spell he underwent treatment in hospital. His old trouble, however, was creeping up on him again and, hemmed in as he was, he saw no prospect of gratifying his necrophilia. Just before

Christmas 1952, he managed at least to get Ethel out of the way by strangling her in bed and burying her under the floorboards in the front room. This occasioned him some embarrassment in explaining to her relatives why Ethel did not write to them at Christmas, but it left him a good deal more free time afterwards to get on with his murderous hobbies. As a result, in the course of 1953, he murdered three other women in quick succession. The garden was getting pretty full by now, and Ethel was buried under the front room floor. So he turned to a deep cubby-hole or alcove that ran from the kitchen behind the washhouse and started to fill this up with dead bodies. The first was Kathleen Maloney, an amateur prostitute, whom he met in a local pub. He strangled her, stripped her, had intercourse with her dead body and then wrapped her in a blanket, and laid her on her back at the far end of the alcove with her legs vertically up the wall. The next was Rita Nelson, an unmarried women three months pregnant whom he offered to abort, and who suffered the same fate as Beryl Evans, her body, when he had finished with it, being stowed alongside Maloney. The last of the three was Hectorina Maclellan, to whom he first offered accommodation and then, when he got her to Rillington Place, killed her, raped her and put her into the alcove, this time in a sitting position (the alcove was about full now), kept upright by hooking her brassiere to the blanket round Maloney's legs. Finally he papered over the alcove door and concealed it by moving a cupboard in front of it. Eventually in March 1953 he sublet the house to a family called Reilly and moved out, leaving the Reillys the possessors of six dead bodies hidden in and around the premises.

The landlord, a Mr Brown, was furious when he discovered the house had been sublet and promptly turned the Reillys out, at the same time giving permission for the tenant of the top-floor flat (another Mr Brown) to use the kitchen. He set about cleaning the place out, trying to locate and remedy the very nasty smell pervading the lower floor. Tapping what he thought was the rear wall of the kitchen he found that it was hollow, and in a few minutes, shining his torch inside, he saw partly-clad female bodies in various stages of decomposition. The police eventually carried out a real search of the house and garden, and all six corpses were brought to light. The sensational news drove everything else from the headlines.

Christie wandered anonymously all over London until he was eventually arrested on Putney Bridge at the end of March 1953.

He was examined both by police officials and by qualified psychiatrists over an extended period; all of them were repelled by his creepy self-righteousness, his precise way of speaking and his puritanical insistence that none of this was his fault. Some of the women, like Fuerst, Maloney, Nelson and Maclellan, he accused of behaving provocatively and indecently, demanding he have sex with them; thus he shifted the blame from himself to them. The others died as a result of his having tried to give them the help they were asking for; Muriel Eady because he was trying to ease her catarrh, Beryl Evans because he was trying to dispose of her unwanted baby, and his own wife who was 'depressed and frightened' because of the 'large number of blacks in the house', so that in a way their deaths were unfortunate accidents. He had no explanation for the fact that he kept in an old tobacco tin samples of the pubic hair he had pulled from their dead bodies; nor did he ever confess to the murder of baby Geraldine (which even he saw there could be no possible justification for) – though he came close to it at one point in his examination. The line he usually took was that he could not remember, and he took to saying to those questioning him: 'You say I did so, so I suppose I must have.' He was always censorious on moral matters and at no time showed any remorse or accepted any responsibility for his actions.

Christie was tried in June 1953 in the same court as had been used for Evans, and like him was imprisoned in the same prison. His case lasted four days, during which time he was regarded as a monster, capable of the most revolting perversions; most of those in court could hardly bring themselves to look at him. He was found guilty and condemned, lodged in the same condemned cell as Evans, and in July 1953 was hanged by the same hangman.

Public indignation ran so high at police bungling, judicial incompetence and the abominable possibility of an innocent man being hanged in error that the Conservative Home Secretary set up an official Enquiry to examine the verdict in the Evans case, so to allay public disquiet. Unfortunately the Report of this Enquiry by Scott Henderson, QC, bore all the hallmarks of a whitewash. It completely sustained the verdict on Evans, and was at least partly intended to restore public faith in the absolute infallibility of the judicial system. Nonetheless, it was conducted in haste, made only a superficial examination of the evidence, dismissed anything not in line with the original verdict, and left until it was too late submissions from those who had real contributions to make towards a genuine re-evaluation of the case. The furore this Report provoked in Parliament was so long and persistent that Scott Henderson was obliged to produce a Supplementary Report at the end of August 1953, but this said much the same as the original, and hence received no better a reception. In refusing to admit even the remotest possibility of error in the Evans verdict (unlike Chuter Ede – now of course out of office – who conceded regretfully that he had been wrong not to grant a reprieve) it was full of assumptions and unanswered questions, and seemed chiefly concerned to defend the findings of the first Enquiry. The public simply refused to swallow the monstrous coincidence of two quite separate murderers operating according to identical methods from the *same single property* in London, or to go on believing that Evans had really committed the crime he had been hanged for. The possibility of judicial error, and in particular *this case*, was one of the main arguments employed by those in favour of abolishing the death penalty, so that Parliament voted for the abolition of hanging in October 1965 and finally made this abolition permanent in December 1969.

Was the hanging of Ruth Ellis justified?

Ruth Ellis was in 1955 the last woman to be hanged in Britain. Her execution, for murder, hotly debated at the time not only for its lack of mercy but also for its conspicuous lack of justice, was passed through the courts and hurried on by the political authorities for fear of encouraging the wider debate on the whole question of the appropriateness of the death penalty. As the law stood at the time, her condemnation was correct; but the circumstances of her conviction were so tragic and so scandalous that in the minds of the public they reflected more on the state of the criminal law than they did on the guilt of the accused.

On the evening of Easter Sunday 1955 Ruth Ellis, a glamorous nightclub hostess, waylaid her lover in a London street, shot him as he was about to get into his car, and then, as he lay at her feet, emptied all the remaining five chambers of her revolver into his body, inflicting multiple injuries and killing him almost immediately. Her victim was the public-school educated David Blakeley, man-about-town and rather unsuccessful driver of racing cars, indulged by his wealthy parents and continuing as a racing driver even though he never won a race. He had been her lover for eighteen months in a squalid and tempestuous affair. After her arrest, the solicitor she chose was John Bickford, middle-aged and undistinguished, who recommended for her defence the well-known criminal lawyer Melford Stephenson, QC, and as his junior the man who later became Lord Rawlinson and Attorney General. The leader for the prosecution was the talented and sometimes unscrupulous Christmas Humphreys, QC, who had scored a string of successes in a large number of well-publicized criminal cases. When her counsel met Ruth Ellis before the trial, they found her shabby and unkempt. In prison she lacked the bleach which kept her a stunning platinum blonde, so her hair had become pale brown and patchy. Worse still she seemed depressed and defeatist. She had done wrong, she felt, and wanted to be hanged so that she could 'rejoin David'. She had committed murder, the ultimate crime, and believed she *should* hang – it was a matter of 'an eye for an eye', she said. With difficulty she was prevailed upon to plead not guilty, not because there seemed to be much chance of an acquittal, but chiefly so that her whole story could be brought out in court.

She came up at the Old Bailey towards the end of June, before Mr Justice Havers, not known as a 'hanging judge', and with a jury of ten men and two women. The defence proposed to concentrate on the way the victim had treated her, as extenuation of her behaviour. Humphreys' approach was simpler. He simply asked Ruth Ellis if she had shot David Blakeley, and when she said 'yes', he asked her if she meant to kill him. Again she said 'yes'. At this point the judge stopped the trial, sent out the jury and interviewed both counsel *in camera,* reminding them that the penalty the law prescribed for murder was death, and that the earlier conduct of the victim was irrelevant to the case. He therefore ruled that evidence of provocation was not admissible. The defence team were effectively at a loss, Rawlinson being forced to admit that he could not ask the questions he had planned without inviting the jury to ignore the judge's ruling. The trial was over in 1½ days, and the jury took just 14 minutes to find the prisoner guilty. Not having heard of the provocation the accused had suffered, they made no recommendation for mercy. The judge put on his black cap, and pronounced sentence of death. In the light of the law at the time, this was quite proper.

Today, the defence of provocation could, and would, be brought in court. Ruth Ellis might well have escaped conviction. Even if the jury had produced a guilty verdict it would have recommended mercy, and the judge would have taken this into account in the light of today's much more flexible sentences. But at that time there was no such latitude either in the conduct of the case or in the sentence imposed.

Behind the hard and brittle surface of Ruth Ellis as a club 'hostess' lay a tragic personal story. She came from a needy South London family, her father an itinerant musician forced by the decline of the music-halls to take poorly-paid menial work. The family settled in Brixton in the early 1930s. Her mother was a staunch Roman Catholic forced by her circumstances into periodic fits of depression. Ruth had three sisters and two brothers. During protracted spells of unemployment, her father took out his frustration on his children, knocking them about and abusing at least two of the girls, Ruth and her elder sister Muriel. The elder girl claimed that he began abusing her sexually at the age of ten, when he forced her to sleep with him and submit to his attentions. Muriel eventually became pregnant at the age of fourteen, and produced his baby. Although her mother knew that Muriel had not been associating with other males, she refused to believe that it was her husband who was the father of her daughter's child. After this episode he left Muriel alone, but transferred his attentions to Ruth, who was forced in the same way to sleep with her father.

At the outbreak of the war, Ruth was a teenager and beginning to grow up. She enjoyed going out dancing with Allied troops in London. By the time the war ended she was seventeen and going steady with a Canadian serviceman, and in due course bore him an illegitimate son, André. When he returned to Canada after the war he promised to return to fetch her, but he never did, and later she learnt that he was a married man with three children. She and Muriel went to work for £2 a week in the local Oxo factory, but this soon palled for Ruth, and she moved on to do waitressing in Lyons' teashops in the West End. She was already a smart and personable young woman with startlingly peroxided blonde hair. Ruth was soon invited to pose for what were euphemistically called 'glamour photos', and went to work as a hostess in a sex club, serving drinks, chatting with the clients, and, at £20 a week (nearly ten times what she had been earning before, and the height of luxury), steadily beginning the slow slide into what effectively was prostitution. In the club she met and fell for George Ellis, a successful dentist. The two were married, but he soon showed himself too fond of drink and when he came home was often violent with her. Ellis tried to counter his addiction by taking treatment at a local centre for alcoholism, but Ruth thought his periods of absence meant he was having affairs with other women, and like her mother began to suffer from fits of depression. Hence she was prescribed the anti-depressants which she took for the rest of her life. Soon afterwards she decided to leave him.

In August 1953 she resumed her career as a hostess in the Cavell's *Little Club* in London's clubland. It was here she first met and fell for David Blakeley who showed himself chiefly interested in women, drink and racing cars. He moved into her flat 'above the shop' and entered into a deeply passionate affair with her. He was good-looking but with a weak, selfish character and something of a cry-baby. The two would quarrel violently, separate, and then in floods of tears be reconciled, with Blakeley buying her gifts and promising not to quarrel again. Bystanders soon came to the view that Blakeley really thought little of Ruth and was merely using her for the sexual satisfaction she gave him.

In February 1955 she met at the club Desmond Cussens, the other man in her life. He took her part and became increasingly smitten with her. In June, whilst Blakeley was away racing at Le Mans, the two became lovers. Cussens looked, after her: he paid her son's school fees, and when Ruth was forced to move he paid for her new flat. When Blakeley found out, he was furious and quarrels thereafter became more frequent and more vicious. Ruth became pregnant again in March, but during a particularly violent quarrel, Blakeley punched her in the stomach, the baby died and she miscarried. Showing no remorse he walked out on her, this time going to lodge with Carol and Antony Findlater in Hampstead. She was a former lover of Blakeley's, he Blakeley's mechanic at the garage. Blakeley eventually sent Ruth a card, the two were reconciled and he promised to come back to spend Easter with her. However he did not show up, and Cussens offered his help in pursuing him. On Easter Sunday, she went round to the house in Hampstead, knocked repeatedly on the door, and when she got no response began to bang on his car parked outside, doing some minor damage to the paintwork. Findlater appeared, told her to leave, and then the police arrived and moved Ruth away. Later that evening, about 7.30, Cussens drove her round there again, and this time she waylaid Blakeley as he left the house, shot him and killed him.

At her trial, Cussens was not even questioned about Blakeley's treatment of the accused, nor was any attention paid to where Ruth Ellis got the gun. The psychiatrist called to give evidence on her mental state was unhelpful and woolly in his testimony, and alienated the sympathies of the judge. Ellis seemed to go out of her way to incriminate herself, and appeared almost relieved when sentence was passed on her. Afterwards, in Holloway, John Bickford her solicitor could not persuade her to appeal, and even after a visit from George Rogers, an MP and a pioneer in advocating the abolition of the death penalty, he found it hard to get her to change her mind. For her son's sake she eventually consented to appeal, but Bickford so fumbled her case that in a fit of irritation she sacked him, choosing in his place the youthful Victor Mishcon, at this time embarking on his distinguished legal career. He tried to arrange an appeal, and, when this failed, to apply for a reprieve.

The Home Secretary at the time was Major Gwilym Lloyd-George, mediocre son of the former great Prime Minister. He was timid and hesitant, afraid to act too decisively for fear of precipitating a full-scale debate on the future of the death penalty. It was his view that if Ruth Ellis were reprieved it would be difficult ever again to hang a woman, or perhaps anybody. At first she refused to give her full co-operation to Victor Mishcon, not seeming to care whether she got a reprieve or not. In particular she would not say where she had obtained the gun. Only later she broke down and confessed, as Mishcon suspected, that it had been given to her by Desmond Cussens, and that, even if he had not actually incited the murder, he was her accomplice not only during, but before, the crime. The two had sat together for the whole of the afternoon in question, commiserating with each other and drinking Pernod, until eventually he drove her to Hampstead later that evening, when the murder took place. She took the view that the murder was her responsibility alone; she was going to hang for it, and she did not wish that Cussens should have to go to prison too. Nevertheless, Mishcon decided to ask for a stay of execution until Cussens should have been examined, and the extent of his complicity revealed. Time, however, was getting short. Unusually, Ruth Ellis's words in her interview with her solicitor in Holloway were disputed – on the grounds that a female warder present during the interview had made a statement to the police which did not fully tally with Mishcon's own notes on it. When the police decided to act they did so half-heartedly, looking for Cussens for a couple of days to question him, and then giving up. So Mishcon did not apply to the Home Secretary until literally the day before the execution was scheduled. Unfortunately, when he did, Lloyd George was at the races and could not be contacted. Home Office civil servants asserted that even if he had been contacted it would have made no difference to his decision: when very late the application was referred to him, he simply refused to grant a reprieve.

So Ruth Ellis was hanged, and the whole sorry story reached its seemingly inevitable conclusion. The administrative bungling behind it did not become public knowledge until much later; when it did, it reinforced the indignation many felt that she should have suffered death in such questionable circumstances. Certainly, at the time, the public expressed its deep shock and horror at the scandal of her execution, and the case helped to shock the nation in the direction of the final abolition of the death penalty.

Tony Martin and the Norfolk farmhouse shootings

In August 1999, after the election of Blair's New Labour Party to government in 1997, with its pledges to be 'tough on crime and tough on the causes of crime', Tony Martin, a Norfolk bachelor in his middle 50s, disturbed two intruders in his lonely farmhouse during the night. He came downstairs with a loaded shotgun and wounded one by peppering him in the legs, and shot the other, a sixteen-year-old youth, in the back as he fled, and killed him. In April 2000, he was tried in the Norwich Crown Court before a local jury of six men and six women, convicted of murder and sentenced to prison for life.

The isolated and dilapidated farmhouse, appropriately named 'Bleak House', was situated in the Norfolk Fens in a remote area at Emneth Hungate, a village of about 200 people about three miles from Wisbech. The farmhouse was originally a red-brick Victorian structure, but was rambling and run-down, full of 'improvements' which had been begun but never finished, and was now overgrown with foliage and in a poor state of repair. The farm itself, originally a smallholding, had been added to over the years, so that now it extended to about 350 acres. Its owner, Martin, was a solitary figure. He had quarrelled with his brother Robin Martin in 1976, who subsequently went to live in Spain, and the two had not spoken since; but he often visited his mother, who lived in Elm, a few miles down the road.

Martin felt cut off, living alone, and had been robbed or burgled on no fewer than ten previous occasions. He lived alone in a ramshackle house, with belligerent views on his day-to-day security and the need to protect his property. He was thought by the locals to be something of a 'nutter'. He often said he was seriously upset by police inability or unwillingness to give him the protection he needed. Police patrols were sporadic and infrequent; if police were summoned, they were slow to arrive or else failed to arrive at all; and they did not seem very interested in recovering his property. Sometimes he could not even get them to come to the telephone, and had to make do with talking to the operator at the station, a woman who was only a civilian, who duly listed what was missing and passed it on to the officers. The last time this happened before the fatal day, in May 1997, he had been so infuriated at her nonchalance that he had threatened, 'Look, if they come back, I'll blow their heads off!' So he set about preparing himself to defend his property, as he thought it right to do. He secured another gun (though he carelessly neglected to license it) so that he had several, one a pump-action shotgun that could take up to six cartridges without reloading, which he kept under his bed, the other a more conventional double-barrelled shotgun, which he kept in an outhouse. He also owned a single-barrel shotgun and a .22 rifle. He converted outlying buildings into look-out posts, with ladders up to the roofs, installed steel bars at the windows, strengthened the doors, and booby-trapped his staircase by removing the treads at the top and at the bottom of the stairs. Not having a wife to object to his behaviour, he even took to sleeping in his clothes, with his boots still on, so as to be ready for any encounter with burglars. He also kept three fierce Rottweilers as guard dogs roaming about the place for further protection.

The cause of concern for the locals was the marauding activities of numbers of itinerant workers who drifted from area to area seeking seasonal work. They were often useful in lifting potatoes in the autumn, or in strawberry-picking in the summer, which kept the local jam factory going in Wisbech, a town of some 12,000 people. But they plagued the Fenland with their lawlessness and their pilfering, and came to be resented and were referred to as gypsies,[1] in much the same way as the 'travellers' were in other rural areas.

---

[1] The true Romany Gypsies (with a capital G) were a distinct, highly principled ethnic group who had started their move westwards from Egypt and the Balkans in the fifteenth century. Their language has some affinities with Punjabi, and they may have originated in India. But some had intermarried with the locals and were referred to as 'diddies' (the word 'didicoi' in Romany meant 'half-caste'). They were further diluted by Irish elements, some descended from the nineteenth-century 'navvies' who had built the railways. Some had settled, but many were still itinerant and were constantly being moved on from one campsite to another by timorous local authorities. Martin used a variety of abusive words to describe them, including the term 'pykies'.

The ringleader of the trio who set out to burgle Bleak House on that August night was Brendan Fearon, who had settled in Newark, over seventy miles from Wisbech, and who had appeared in court thirty-five times for a variety of offences, and had served several jail sentences, though he was still only thirty. He arranged with Darren Bark, another traveller, aged thirty-four with fifty-two court appearances to his name, for him to serve as getaway driver in his white Ford Granada. On their way they picked up the youth, sixteen-year-old Fred Barras, expelled from school at the age of thirteen, and sentenced to a term in a young offenders' institution at fifteen, and already with twenty-eight court appearances on his record. He said he picked him up 'to keep him out of trouble', although how taking him on a burglary expedition was going to keep him out of trouble he never quite explained. Outside Newark, in a surreal incident, they were stopped by a traffic policeman who asked to see Bark's driving documents, his licence and insurance, none of which he had. In the car boot were the tools of his trade, screwdrivers, various hammers, an iron bar, a jemmy and three empty hold-alls for the loot; but these passed over unnoticed and the policeman merely gave the driver a form to fill in, together with a request to produce his documents at a time convenient to him. They arrived outside the farm at half-past nine. Fearon and Barras got out of the car, leaving Bark to park the car out of sight in a nearby lane. He did so, and waited. Later he heard shots and promptly made off, leaving the two burglars to their fate. Concerned about his mates' fate, he returned next day to the scene, where the police arrested him.

About the same time, Martin, having bid farewell to his mother in Elm shortly before, went upstairs to bed and promptly went to sleep without bothering to undress. At about ten o'clock, however, he was disturbed by sounds of someone moving about downstairs. He froze apprehensively, then quietly took his gun, loaded it, and went to the head of the stairs, where he cautiously started to descend. He could hear the intruders whispering and the occasional clink as they dropped one of his antiques into their bag. He had no idea how many of them there were, and he was shaking with fear. One of the stairs squeaked as he crept downstairs, and the burglars turned and shone their torches on him as he stood over them. He was blinded by the sudden light, and fired low, several times, from the hip. They panicked. They tore out the window frame they had come in by as they left, the older man bleeding profusely from the upper leg, the younger boy whimpering, 'He's got me!' and calling for his mother. Both made it outside, but Barras died immediately afterwards on the long grass outside from a two-inch hole blown in his lower back. Fearon made his way to the door of Martin's nearest neighbour about half a mile away, and asked for a drink of water. The neighbours were nervous about admitting him and, ringing the police, were told to leave him outside and have nothing to do with him. Fearon was directed to an outside tap, but collapsed from shock and loss of blood, and the two neighbours were bold enough to ignore police instructions and go to his assistance. He was bleeding profusely, and asked for a blanket because he felt cold. In the meantime, Martin was unaware whether he had hit the burglars or not. He thought there had been three of them. He said, 'They just dropped their rucksacks and ran. I don't know whether I hit anybody.' It was not until 2.40 the following afternoon that Barras's body was found by the police, lying dead only a few yards from the house.

Martin, meanwhile, had left his gun in the outside lavatory at his mother's house, had gone to a hotel in Wisbech with whose proprietress he was acquainted, and had spent the night there. Armed police came to arrest him the following morning just after 6am. They also went to Bleak House to search it, but were kept at bay by the Rottweilers, so that it was not until nearly three o'clock in the afternoon, when a local farmer had rounded up the dogs, that Barras's body was found. Martin was kept in custody, and later transferred to a 'safe house', as much in the interests of protecting him from traveller retaliation as of detaining him.

In April Martin was charged in court with the murder of Fred Barras, the attempted murder of Brendon Fearon, or of wounding him, and of possessing a firearm with intent to injure life. To these four charges he pleaded 'Not Guilty'. To a fifth charge, of possessing a Winchester pump-action shotgun without a firearms certificate, he pleaded 'Guilty'. The trial lasted for upwards of a week, and included a full visit by the judge and jury to the farm. When they retired, the jury found Martin not guilty of attempting to murder Fearon, not guilty of possessing firearms 'with intent to endanger life', but after a further ten-hour retirement, found him guilty by a majority verdict of 10–2 of the other two charges, of 'wounding Fearon with intent to do him bodily harm', and of murdering Fred Barras. As the result, Martin was sentenced by Mr Justice Owen to imprisonment for life (the same sentence as was given to the Yorkshire Ripper), and was sent to Bullingham Prison, Bicester.

The trial was properly conducted, though criticism was made of various other features of the case. Members of the jury felt intimidated in the conduct of the case; a number of them complained of the hostile stares in court of members of the travelling community, who they claimed were attempting to 'put the evil eye' on them; some afterwards said they had received threatening mail from them during the trial. Police believed that keeping Martin in a 'safe house' had probably saved his life, and admitted that they had discovered that someone had offered £60,000 to have Martin killed. It might have been better to transfer the case, say, to the Old Bailey, rather than leave it in Norwich. The case certainly led to widespread press[2] and public interest in the issues it raised, most of it supportive of Martin's case. Some could not understand how the same jury could find Martin not guilty of attempting to murder Fearon, but guilty of murdering Barras, when the two were shot in the same way and at the same time. Many were outraged by the sentence and agreed with Martin's comment that, 'Out there you are on your own. The police are a waste of time.' Anthony Bosanquet, of the Country Landowners' Association summed up the same feeling more tactfully when he said: 'Effective policing cannot be carried out from a distant urban station. Extra resources must be given to rural areas so that people do not have to live in fear.'

Political leaders also found themselves taking sides over the issue. The leader of the Opposition, William Hague, said that a future Conservative government would re-balance the justice system, 'with a strong presumption that the state will be on the side of people who protect their homes against criminals.' Many thought it was contrary to the principles of 'natural justice' that people like Martin should be penalised while judges bent over backwards to be fair to criminals. Politicians of both main parties promised to try to define the principle of 'reasonable force' that could be used against offenders in such cases. The home

---

2 *The Sun, The News of the World, The Mirror* and *The Mail on Sunday* supported Martin and thought he should not have been jailed; *The Guardian* also gave general support to his cause; *The Times* was generally in favour, though one of their writers thought Martin was a 'deeply unpleasant man'. Only *The Scotsman* supported the sentence, calling Martin 'murderously obsessive'; and asserting in face of all the evidence that 'he has few soulmates in many of Britain's rural areas.'

Secretary, Jack Straw, attempted to do this, but the new formula was not much better than the old one; if anything it made reasonable self-defence more problematic than it had been before. The feeling grew up that the state was more concerned with protecting its own monopoly of law enforcement than protecting its own citizens.

Meanwhile Martin, who had been transferred to high-security Gartree Prison, Leicester, changed his legal team in 2001 to make an appeal against his conviction. Justice Owen, the trial judge, and LCJ Lord Woolf had already defined his life sentence as one of eight or nine years, but now, on appeal, his sentence was reduced in 2002 to one of five years on a manslaughter charge. There was general public satisfaction that the judiciary had at last seen sense. Martin was released from prison at the end of July 2003, having served two-thirds of his sentence.

FINANCIAL AND ASSOCIATED SCANDALS

John Law:
fraudster or honest banker?

By a remarkable coincidence the year 1720 saw unrelated financial crises in both Britain and France. The two had similar features: a mad scramble for shares, financial peculation, unsustainable share prices and their inevitable collapse. In Britain the crisis was triggered by the ambitious directors of the South Seas trading company; in France it was triggered by the advanced financial ideas of a Scottish banker, John Law. It is fashionable for historians to ridicule John Law and his fanciful financial notions, but his ideas were not completely unsound, and it is arguable whether he deliberately set out to defraud.

John Law was born in 1671, the son of a wealthy Scottish goldsmith. His father's occupation gave him the opportunity to gain expertise as a banker, and his father's wealth gave him the means to travel extensively in Europe and to study foreign banking practices at close hand. By 1705 Law considered himself sufficiently experienced to publish a treatise expounding his monetary theories, and he followed this with another in 1707. At a time when economics was in its infancy, and even less of a science than it is today, many of Law's ideas seem remarkably modern. He believed that trade was severely hampered by shortage of currency (gold and silver) and advocated a paper currency backed by state credit. He even put forward the idea that the volume of trading activity depended, not only on the amount of currency in circulation, but also on the speed (velocity) of its circulation. Even more modern was his notion of paying off state debts with depreciating currency – a ploy most states were to resort to in the twentieth century. Yet he remained firmly Mercantilist in his advocacy of monopoly trading companies supported by the state. Law attempted to interest a number of European countries in his ideas, but they were all too set in their ways to listen to him. Nevertheless Law visited Paris where, weighed down by bags of gold, he would make his appearance in its notorious gaming dens. Here he met the Regent Orleans, and soon Law's success at the tables made Orleans a ready listener. Orleans's concern was not so much his own lack of luck at the tables, but France's economic decline after the extravagances of Louis XIV's wars. Having tried every expedient without success, Orleans watched in jealous admiration as Law in 1716 set up a bank in Paris. This engaged in normal banking activity: discounted bills at a profit, issued its own notes, did not speculate or take risks, and made substantial profits. With these profits, and the public confidence his bank inspired, Law proposed to undertake the development of Louisiana, France's huge territory in North America. In 1717 Law was granted permission by Orleans to transform the company of the West into the Mississippi Company (Le Mississippi). In return for a massive loan to the government the company was given monopoly rights to trade with Louisiana and to colonize it. In 1718 the bank became a state bank, and its banknotes were state-backed, and authorized for general circulation and exchange. Soon 'Le Mississippi' had swallowed up the French companies of Senegal, South Seas, India and China, and such was the confidence inspired by the Company that people rushed to exchange their government bonds for shares in the company. Demand for its shares rose inexorably.

In the meantime Law had been appointed Controller of the Finances (January 1720), and this enabled Law to embark on major fiscal reforms, such as merging direct and indirect taxes, and the imposition of a new universal tax, the *dîme royale,* from which the nobility were not exempt. There was, at this stage, no financial impropriety in Law's activities. His bank was a great success, and his trading companies were legitimate businesses. But it was a grave financial misjudgement to link the bank, with its legitimate financial activities, to the companies with their speculative commercial ones. Fired by confidence in all that Law turned his hand to, investors exchanged their state fixed interest bonds for shares in Law's companies, where they expected to see ever rising returns. In short, Law's bond issue of 1,500 million *livres* (issued at ten times over their face value) enabled him to buy out the entire French national debt.

Thus Law's success raised economic and financial activity to fever pitch. It created new trading cities such as Lorient in France and

New Orleans in America. It also created vast numbers of people eager to make their fortunes. These varied from the shrewd speculator to the financially ignorant widow or farmer. As owners of government bonds traded them in for shares in Law's companies, France's National Debt fell spectacularly while demand for shares in Le Mississippi soared. Law's house was besieged by those who believed that he could personally provide shares. His windows were broken by those trying to gain entry. One enthusiast got stuck in his chimney trying to reach Law's bedroom. A Duchess feigned illness outside his house in order to gain admittance. And the price of the shares soared, until they were changing hands at forty times their face value. Law's critics and enemies hastened to point out that Law's bank and companies could not possibly provide enough dividends to justify so high a share price. The Farmers-General (leading French financiers in charge of tax-collecting), who had been outbid for the tax-collecting monopoly by Law, were vociferous in their criticism, and English agents, whose government was alarmed at the prospect of French economic revival, hastened to support the hostile rumours. Law and his associates took fright. To sustain the share prices they encouraged rumours of mountains of solid gold and rocks of solid ruby in Louisiana, and they put it about that the native Huron Indians would be willing to hand over such wealth in exchange for trifling merchandise of little value. Such tactics did not work. Nor did artificially lowering the share price, and demonetising gold and silver coin. By the end of 1720 Law's banknotes were worth only 10% of face value, and Law had found it expedient to quit France in a hurry.

With his departure Law's work abruptly ended. The bank was closed, the Farmers-General recovered their former privileges, the *dîme royale* was abolished and the companies were reorganised. There was some lasting legacy: Lorient and New Orleans slowly grew and prospered, and after 1720 there was a significant period of French economic expansion. As for Law, soon after he left France he appeared in London, where it is said he attended a performance of *The Alchemist* at Drury Lane. But Law had not been trying to change base metal into gold. He had been trying to run France's economy on what he believed to be sound economic principles. The only questionable action he can be accused of was his attempt in the summer of 1720 to talk up the shares. With the collapse of his companies went the collapse of his personal fortune. He was, as late as 1723, still being consulted about the running of the French East India Company, but his ideas had been largely discredited. France was prejudiced against a state bank for nearly another hundred years. Those who lost money through Law's companies made much noise; those, like the Duke who needed two carriages to carry away his gold, wisely kept quiet. In 1729 Law died in Italy a pauper, himself as much a victim of the events of 1720 as those who had every right to denounce him.

The Highland Clearances: development or genocide?

Many Scots continue to regard English policy in their country after the Union in 1707 as a scandal, inspired by racial intolerance – even hatred. Nowhere is this clearer than in the case of the so-called Highland Clearances.

The ending of the clan system and the clearing of large areas of Highland Scotland, allegedly for the purpose of agricultural improvement, were significant features of Scottish history in the later eighteenth and the nineteenth centuries, and yet they scarcely merit a mention in most English history books. Perhaps the omission is the result of England's shame at the distress these 'improvements' brought in their train. Certainly the clearances brought with them considerable economic dislocation and social suffering. Indeed the whole episode betrays a quite scandalous harshness, and illustrates the indifference, if not the contempt, that the English felt for Scottish feelings. It also explains why many Scots even at the present time see the episode in terms of their national humiliation at the hands of the occupying foreigner.

On account of his Highland clearances, George Granville Levenson-Gower, first Duke of Sutherland, made himself one of the most hated men in Scotland in the later eighteenth century. Regarding himself as an individual of high culture, he followed the fashion of his day as an 'improver' of his estates in Staffordshire, where he improved farming methods, cattle and crops, encouraging his tenants to be as progressive as he was. In making these changes he rode roughshod over local resistance, paying scant attention to the feelings of his tenants, or those of the yeomen farmers of the area. Such attitudes were typical of the high-handed methods of the landed gentry of the time, who forced through their changes willy-nilly. Those who resisted him he regarded as purblind opponents of a newer and more scientific system of agriculture, their stance comparable to that of the labourers who sabotaged the introduction of machinery into the industrialised cotton mills in the course of the industrial revolution.

He inherited by marriage over a million acres in Sutherland, and set himself the task of 'improving' these, too. Two key events enabled him to set about this task. In 1746, the Highlanders had been defeated at Culloden, and the old Scottish way of life had been destroyed; and, in 1792, the hardy breed of Cheviot sheep was introduced into Scotland, producing twice the mutton and three times the wool of the scrawny native breed. As English historians saw it, the destruction of the clan system was a constructive step. The English regarded the authority of the laird as an obstacle to order and progress: his 'heritable jurisdiction' gave him the right to exercise judicial authority outside the courts of law, whilst at the same time he was able to insist on military service from his followers and tenants. One English historian wrote that the destruction of the clan system, 'however unpopular', was 'an essential preliminary to the pacification and the modernization of Scotland.' The Scots, on the other hand, regarded the English action as the action of a vindictive foreign garrison, and on a par with the English banning of the kilt and the tartan.

Over a period of nine years, the duke drove out 15,000 of his tenants from their holdings to make way for his sheep, compelling them to resettle on a narrow strip of coastal land and eke out a desperate living from inshore fishing and from harvesting a type of large brown seaweed known as kelp, which had important industrial uses as a source of soda and iodine. Nothing now remains of the homes of hundreds of peasant families. Strathnaver is a long, lovely but empty valley, where only the foundations of farmsteads and cattlesheds can be traced in the ground.

The duke's agent, the ruthless Patrick Sellar, burned their houses and drove the peasants from land that they and their ancestors had held for generations. Eventually brought to trial in Inverness in 1816 and charged with culpable homicide, Sellar was placed before establishment judges who saw the whole situation through English eyes, so that he was, unsurprisingly, acquitted.

Some Highland chieftains gathered their kinsmen together and sailed abroad to seek a new life in the colonies. The Earl of Selkirk, for example, took a boatload of his clan to Canada to found the Red River

Settlement near a place now known as Winnipeg. In the second half of the eighteenth century nearly 50,000 Highlanders left their lands. In the nineteenth century this figure was dwarfed by those leaving when kelp and cattle prices collapsed. Those remaining were forced to rely on the potato and starved when blight struck. The refugees flocked to the factory towns of lowland Scotland, where they provided the cheap labour on which the Scottish industrial revolution was based.

By 1850 about a million and a half Scots had perished or had fled the country. And while England during the first half of the nineteenth century – whether as an indication of the country's stability, its stolidity or merely its forelock-tugging social deference – enjoyed the benefits of reasonable social and political tranquillity, both its Scottish and its Irish neighbours, both more volatile, underwent seismic changes which transformed the whole future of their country. Indeed, England's population, 1801–1821, went up to over twenty million, but Scotland's only to three, while the population of Ireland actually fell by about half.

At the present time, two and a half centuries after the defeat in battle of Prince Charles Edward, the memory of this scandalous exploitation of the Scots by the English continues to rankle. However, the fact that the new Scottish Parliament has so far taken no steps to redress this grievance by bringing forward proposals for the radical reform of land ownership in Scotland may be evidence that the Scots have at last taken note of the fact that their English neighbours brought great suffering on the country, as they did on their own, for the best of motives, and that once these changes have been made they cannot easily be unmade.

The scandalous adventures of Edward 'Ned' Kelly

Ned Kelly, storybook villain of Australian legend, was a minor layabout whose history has been magnified beyond all recognition. He was not really anything like as black as he was painted. A bushranger and outlaw of the wildernesses of New South Wales and Victoria states, he provided the sort of material which mothers introduce into their bedtime stories to discipline and to subdue their unruly offspring. Over fifty books, a number of paintings by an artist called Nolan, a play by Douglas Stewart and a modern film still celebrate the legend of this extraordinary desperado, outlawed in north-eastern Victoria in 1878 and caught and hanged whilst still only twenty-five years old in 1880.

His father, John Kelly, was born in Tipperary, Ireland, in 1820, a man with all the blarney and predatory instincts of the stereotypical Irishman. John's mother had been Mary Cody, a cousin of William F. Cody ('Buffalo Bill'), the circus-master and wild western hero of the United States. Transported to Van Diemen's Land in 1842, John served out his sentence, then crossed to Port Philip where he married Ellen Quinn who had emigrated to Australia from County Antrim in 1841. Their home was about thirty miles north of Melbourne, where Ellen inherited about 700 acres of land. Later they moved to Avenel, forty miles further north; close by in Beveridge in 1855 Ned was born, the third of nine children. Ned attended school until he was eleven, when his father died, and the family, in poverty, moved into a slab hut[1] at Eleven Mile Creek in the 'outback'. Close by, at Glenmore, Ned's grandfather James Quinn

---

1 A 'slab hut' is one whose walls are constructed out of piled-up squares of turf.

owned a cattle-run of 25,000 acres, though in this wild and scorching country none of them was out of trouble for long; several of the Quinns and their relatives, the Lloyds, were sentenced to jail-terms for their involvement in rustling and brawling. An area of several hundred square miles around Benalla, Wangaratta and Beechworth, including the King River and the plains and mountains nearby, was known as 'Kelly country' and became notorious for horse-stealing, cattle-rustling and robbery, with its headquarters at Mrs Kelly's home at the shack at Eleven Mile Creek. She remarried in 1874 a George King, an emigrant from California, an accomplished horse-thief, and there were four further children from this marriage, most of whom took readily to the family trade of brigandage. They treated the local police with contempt, for they were for the most part poorly-paid immigrants unskilled in bushcraft and poorly mounted; and the police for their part soon tired of them. The local Superintendent, a Scot called Nicholson, believed 'they should be rooted out of the neighbourhood', saying, 'even a paltry sentence would take the flashness out of them.'

Kelly early on conceived the not entirely mistaken idea that the police were after him, determined to pin on him any offence they could find. In 1869, at the age of fourteen, he was locked up briefly for assaulting a Chinaman and then again as the accomplice of the bushranger Harry Power, but neither charge stood up in court and his feelings of victimization increased. He was tried and convicted at the age of fifteen for assault, serving six months, and then for horse-stealing, for which he served three years, in spite of his vigorous protests of innocence. Released in 1874, Kelly worked for a time in a sawmill, but by 1876 had resumed a criminal career by joining his stepfather, George King, in stealing horses over the Murray River. He later claimed to have stolen over a hundred of them. The so-called 'Kelly War' broke out in early 1878, when a newly enlisted constable by the name of Fitzpatrick returned from the bush with a slight wound to the wrist, and reported that Kelly had shot him. A posse of police was dispatched to deal with the troublemakers. Mrs Kelly was arrested at the shack, together with two associates; she got three years in prison and the men six years each. Ned Kelly and a number of others went on the run with a price on their heads. For a time they took refuge at Stringybark Creek, working the creek for alluvial gold and brewing illicit grog, but before the end of the year the police had caught up with them, and in the inevitable shoot-out a number of policemen were shot dead. By November they were proclaimed outlaws and a price of £500 placed on the head of each of them.

There followed several months of something like a guerrilla war in the bush. The police exercised their powers of entry, search and arrest and of commandeering food and horses pretty indiscriminately, giving rise to considerable local resentment on the part of locals who were detained on remand for long periods before release. The Kelly gang led a charmed life, often helped by sympathisers who were victims of police harassment. It was their boast that they never harmed a woman or robbed a poor man; but they certainly did everything else. They detained 22 persons near Euroa while they robbed the National Bank there and got away with £2000 in notes and gold; shortly afterwards they detained sixty persons in the Royal Hotel, Jerilderie, 'arresting' two local policemen by a ruse and robbing the Bank of New South Wales of another £2100 while still masquerading as police. Thereafter the reward offered for them was increased to £2000 per head, but the outlaws disappeared from view and spent sixteen months in hiding after February 1879.

The end came in June 1880. Flushed out by police spies, the gang took possession of Glengowran township, detaining thirty people at the hotel, and tore up a length of the railway to wreck the train they knew to be bringing gold and police reinforcements late at night. Unfortunately they then got drunk, and the local schoolmaster was able to stop the train before it was derailed – but its whistle alerted the stupefied party and they staggered out in the early hours, wearing grotesque armour cobbled together from agricultural equipment. Kelly's armour weighed ninety pounds and consisted of a cylindrical helmet and a breastplate with apron and a back plate laced together with leather thongs. There was a stiff fight between 5 and 7am and many of the Kelly gang were killed, or killed themselves rather than submit. Two took poison after police set fire to the building they were sheltering in. The police took Ned Kelly alive by shooting at his legs, though when he was taken he had several wounds in other parts of his body. He was tried, convicted and hanged at Melbourne Jail in November 1880. His mother lived on, dying at a ripe old age in 1923.

'Such is life!' was the aphorism with which it is said he went to the gallows. But much as he liked to find excuses for his short and disastrous career, there was no doubt that Ned Kelly was the chief architect of his own misfortunes, and this perhaps helps to explain why Australian mothers hold him up as a dreadful bogeyman to their children. Whereas other men in similar primitive circumstances worked hard and in some cases made their fortunes, Kelly took what seemed the easy way out and during his short lifetime preyed on his neighbours. There are more than a few parallels between life in the Australian bush and that in the American 'Wild West', where violence and banditry seem also to have been endemic. Yet at the same time there was much consistent endeavour, hard industry, honest enterprise and even Christian principle demonstrated by cattlemen and settlers in the pioneering days, and Edward Kelly must remain as much to be blamed as to be pitied.

Who made a killing out of the Marconi scandal?

In the summer of 1912 there took place not by any means the first, but, all the same, a resoundingly scandalous case of blatant 'insider dealing' in the trading of commercial shares. In March, the Postmaster-General, Herbert Samuel, accepted a tender from the English Marconi Company for the construction of a network of wireless (or radio) stations linking Britain's possessions in the Empire. This tender, together with the dramatic publicity afforded to radio by the sinking of the Titanic *after its collision with an iceberg in the Atlantic on April 10, produced a sharp rise in the market value of the company's shares on April 18.*

The managing director of the English Marconi Company was Godfrey Isaacs, who in turn was brother of the Attorney-General, Sir Rufus Isaacs, and managing director of the legally independent American Marconi Company. He decided to expand the American wing of the business by floating a new issue of shares on April 18. Over a week beforehand he invited two of his brothers, Harry and Rufus, to purchase a large block of shares at a price considerably cheaper than the market rate. Between them they bought 56,000 shares, reselling 1000 of them to each of Lloyd George, who was Chancellor of the Exchequer in Asquith's Liberal government, and to the Master of Elibank, who was Liberal Chief Whip. The figure paid was about £2 per share. When the issue was floated the share price jumped immediately to £4, and the three ministers resold their holdings at an easy and very handsome profit.

Rumours swiftly spread in the city of the deal, and the rabidly anti-Semitic journal *Eye Witness,* edited by Hilaire Belloc and Cecil Chesterton (brother of the unlovely 'G.K.'), featured this piece of insider dealing in abusive terms. Samuel, though entirely innocent of any wrongdoing, shared in its strictures because he was a Jew. The Prime Minister, though privately very angry, tried to hush the affair up, thinking that the circulation of the journal was small, and that more damage would be done by denying the report than by ignoring it. He was wrong. In early October Samuel secured the appointment of a parliamentary Select Committee to investigate the Marconi scandal, and in the ensuing debate both Isaacs and Lloyd George specifically denied having any dealings with 'the Marconi company'. They were careful, however, to extend their denials solely to the English company, but did so in such a way as to give the impression that they were referring to the whole company. This piece of sharp practice satisfied their critics for the time being until, early in 1913, both Isaacs and Lloyd George admitted, in the course of a legal action against the French *Le Matin* that in fact they *had* bought shares, though in the American company. This unleashed fresh furies on both sides of the Commons. It also came out that the Liberal Chief Whip had also put £9000 of Liberal Party funds into the company. The Committee naturally wished to question him further about such a use of party funds, but instead of doing so he betook himself on a trip to the remote township of Bogota in rural Colombia and consequently was unavailable for some weeks. Thus, when the Select Committee reported in June 1913 after a good deal of ill-tempered debate, it split on strictly party lines, and so the Liberals, with their big parliamentary majority, won. Ironically, Isaacs later won promotion to be Lord Chief Justice, and went on as Lord Reading to become British Ambassador to Washington and subsequently Viceroy of India, whilst Lloyd George continued his pose as the innocent victim of the Marconi scandal, and during the First World War in 1916 (some said by methods scarcely more reputable) became Prime Minister after Asquith.

The affair seemed to have little injurious effect on Lloyd George, who remained as Teflon-coated as he had ever been, but it did not do much good for the harmonious working of British government or for the reputation of parliamentary democracy. Memories of Lloyd George's involvement may, however, have given some small consolation to disgruntled Unionists, frustrated Irishmen, and to red-faced World War generals obliged to listen to his homilies on their moral shortcomings.

Horatio Bottomley:
patriot or con man?

An orphan from London's East End, the patriotically-named Horatio Bottomley was born in 1860. He was sharp and intelligent and as he grew older he learnt to live on his wits. By the time he was twenty-four he had a shrewd idea of the importance of good public relations and was able to establish the newspaper the Hackney Hansard, *becoming a self-made millionaire by 1900. Nevertheless, many of his business dealings were on the shady side of the law. He was always adept at raising money, but often dishonestly. For example he was charged with fraud twice, in 1891 and 1909, but was acquitted on both occasions. At the same time, few shareholders in the numerous companies he promoted ever received any dividend, and a number of those who lost most money quoted his name in their bankruptcy petitions. To him the publishing world seemed the most glamorous, and he added to his early success in Hackney by founding in 1906 the magazine John Bull, which brought him wide national recognition, and retained a large circulation until the Second World War. Pulling a number of financial strings, he managed to get himself elected MP for South Hackney in the same year.*

The course of his business career, however, never ran very smoothly, and he went bankrupt in 1912, when at the same time he applied for the Chiltern Hundreds in the House of Commons as a way of seeking his political exit. But the War enabled him to play his populist role even more successfully than before. If there was a populist cause, Bottomley would champion it. In 1917, for example, he contrived to combine denunciation of the reduction in licensing hours, the weakening of the strength of beer and other liquor controls put forward by Lloyd George with a stirring appeal for the more energetic conduct of the war, which had been the reason behind these controls in the first place. He also organized and attended a series of recruiting meetings at which he called for volunteers and solicited financial contributions to the war effort. It is said that he measured the success of his oratory by the size of his takings; he recited a poem containing the line, 'This is more than a war, mate – it's a call to the human race', and shovelled the fivers into his pocket at the end of the meeting with an enthusiasm that suggested that the war effort was not the only beneficiary of this largesse. Altogether he raised rather more than £900,000. In the gloomiest days of the U-boat war, the war cabinet solemnly consulted with Bottomley – the 'soldiers' friend' – about how to reassure public feeling, and Lloyd George was only narrowly persuaded against offering him a place in the government. When the war was over, Bottomley, now self-confidently back in the money, was able to discharge his bankruptcy and get himself elected to Parliament once more as an Independent MP. He never failed to offer Lloyd George advice on any subject of war-making or peace-making; for example, he buoyantly offered his views on the future disposition in the peace settlement of lands – though he had probably no more idea than Lloyd George himself where Teschen was, or what was the geographical difference between Silesia and Cilicia.

In 1922, however, he came another cropper that finally removed him from public life. In May 1922 he was caught in the trap of one of his ingenious swindles and was sent to prison for five years for fraudulent conversion. He had initiated a neat little scam by which he invited small subscriptions which would be clubbed together for the purchase of Victory Bonds, whose interest was to be distributed amongst the subscribers as prizes. Most of the contributions, however, were never invested at all, but went instead into Bottomley's capacious pockets. Some were used to buy off those contributors who complained that they had been diddled. But his expression remained always quite untroubled, and he was always frank and open about his mischief. When an acquaintance found him stitching mailbags in prison and said to him: 'Ah, Bottomley, sewing?' he is reported to have replied: 'Unfortunately, no – reaping'. After serving his time, he never succeeded in recovering his former standing and respect and faded into obscurity. Bottomley died a pauper in 1933.

The anecdotes about his scandalous career were the stuff of popular recollection and entered into the half-affectionate proverbs of folk history. There seemed to be little resentment at his appalling behaviour or at his unrepentant lack of morals; even to those he had cheated Bottomley remained always a 'card'.

How did the 'Ohio Gang' pull off the Teapot Dome scandal?

Warren Harding is among the worst Presidents that the United States has ever had. The best thing that can be said of him is that the Teapot Dome scandal, a swindle relating to an outcrop of land in Wyoming rich in oil reserves, took place without his knowledge or direct involvement, and came into the public arena only after he was dead. But that it happened at all was entirely due to his ignorance and neglect, and was the result of his failure to grasp the essential duties of his office, as the result of which he spent his life on the golf links, attending baseball games, playing poker with his cronies, or making love to his mistress, Nan Britton, in the room behind the Oval Office.

Harding was an amiable and rather indolent man who seems to have drifted into the US Presidency almost by accident. He was handsome and good-natured, and his firm handshake, his square jaw and his genial smile were great assets to him. At the same time they concealed his essential mediocrity. Born in the small mid-west town of Corsica, Ohio, in 1865, he made unsuccessful efforts to become a school teacher and later a lawyer, and finally went into publishing when he bought up a local newspaper on the verge of bankruptcy in the nearby town of Marion in the early years of the century. At the time he met Florence Kling de Wolfe, daughter of one of the leading local families, who took a shine to his winning ways and, in spite of her father's opposition to the match, married him. His success dated from this time, for his wife supplied the energy and acumen which soon made her husband and the Marion *Star* a success, driving Harding, essentially an unenterprising and rather lazy individual, towards a high-powered career.

He had no very clear political intentions, but as a newspaper editor – especially one with an ambitious wife – he met large numbers of politicians, one of whom was the Republican Harry Daugherty, a man with definite career intentions, but lacking the charisma to carry them out. Harding, on the other hand, looked the part, so Daugherty, along with Florence, determined to be the power behind the throne. With Daugherty's backing as campaign manager, Harding soon became Republican senator for the state of Ohio, and shortly after Lieutenant-Governor of Ohio. This was really as far as Harding wished to go, but Daugherty continued to push him until, rather to his surprise, he found himself elected to the White House in 1920, successor to the formidable Woodrow Wilson.

In some respects Harding was an improvement on his predecessor. Wilson was rigid, puritanical and self-righteous, but Harding was accessible and clearly a good chap. It was typical of the new regime that Harding immediately opened the White House grounds to the admission of the public; Wilson had had the gates locked and kept the public at arm's length. Unfortunately the new President was no more than just a good fellow: he was weak, easily led and always willing to oblige his friends. But the workings of the US economy were a closed book to him and his knowledge of external affairs was almost non-existent – unlike Wilson, whose grasp of the post-war world was excellent. He was happy to drink illicit whisky and play poker in smoke-filled rooms with his friends, whilst they, the members of the so-called 'Ohio Gang', as his cronies were known, got their hands on the loot.

His presidency, however, started rather well. His Secretary of the Treasury, Andrew Mellon, was one of the ablest of American financiers between the wars, whilst Charles Evans Hughes as his Secretary of State and Herbert Hoover as his Secretary of Commerce both were able to manage well areas of government where Harding's own abilities were found to be lacking. Unfortunately some of his other appointments were less satisfactory, such as Albert B. Fall as Secretary of the Interior and Harry Daugherty himself as Attorney General.

Harding shied away from difficult questions relating to the post-war treaties and disarmament, to the world's monetary problems, even to tariff and tax proposals, all of which he found far too complex and boring: he preferred to entertain and be entertained in the Oval Office, to sit with his waistcoat unbuttoned, his feet up on the desk and a spittoon by his side. The members of the 'Ohio Gang', however, set up what was almost an alternative White House on K Street, with Fall and Daugherty as the key figures, and Jesse W. Smith as the 'gofer' who helped to 'fix' the deals his colleagues wanted. Smith was a coarse, expansive man with a loud voice, who liked to sing: 'My God, how the money rolls in'.

Soon, ugly rumours began to spread about the 'Ohio Gang'. Colonel Charles R. Forbes, whom Harding had appointed Director of the Veterans' Bureau, the body set up to safeguard the interests of disabled ex-servicemen, misappropriated millions of dollars from the Treasury. Hospital supplies bought with public money had been promptly sold off as war surplus, Forbes pocketing the cash they produced: thus sheets bought at $1.35 a pair were sold off at 27c, and a million towels bought at 34c each were disposed of at 36c per dozen. He also received 'kick-backs' for the award of hospital contracts, and others from real estate dealers who sold land for hospitals at far more than its market value. Secretary of the Interior Fall also had his fingers in the till. He was said to have leased out naval oil reserves at Elk Hill, California, and at Teapot Dome, Wyoming, to his friends. Earlier, President Wilson had decided that these oil resources should be held in reserve in case of future emergencies, and had placed them under the control of the Navy Department. Secretary Fall, however, persuaded the Navy Department to hand them over to his own Department, the Interior. Later he disposed of the government's rights in Elk Hill to one of his cronies, Edward Doheny for $100,000, and in Teapot Dome to Harry Sinclair, an oil tycoon, for $14 million. It is hardly surprising that he was able to pay off years of back-taxes, buy an enormous ranch in New Mexico and stock it with prize cattle. Soon the rumours of corruption were too insistent to ignore. Harding's health was already beginning to crack – a decline, no doubt, accelerated by the amount of bourbon he had been drinking. Seizing Forbes by the throat in a corridor in the White House, he got rid of his Head of the Veterans' Bureau, calling him 'a dirty double-crossing bastard'. Forbes later went to Paris on an extended trip, and sent in his resignation 'for health reasons'. Harding went on to grill Jesse Smith about the shenanigans in K Street. When he learnt the full story, he sacked him on the spot, telling him he would be arrested the next day – but Smith went back to his hotel room and shot himself before that could happen. Harding was due to make a trip to Alaska in 1923 and he decided the time was right to be absent from Washington for a while. But on his way home down the Pacific coast he was taken ill. His doctor put his illness down to poisoning from crab meat, and briefly he seemed to recover; but when he got back to Washington he died suddenly in August of what was said by some to be a fit of apoplexy. His wife died in the following year.

Retribution was not long to follow. A Senate Investigating Committee examined the dealings of the Harding cabinet; as a result, both Fall and Daugherty were heavily fined and spent some time in jail. There was no suggestion that Harding himself had been dishonest, but only slack and pitifully weak in letting his Ohio friends play their corrupt games. The Harding Memorial Association raised $700,000 for a monument in Marion, Ohio, where the President was buried, and the design produced was for a cylindrical building with a marble colonnade. Others preferred a design more like a sphere, but this was dropped when it was suggested that all it needed was a spout and then it would look exactly like a teapot.

POLITICAL SCANDALS

How did Titus Oates try to save England from the Popish Plot?

The story of the Popish Plot against the Protestant kingdom of Charles II in the late seventeenth century is one of the most sordid fictions of late Stuart England, and the ingenuity of Titus Oates in inventing it an example of the scandalous exploitation of the popular religious gullibility current at that time.

The strength of popular feeling against Catholicism is easy to imagine. Tudor England had witnessed Queen Mary's attempt to restore Catholic worship and Papal power, and Elizabeth's reign had been frequently rocked by similar plots. More recently there had been an attempt to blow up the King and both Houses of Parliament in the Gunpowder Plot in 1605. Charles I, who had a Catholic wife and was suspected himself for being of Popish inclinations, had fought a civil war to preserve the royal despotism, if not actually to restore the Catholic faith; and he had invoked the armed support both of the Scots and the Catholic Irish to subdue his own countrymen. His son, restored to the throne in 1660, had married the Portuguese Infanta, Catherine of Braganza, also a Catholic; he, too, was on bad terms with Parliament and was thought to harbour Papist intentions (his heir and younger brother, James Duke of York, the future James II, eventually allowed himself to be converted to the Catholic faith). In 1666, Catholic plotting was widely believed to have been the cause of the Great Fire of London. After the Secret Treaty of Dover in 1670, Charles was suspected of being the puppet and pensionary of the Catholic Louis XIV of France when he agreed to support the French against Protestant Holland in return for substantial subsidies. The French king at this time showed the harsh face of Catholicism in his wars with his Dutch neighbours, and in his expulsion of hundreds of thousands of Huguenot Protestants, many of whom, when they landed in England, told of their horrifying experiences at the hands of Louis's *dragonnades*. Public paranoia about the Catholic threat was as understandable as it was widespread. A Cold War atmosphere prevailed throughout the whole country.

It was this ignorant and rather brutish prejudice which Titus Oates turned to his own advantage, presenting his alleged Popish Plot as part of a systematic effort on the part of disloyal Catholics to subvert the kingdom and restore it to Rome. As in the case of the American Senator Joseph McCarthy over three hundred years later, no one at first enquired into Oates's background, or his fitness for his assumed role as saviour of his country; it was only after his sudden fall from pre-eminence that the seamier side of his career came to light.

Titus Oates was born in Norfolk in 1649, son of a former chaplain in the New Model Army who served time in Colchester Jail and after the Restoration became an Anglican and finally a Baptist. The young Titus went to Merchant Taylors' school and later to Gonville and Caius College, Cambridge, but was speedily expelled from both institutions both for his behaviour and for his conspicuous lack of academic ability. His inadequacies, however, did not prevent him from entering the Church. He held a series of minor clerical appointments, but did not last long in any of them, being accused by his congregations of drunkenness, blasphemy and petty theft. Facing a perjury charge in Hastings after accusing a local schoolmaster of sodomy, he was imprisoned briefly in Dover Castle, but escaped to enrol as a naval chaplain in the Tangier-bound *Adventure* in 1675. On his first voyage, however, he was expelled from the navy for homosexual practices, and was imprisoned again. Once again he escaped. He was on the run in London, and though he was an Anglican clergyman, soon fell in with a Catholic actor named Medburne, who introduced him to the disreputable *Pheasant Club* in Holborn. As the result of Medburne's introduction he became chaplain in the household of Henry Howard, Duke of Norfolk, England's leading Catholic family. The numerous contacts he made here he later exploited as unwitting participants in his so-called Popish Plot, and he did not hesitate to accuse, disgrace and ruin many of them in the process. He also fell in with the Reverend Israel Tonge, Rector of St Mary's in Steyning, a fanatical polemicist on the subject of Catholic infiltration into England who had written numerous books on the alleged designs of the Catholics to take over the Establishment, and who readily interested Oates in spying on the Catholics. As the result of these influences, Oates was received into the Catholic faith in 1677, though he later claimed that his conversion had been feigned as a means of finding out information useful to his country about the Jesuits.

Oates enrolled first at the Jesuits' English college at Valladolid in Spain and after his expulsion from there after four months, went to the St Omer College in Flanders, whence he returned under a cloud in June 1678. He learnt absolutely nothing about any Catholic plot against England (indeed, since there was no plot there was nothing to *be* learnt), but he fraudulently turned the experience to his advantage by claiming that he had been made a Doctor of Divinity by Salamanca University, and referred to himself as 'Dr' Oates thereafter.

Oates did not delay to regale the credulous Tonge with tales of a Jesuit conspiracy to organize a Protestant massacre in London, to stir up disaffection throughout the three kingdoms and to assassinate the King in favour of the Catholic James. He had, he claimed, 'irrefutable proof' that the Fire of London had been caused by a Popish conspiracy, that he had 'seen' a Papal Bull detailing the administrative arrangements to be made for England after its restoration to the faith, and that he had 'overheard' his old friend Medburne and others plotting to waylay Charles II with pistols and daggers in the park to assassinate him. These tales lost nothing in Tonge's retelling of them. Before long, the Earl of Shaftesbury, one of Charles's opponents in Parliament, seized on anti-Catholic prejudice as the chance to bring pressure on the government. At the same time popular opinion quivered with apprehension.

Charles asked his chief minister, the Earl of Danby, to investigate, thus beginning the process whereby Oates's rumours were given wider and now semi–official currency. At first, Oates himself remained in the background, but in September 1678 he was indicted before a popular London justice, Sir Edmund Berry Godfrey, and swore to the truth of his allegations. Numerous arrests were made of those he named, of whom eight were tried and executed. Oates tried to avoid provoking the King by impugning persons close to him, but he risked criticizing Richard Coleman, private secretary to James's wife, the Duchess of York, by accusing him of treasonable correspondence with Pierre de la Chaise, Louis XIV's personal confessor. These letters did in fact exist, and, since Coleman had believed that they were confidential, it required no great leap of Oates's imagination to guess at the kind of language they contained. Coleman was arrested on a charge of treason, and, shortly afterwards, the popular Godfrey was found dead, strangled and run through with his own sword. Popular indignation knew no bounds. So hostile was the London mob when they mistook Nell Gwyn's carriage for that of the Duchess of Portsmouth, the King's Catholic mistress, that Nell was forced to remonstrate with them: 'Be silent, good people! I am the *Protestant* whore!'. In connection with the Godfrey murder, a young Catholic silversmith, Miles Prance, believed to have been implicated in the murder, was dragged from his workshop and tortured into a confession of guilt, as the result of which three others were condemned and hanged.

In October 1678, Oates was summoned to appear before Parliament, where he gave further detailed and damning testimony of the 'Plot'. The Whig opposition, led by Shaftesbury, seized the opportunity to push through a Bill barring Catholics from membership of both Houses – a bill which was not repealed until 1829. He also introduced a Bill excluding James from the succession; but this was too much for the King, who dissolved Parliament rather than see it put on the statute book. Suspending Parliament, however, brought an immediate shortage of royal income, and Charles was obliged to invoke the secret clauses of the Treaty of Dover which promised him a substantial private subsidy if he agreed to convert to Catholicism before he died. So, ironically, Oates's groundless ravings had in reality created the very thing they had for so long predicted – a Popish Plot!

Meanwhile Oates, knowing nothing of this, went from strength to strength. He was installed in sumptuous apartments in Whitehall, protected by a small army of bodyguards and furnished with a huge pension. He also had the temerity to submit an expense account of nearly £700 for his work in uncovering the plot, and this bill Parliament unquestioningly paid. As the result of his denunciations, over thirty more-or-less innocent Catholics were arrested, tried and executed, including Edward Coleman, sentenced by the Lord Chief Justice to be hung, drawn and quartered, a monstrous sentence for his trifling indiscretions. Some of the other accused were very high-profile people indeed. William Howard (Viscount Stafford and the Duke of Norfolk's younger son) was executed in 1680, and Oliver Plunkett, Archbishop of Armagh (later canonized by the Catholic Church), in the following year.

Emboldened by his success, he extended his accusations to include five further Catholic peers, and went on to denounce the Queen (whom he ungallantly dubbed 'Dame Short-arse') for plotting to murder her husband. Public apprehension continued at such a high pitch that the London militia were even empowered to halt funerals in order to search coffins for hidden armaments!

The period of what is known as the 'Exclusion crisis' went on throughout this time, with the King dissolving Parliament three times in order to block Shaftesbury's bill to prevent the Duke of York's succession. Then, suddenly, the wind changed. The courts discharged a few of those accused by Oates and his supporters for want of real evidence, and in 1682 Charles felt strong enough to cut off Oates's pension. Indeed, none of those accused ever confessed, or gave any indication that a Popish Plot really existed. No English Protestant ever had his throat cut. The Catholic risings in Ireland and Scotland never materialized. Other instances of Oates's perjury began to crop up, and his other rather feverish allegations began to be disbelieved. In 1684 he was accused of slandering the Duke of York by referring to him as 'that traitor James', was tried by 'Hanging' Judge Jeffreys and sentenced to an enormous fine of £100,000, his failure to pay which led to his imprisonment for debt. James also later charged him with perjury.

The following year, Charles died and James succeeded peacefully to the throne. The evil deeds predicted for the new king did not materialize; there was no great purge of Protestants, and Oates's predictions suddenly began to look empty and foolish. Shaftesbury died, and both the Scottish and the English parliaments continued in existence with royal approval. Oates appeared before Judge Jeffreys a second time and was fined a further 2,000 marks for his perjury. In the dock he was roundly denounced by Jeffreys for the injustices for which he was responsible (the Judge conveniently forgetting his own part in condemning those Oates had accused). His punishment was severe. He was defrocked, pilloried at Westminster and led round Westminster Hall under a placard saying *Titus Oates convicted upon evidence of his two horrid perjuries* (Monday 18 May 1685), was pilloried again on the next day in front of the Royal Exchange; on Wednesday he was flogged from Aldgate to Newgate, and (after a day in which to recover) he was whipped again on Friday from Newgate to Tyburn. Miraculously he survived his ordeal, but as the concluding part of his punishment he was to be afterwards imprisoned for life. For good measure, he was to be pilloried annually for the rest of his life in different parts of London on four days in April and August.

But not even this experience fully quenched his energy: indeed, he was supposed to have fathered a child after a brief liaison with his prison bedmaker. Nonetheless, the 1688 Revolution which brought the overthrow of James II was good news for Oates. He was released from prison in the autumn of that year, and in the following March petitioned Parliament for redress. The Lords were not prepared to clear him of perjury, though they so far sympathized with him as to release him from prison and grant him a free pardon. He surprised everyone (especially those convinced of his homosexual proclivities) by marrying an heiress shortly afterwards, but within a few years he ran through her fortune and was obliged to serve a sentence in a debtor's prison. He died a poor and lonely man in 1705. The whole episode illustrated very painfully how an atmosphere of dread and terror could be exploited by an unscrupulous demagogue, not in any genuine cause, but solely for purposes of his personal aggrandisement.

Did John Wilkes deserve Parliament's treatment of him?

The story of John Wilkes is usually regarded as scandalous on two counts. First the character of Wilkes has been deemed disreputable even by the tolerant standards of the eighteenth century, in spite of his public pose as the 'champion of liberty'; and secondly the treatment of him by government, Parliament and erstwhile friends was regarded by many contemporaries as utterly despicable. Does he deserve his licentious reputation, and how despicably was he handled by the authorities?

John Wilkes was born in 1727, the son of a wealthy whisky distiller. His background gave him the wealth but not the breeding to move in high society. He was educated at Leyden University in the Netherlands, and on his return married a wealthy heiress twelve years his senior. It was hardly a love match: Wilkes was pushed into it by his father; and Wilkes, despite his reputation for womanising, was notoriously ugly. Nevertheless they did have a daughter, Polly. Wilkes rewarded his wife by frittering away her fortune and then abandoning her in 1757. In the meantime he had become mixed up with a group of young men with hedonistic interests. One was Thomas Potter, MP for Aylesbury and son of the Archbishop of Canterbury. He introduced Wilkes into political circles and, for £7000, managed to secure Wilkes's election to the second of the two Aylesbury seats. Their hedonism led them to join the Hellfire Club, founded in 1745 by Sir Francis Dashwood. Its members used to meet in the ruins of Medmenham Abbey where there was much drinking and many flimsily clad young maidens. There was probably more wishful thinking than actual immorality among some of its more elderly clientele, but the younger members, including Wilkes, indulged in activities that shocked respectable society. Even worse than the Bacchanalian revels in the eyes of many were the blasphemous 'black masses' whose mocking rituals were obscene parodies of those of organised religion. Among the Club's members at one time or another were many of the political figures of the day, including Lord Sandwich,[1] the Earl of Bute and Lord Temple, the Elder Pitt's brother-in-law. The improprieties at Medmenham were often publicly denounced by those who indulged in them in private, so there was always an element of hypocrisy in the vigorous contemporary strictures on Wilkes's morals as justifications for his political destruction.

Wilkes's first clash with political authority was opportunist and self-seeking rather than based on principle. At the same time as he, with Charles Churchill, was founding the newspaper the *North Briton* in June 1762, he was attempting unsuccessfully to secure for himself a foreign office appointment to Constantinople, and so perhaps was not fully committed to finding out just how far the liberty of the press extended. His association with Temple and the Grenvilles marked him out on the side of the opposition, and the *North Briton* had an easy target in the Prime Minister, the Earl of Bute. He was Scottish; hence the aptness of the title the *North Briton,* and he was excessively sensitive to criticism. Wilkes's barbed and witty taunting of him made little impact on the public, but was probably one of the factors which brought about Bute's resignation in April 1763. Nevertheless the Peace of Paris which ended the Seven Years' War in March 1763 was Bute's peace, and Wilkes lost no time in ridiculing it. In Number 45 of the *North Briton* Wilkes attacked the King's speech from the throne in which George III read the government's words commending it to Parliament. Wilkes described the King's speech as a falsehood, asserted that the King was merely the mouthpiece of his ministers, but yet went on to remark that 'every friend of his country must lament that a prince of so many great and amiable qualities can be brought to give the sanction of his sacred name to the most odious measures, and to the most unjustifiable public declamation from a throne ever renowned for truth honour, and unsullied virtue.' The gentle sarcasm of this remark was not lost on the ministers, and George was furious. Even though the new Secretaries of State, Lords Halifax

---

1 He it was who could not tear himself from the card table long enough to take sustenance, and, when hungry, required a slab of meat to be brought to him between two slices of bread. So the 'sandwich' was invented.

and Sandwich, had, when in opposition, been close allies of Wilkes, the government decided that Wilkes must be brought to book. So Halifax issued a General Warrant 'against the authors, printers and publishers of the *North Briton*, No. 45'; this enabled Halifax to arrest suspected persons without having to name them.

The legality of General Warrants was uncertain, although they had been used before with reasonable discretion, and were to be used in the future as late as 1936 and even later in wartime. But whether it was really necessary in this case to proceed by General Warrant when the names of most of those involved in No. 45 were known to the government is debatable. Perhaps it was hoped that by General Warrant a few more of the guilty ones would be scooped up, and in fact forty-eight persons were arrested under this rare procedure. But the government made matters much worse by using the Warrant to summon Wilkes before Halifax, who lived in the same London street, and then having Wilkes conveyed to the Tower, where at first he was allowed no contact with the outside. In the meantime his house was searched and a number of his private papers were seized. Whatever the legality of General Warrants, the seizing of Wilkes's papers was an illegal infringement of Wilkes's rights.

Wilkes's friends soon organised his release on a writ of *Habeas Corpus*. Wilkes, in his address to the judge, claimed that he was not seeking redress merely for himself, but also for 'all the middling and inferior sort of people'. Sir John Pratt, the chief justice, ruled his imprisonment infringed the privileges of Members of Parliament, and that the legality of General Warrants would have to be determined later. And he did so determine, a few months later, that General Warrants of the kind issued by Halifax were illegal, and awarded Wilkes a welcome £1000 damages against the Undersecretary of State, Robert Wood. Wilkes now had new allies. He had not been afraid, when in court, to champion the rights of the 'middling and inferior sort' when he had in fact been seeking redress for his own treatment at government hands. The middling and inferior sort now rallied to Wilkes. A Club founded in Wapping for the purpose of members drinking themselves senseless on Wilkes's birthday celebrated every day as his birthday as they did not know the precise date. At Wilkes's original arrest he had gone to Lord Halifax's house in a sedan chair followed by adulatory crowds. Wilkes was now in a position to call out the London mob on whatever pretext. He did not neglect to do so. Moreover, since no printer dared handle it, Wilkes had set up his own printing press, and the No. 45, which originally had had only a closed circle of readers, was now avidly snapped up by a much wider public.

The government could not allow Wilkes's triumph in court and the reprinting to go unchallenged. Having secured parliament's condemnation of No. 45 as a 'false, scandalous and seditious libel', it now resorted to further illegality. Amongst the papers seized in Wilkes's house had been several copies of *An Essay on Woman*, an obscene parody on Pope's *Essay on Man*, made the more hilarious and improper by the footnotes which pornographically imitated the footnotes of Bishop Warburton to an edition of Pope's works. This composition had never been published, although a few copies had been circulated privately. Its authorship was long in dispute, but it seems that the original was the work of Thomas Potter in collaboration with Wilkes. Although it had been dedicated to Lord Sandwich, and it would be embarrassing for him to read such an obscenity publicly, it was he whom the government called upon to read out in the House of Lords, the somewhat updated version which had been found in Wilkes's house. (Potter died in 1759, and the poem Sandwich read contained later political allusions). The House tut-tutted its disapproval. Yet Sandwich was a well-known old reprobate who had been an active member of the Medmenham brotherhood, and his defence of propriety was patently ridiculous. Even so, hearing what had happened in the Lords, the House of Commons was persuaded to condemn Wilkes for publishing obscenities – yet the poem had been obtained illegally, and in any case had never been published. The government went even further in persuading one of its supporters, an MP named Samuel Martin, to pick a quarrel with Wilkes, and challenge him to a duel. Wilkes was seriously wounded, and, rather than face court proceedings on the charges of sedition and obscenity, hastily moved to Paris to be with Polly and to recover from his injury. He had, originally, every intention of returning when recovered, but the fleshpots of Paris were too attractive and he was to remain in Paris for four years.

This did not excuse the measures now taken against him. Since he was not available to answer the charges, Parliament expelled him, and the courts declared him an outlaw. A few weeks later Lord Justice Mansfield entered judgment against him for the seditious and obscene libels. So Wilkes had been condemned by both Parliament and courts without a word being heard in either place in his defence, and his plea of ill-health, not unreasonable on account of the duel, had been rejected. It is not really surprising that he extended his stay in France. The vendetta, pursued against Wilkes by the government, was scandalous, even by eighteenth-century standards, and to most contemporaries his self-enforced exile in France was a disgraceful outcome for which the ministers were wholly responsible.

Worse was to come. In the spring of 1768 there was to be a general election. Realising that his former friends were quite content to see him stay in exile – one friend, the Duke of Grafton was now Prime Minister – Wilkes decided to take a gamble and try to re-enter politics by becoming an election candidate. Sympathisers got him into a city company to enable him to stand for the City of London, but here he was defeated. Polling took place a little later in the county of Middlesex, and immediately after his London defeat Lord Temple gave him land to qualify there. He was aided by the radicals Horne Tooke and the lawyer Serjeant Glynn who used their considerable influence in Middlesex to whip up votes for Wilkes. He secured nearly 1300 votes to his nearest rival's 800 (March 28). For nearly a month he revelled in his victory. He holidayed in Bath for a week and on his return to London waited to be arrested as an outlaw. Grafton's government was not immediately anxious to become embroiled with Wilkes, so on April 20 Wilkes insisted on surrendering to the legal authorities. A week later Lord Mansfield cancelled his outlawry on a silly technicality, but he was returned to his prison in St George's Fields to await trial on the issue of the seditious and obscene publications. When the new parliament assembled large crowds appeared outside the prison to convey Wilkes in triumph to take his seat. The Scots Guards sent to guard the prison were involved in a skirmish with the rioting crowds and several of the crowd, including a spectator, were killed. Wilkes capitalised on this by publishing letters on the riots, and accusing ministers of using Scottish soldiers to butcher freeborn Englishmen. There were even greater riots later, although only one fatality, when Serjeant Glynn gained the other Middlesex seat in a by-election. In the meantime Wilkes was fined £1000 and sentenced to twenty-two months imprisonment on the outstanding charges. The government had determined from the moment of Wilkes's election that his membership of the House of Commons would be intolerable. Now that he was in prison there was no immediate haste, but in January 1769 Parliament voted that Wilkes's comments on the government's responsibility for the

St George's Massacre was a seditious libel and a few days later expelled him from the House. Many members spoke in his defence. Edmund Burke commented that Wilkes's treatment by the Ministers was for the benefit of Wilkes and at the expense of the Constitution.

The House of Commons has always had the undoubted right to expel members who transgressed, but it now played into the hands of the radicals and reformers by attempting to determine its own membership and by rejecting the decision of the electors. No one was brave enough to stand against Wilkes at the new election, so thirteen days after his expulsion Wilkes was re-elected without opposition. MPs once again debated Wilkes's expulsion. One member ridiculed the argument that Wilkes's morals debarred him from membership. 'Even in the Cabinet, that pious reforming society,' he said with heavy irony, 'why, were Mr Wilkes to be judged there, and the innocent man to throw the first stone, they would slink out one by one, and leave the culprit uncondemned.' But by an overwhelming vote Wilkes was again expelled. For the third election government supporters had managed to find a candidate, but large mobs shouting 'Wilkes and Liberty' frustrated the challenge, and Wilkes was again returned unopposed. Preparations were made for a fourth election and this time Colonel Luttrell, MP for Bossiney decided to challenge Wilkes by standing against him. Two others, emboldened by Luttrell's example, entered the contest. This time the election was unexpectedly quiet, but the result on April 13 was foregone. Votes cast for Wilkes were 1143, for Luttrell 296, and for the other unfortunate candidates 5 and 0 respectively. The government decided on a new tactic. The Middlesex sheriffs, after some delay, presented the poll result to the House of Commons, which declared that Henry Lawes Luttrell Esq., *ought to have been* returned, and on May 8 Luttrell was confirmed by the House as the new MP. So the House of Commons not only claimed the right to expel from its membership, but now it claimed the very new right to overturn the wishes of electors and to appoint its own nominee as a Member. Thus the House of Commons was on the way to making itself a self-perpetuating oligarchy.

After this Wilkes's career was something of an anticlimax. He served the rest of his twenty-two months' sentence in comparative luxury, supported by funds from the Reform societies and from the Americans, both of whom believed that he was committed to their cause. So long as the money came in he gave them verbal support, but little else.

He managed to get himself elected alderman of the City of London, and got his revenge on the House of Commons in 1771 by arresting the House messenger who had entered the City in order to apprehend printers who had printed parliamentary debates without permission of the House. After several failed attempts, he became Lord Mayor in 1774. He took his seat in the Commons after the 1774 election because Lord North, the Prime Minister, considered rightly that Wilkes was less of a nuisance inside Parliament than outside it. In the Commons Wilkes spoke in favour of reform, defended the Americans and advocated further religious toleration for Roman Catholics and dissenters. But he was not an orator, and he failed to stir the House; nor could he maintain the white heat of mob support outside it. Time worked against continuous agitation. In 1780 he turned against the mob when, after some hesitation, he was vigorous in organising the putting down of the Gordon riots. So he ended his life as a conventional politician, not as a radical. On one of his last trips to his house in the Isle of Wight he turned on an old lady who shouted 'Wilkes and Liberty'. 'Be quiet, you old fool,' he angrily replied, 'That was years ago.'

Wilkes is remembered today for his championship of great causes. But this was almost accidental. He did not seek out these causes; they sought him out. In return for mob support he became an advocate of parliamentary reform; in return for American money he became an advocate of the American cause. He pursued personal grudges, not great causes. Had he not been so abominably treated by government and Parliament he might well have been little more than a footnote in the standard textbooks. His morals, like those of so many of his time, were reprehensible, but in fighting against personal injustice Wilkes had an unwitting hand in protecting and promoting British liberties. And the reputations of those who pursued him and the one–time friends who abandoned him remain tarnished to this day.

Why did two ex-Cabinet ministers fight a duel?

1809 was a bad year for Britain. For sixteen years, with a brief intermission, the country had been fighting Revolutionary and Napoleonic France with little success. By 1809 Napoleon was master of Europe. Of his three continental enemies Austria had been defeated three times, Prussia had been conquered and Russia was an admirer and ally. Only Britain, forlornly looking for a new European coalition to replace the three that had failed, continued to offer resistance, and was maintaining a precarious foothold in Europe with its 30,000 troops in Portugal. The British government was faced with failure abroad and economic difficulties at home. Why, then, did two Cabinet ministers take their personal differences to the point of breaking up the government and risking their lives in a duel?

The British Cabinet was headed in 1809 by the Duke of Portland, seventy-one years old, and lacking in great political skill and intellect. His government was regarded by most politicians as stopgap, but the main opposition, led by William Grenville, had ruled itself out by championing Roman Catholic emancipation, for George III would never accept a ministry committed to it. The better brains of the ministry were in the House of Lords. George Canning, who was in the Commons, regarded himself as political heir to the younger Pitt, and head and shoulders above all his contemporaries. He regarded the office of Prime Minister as within his grasp, especially as he was already holding the important office of Foreign Secretary. If he had a serious rival it was Lord Castlereagh, one year Canning's senior by age, but one year his junior in the holding of political office. Castlereagh's peerage was Irish, so he was able to take a seat in the House of Commons, from which he could pose a considerable threat to Canning's political ambitions. Moreover, as Secretary for War and the colonies, he was responsible for Britain's war policy, and thus, in wartime, was more important than the Foreign Secretary.

Canning had already in Cabinet criticised the Convention of Cintra, 1808, by which the defeated French army in Portugal was allowed to evacuate the country unmolested. Canning wanted Castlereagh to disavow the Convention, but Castlereagh refused. Canning also believed that Castlereagh had been involved in misuse of East India Company funds to buy parliamentary seats, although the charges had never been proved. He complained bitterly that Castlereagh had no interest in the war in the Peninsula, and that he ought to have taken steps actively to intervene in Germany.

In the early spring of 1809 it seemed likely that Austria might re-enter the war against France, and that efforts should be made to give Austria active British support. Castlereagh was thinking of an expedition to the Scheldt, but in March Canning lost patience and wrote to Portland to complain of incompetent colleagues, and to demand a reconstruction of the Ministry. Canning threatened resignation unless this was done, and Portland was left in no doubt that Canning wanted Castlereagh removed from the War Office, but not necessarily removed from the Cabinet; he could be offered some lesser post. Portland, supported by Spencer Percival, did not want to lose either man, and with strong approval from the King suggested that, as a cabinet reshuffle was inevitable in view of Portland's poor health, Canning should wait at least until the end of the parliamentary session. Portland let it be known among some colleagues that they were pledged to remove one of them, and there was speculation concerning who it might be. By now Castlereagh's plans for the Scheldt expedition were well under way, and Portland's colleagues insisted that Castlereagh should be given time to put them into effect, thus postponing any reshuffle. The expedition set sail in July, just as the army of Austria was overwhelmed by Napoleon at Wagram. Most of the troops were landed on the very marshy Walcheren Island where they were unable to get to grips with the enemy, and where those not evacuated by sea succumbed to fever. The expedition destroyed the reputation of the second Earl of Chatham who had been given the command, and had, until this debacle, enough political experience to be a rival to Canning.

In August Portland suffered some sort of seizure, and by early September it had become clear that the Scheldt expedition was a failure. Canning decided that he could wait no longer. On September 6 he resigned from the Cabinet when Portland and Percival threatened to resign themselves if Castlereagh's dismissal was insisted upon. Only now did Castlereagh realise what had been going on. He resigned from the Cabinet, and after a delay of thirteen days wrote a bitter letter of complaint about the way in which Canning, knowing that Castlereagh was about to be replaced, had allowed Castlereagh to plan and execute the Scheldt expedition '*with your apparent concurrence and approbation.*' He ended the letter by challenging Canning to a duel. It has been suggested that Castlereagh's challenge was more about revenge than vindication of his honour. On the other hand it might well have been purely political. If Castlereagh did nothing Canning would very likely be invited to join a new Ministry, and Castlereagh could never consent to serve with a minister who had been intriguing against him behind his back. If, on the other hand he issued a challenge, then a duel would take both of them out of the political arena for the time being. From Castlereagh's point of view there was little danger of actual bloodshed. He was an expert shot and could determine where, or whether, the ball would strike. Canning had never fired a pistol, and was almost certain to miss his target, even if, as was unlikely, he was to deliberately aim at Castlereagh.

In his reply to the challenge Canning felt that a lengthy explanation would imply cowardice on his part, and anyway would unfavourably involve Portland, Percival and the King. The seconds (Charles Ellis for Canning and Lord Yarmouth for Castlereagh) met on the evening before the duel to try to sort out a solution, but Castlereagh not surprisingly was unresponsive; he had no intention of leaving the political arena clear for such a devious rival. Duels were common among military officers but comparatively rare among politicians. When duels had a fatal result they often resulted in manslaughter or murder charges, but juries almost invariably acquitted. When duels were given sufficient advertisement the authorities often tried to intervene, but in this case the challenge was so closely followed by the duel that such interference was unlikely, and in the event no attempt was made by the constables to prevent the duel. Canning wrote a farewell letter to his wife, just in case, in which he showed concern that his affairs were in order, but he could not resist the opportunity for self-justification: '*I am conscious of having acted for what I thought best for my country, with no more mixture of selfish motives than the impatience of misconduct in others.*'

The duel took place on Putney Heath at 6am on September 21. The seconds fixed the distance as far as custom allowed, at twelve paces, hoping to minimise injuries. Perversely enough it was Castlereagh who was in the greater danger, since Castlereagh could place his shot with care, while Canning's random efforts might go anywhere. And so it proved. Canning's pistol had to be cocked by his second, Ellis, who explained that Canning had never fired a pistol in his life. With their first shots both missed. Castlereagh refused to accept that honour was satisfied, and Canning replied that since Castlereagh had called him out it was for him to say when the duel was over. With the second shot Canning narrowly missed his opponent, and Castlereagh's hit Canning in the fleshy part of the thigh, fortunately missing bones and arteries. Ellis began to help Canning away but Canning stopped to enquire whether they had finished. Yarmouth assured him that it was indeed over, and Castlereagh came up to assist Canning to Yarmouth's house close by, to which a surgeon had been summoned in readiness.

The duel shocked the political world. The King was angry, former colleagues of the two were appalled. In October the Ministry was reconstructed with Spencer Percival at its head; there was no one else to choose, since by their conduct Castlereagh and Canning had ruled themselves out. There might have been room for one of them after a decent interval, but they regarded the new Ministry as so weak that it was unlikely to survive, and did not wish to be associated with it. Eventually, as the Ministry gathered strength, room was found for Castlereagh in the spring of 1812, but Canning had to wait until 1816 to rejoin a Cabinet, and then in a somewhat minor position as President of the Board of Control.

The duel consigned two able men to the political wilderness at a time when the government was weak and needed strengthening. Castlereagh believed he had no choice but to challenge Canning or his own political career would be at an end. Canning had unbounded ambition and had resorted to intrigue condoned by the Prime Minister and the King. His comment after the duel that he did not know why they had been fighting could only have been feigned naivety. His criticisms of Castlereagh would have been just as vehement had Castlereagh listened to him and landed troops in Germany, or sent extra regiments to Portugal. And the Scheldt failure had more to do with its execution than Castlereagh's planning. Canning's precipitate attempt to clear a way to the top had rebounded on himself, and not until Castlereagh's suicide in 1822 was the shadow of the duel removed. But by then, in Lord Liverpool, a surprising man of strength had been found from among the politicians Canning so despised, and Canning did not achieve the Prime Ministership until he had only four months left to live. His relentless pursuit of Castlereagh can only be justified if it was deserved, which in the main it was not. The duel was Castlereagh's very effective response to a shabby piece of political manoeuvring.

President Andrew Jackson: colossus or crook?

Andrew Jackson, taking office at the White House in 1829, was perhaps the first popular President of the United States. Those before him had been 'easterners', affluent, cultured, a good deal influenced by the example of England and therefore 'toffs'; but Jackson was tough, wiry, an almost completely uneducated vulgarian and entirely a 'westerner'. His nickname – he was the first US President to bear a nickname – was 'Old Hickory', and was taken from the tough wood characteristic of the hickory tree, the hardness of which Jackson himself possessed. He was forceful, uncompromising and had very decided opinions on the Negroes and the Indians. He was an accomplished soldier. At the time of the War of 1812 he became a national hero in the Creek War of 1813–14 against the Indians and in 1815 in his defeat of British forces at the battle of New Orleans. He narrowly escaped censure in his invasion of Spanish Florida in 1817, when he had his first experience of putting down Seminole Indians – and later the Cherokees – and 'resettling' them further west. He nearly won the 1824 Presidential election, winning the largest number of popular votes, but was narrowly pipped at the post by J. Q. Adams, another of the more moderate Presidents who ruled on an eastern power-base. In 1828, however, with the support of his new political organization that later developed into the Democratic Party, Jackson became President. He had the backing of the poorer southern states, and the wild frontiersmen of the developing west; no one could think he was a gentleman.

Adams supporters had already begun criticizing the new President's moral character. He had freely compared their manners to the insolence of the English House of Stuart; now they turned on him as a rather easier target. They accused him of adultery, gambling, drunkenness, lying, theft and cockfighting; they revealed their intolerance of the south's 'peculiar institution' by criticizing his involvement in slave-trading. They even accused him of bigamy – a charge not entirely without truth, since when he married his wife Rachel he did so under the impression that she was already divorced from her first husband, only to find that she was not. There could really not have been a greater contrast than there was between Jackson and the Presidents who had preceded him.

But there could be no question of his popularity, especially with the pioneer settlers of the west, the ordinary farmers of the south and the town-dwellers of the eastern states. They flocked to his inauguration in their thousands. They could not hear his address, of course, since there was no system of public address in those days; Jackson had a poor weak voice, and in any case was not saying anything worth hearing. But they joined in for the party afterwards. It was a very exuberant occasion, bordering on a riot: they cheered him until they were hoarse; they stood on the elegant upholstered furniture to get a better view; they broke a good deal of expensive china and fine glassware, and they did not hesitate to slip into their pockets souvenirs to take home for those unfortunate enough not to have been present.

The populist character of his inauguration was paralleled by the style of his presidency. In his message to congress at the outset of his term he had complained of the inefficiency of the Civil Service under Adams, roundly asserting (rather like Lenin almost a century later) that 'the duties of all public offices are … so plain and simple that men of intelligence may readily qualify themselves for their performance.' But what he was really interested in (again like Lenin) was providing 'Jobs for the Boys'. He instituted in 1829 a complete 'packing' of the new administration: his supporters took all the new appointments from the most important Cabinet offices down to the local postmasterships. This marked the beginning of what came to be known as the American 'spoils system', and created an abuse that later grew to be one of the least attractive features of American life.

Another much criticized feature of Jackson's government was his quite naked 'cronyism'. He was a good deal given to the unofficial discussion of the problems of government with friends who were not Cabinet ministers, so giving rise to the suggestion that he had a 'kitchen Cabinet'. Worse still, one of them was a woman. John Eaton, his Secretary of War and a former senator from Tennessee, was one of his cronies; his wife, formerly Peggy O'Neill, had long been a notorious character in Washington as the good-looking, free-and-easy daughter of a local publican whom Eaton had eventually married. The other Cabinet wives snubbed her at dinners and balls; even Mrs Donelson, niece of the president and mistress of the White House (Jackson was by now a widower), refused to call on her, and when Jackson reproached her, left her job. Such was the unseemly squabbling over Peggy Eaton that Adams and Clay and the other opposition 'Whigs', as they came to be called, had no difficulty in poking fun at the Jackson regime.

The irascible Jackson was always an easy target. He waxed extremely angry, and used quaint archaic oaths like 'By the e-*ter*-nal!' and 'Gol-*darn* it!'. He was even drawn into a duel with a noted pistol shot of the time, Charles Dickinson, whom he rashly suspected of slighting him. When they fought, Jackson took his opponent's ball near his heart, but kept himself upright, fired and wounded Dickinson in the upper thigh, rupturing an artery and inflicting a wound from which he later died. The President was warned against an operation by his surgeons and carried the bullet to his grave, even though the wound bled from time to time.

It was his 'ornery guy' image that helped to maintain his long popularity during the eight years of his office. Honoured by Harvard College whilst on a trip to New England, he presented himself at one of America's most prestigious institutions to receive an LLD at a ceremony in which (in the best traditions of Oxford and Cambridge) he had to respond in Latin. His speech was perhaps the shortest on record, and yet it had a kind of surrealist relevance to Jackson's own political philosophy – it was '*E pluribus unum, sine qua non*'.

At the close of his presidency, his New York supporters sent him a wheel of cheese weighing three-quarters of a ton, which he set up in one of the White House lobbies on Washington's birthday, inviting anyone passing to help himself, if he brought his own utensils; by the end of the day, so great had been the response that not a solitary crumb remained.

Thus, of Jackson's personal popularity there can be no doubt; unfortunately there can be no doubt either about the man's scandalous and quite irredeemable vulgarity. Charles Dickens put his finger very precisely on this feature of American life in the chapters of *Martin Chuzzlewit* which deal with the hero's disastrous trip to the USA in pursuit of a fortune. To the lasting humiliation of the eastern seaboard's aristocratic reputation, Jackson stained the character of the ordinary US citizen for upwards of a century with the commonly-accepted idea that the American was an ignorant, trigger-happy, boastful, loud-mouthed philistine who did not deserve even a fraction of the acknowledgment he demanded as his right. This unfortunate misapprehension for a long time did America's reputation no good whatsoever.

Did Sir Hari Singh bring about the Kashmir question?

At the end of 1947 Sir Hari Singh, Maharajah of Jammu and Kashmir, decided, after protracted uncertainty, to throw in his lot with the newly-established state of India instead of joining the independent state of Pakistan, both of them created by the British Parliament's India Independence Act of July, 1947. Both were originally Commonwealth Dominions, though one became a republic in 1950 and the other steadily declined into a military dictatorship in the course of the 1950s. The Maharajah's choice was made under the pressure of events, and for quite the wrong sort of reasons. Its repercussions, however, continued to shake the whole subcontinent for more than half a century and still rumble on even in the twenty-first century.

The ancestors of the Maharajah had been installed in Kashmir during the period of the British Raj, and largely as the result of British influence in the area, in the middle years of the nineteenth century. At this time, the Sikhs, having lost two wars to the British, offered up Kashmiri territories in lieu of war reparations. The British promptly sold them to the neighbouring Rajah of Ladakh and Jammu, thus creating the modern Kashmir. Sir Hari Singh was the descendant of this despot. Unfortunately he was not the most admirable of men. He was one of a whole galaxy of some 600 Indian princes, nearly all of them Hindus, who, long accustomed to kid-glove treatment by sycophantic British administrators before independence, for the most part unhesitatingly opted to join India after it. Nearly all were immensely rich, effete and idle, and more than a few at least a bit batty. Sir Hari lived in a vast, sprawling palace in Srinagar, the capital of Kashmir, and devoted himself to bear hunting and duck shooting. Educated partly in England like many of his princely contemporaries, he was unique in suffering the indignity of being found in bed with a woman in the Savoy Hotel, and being subsequently blackmailed for thousands by her indignant 'husband'. He was something of a playboy: vain, conceited, extravagant and lazy. Those who knew him said he was as rich and as nutty as a fruitcake. One thing he was not good at was having to make up his mind. It was this hesitancy which, in the end, proved to be the undoing of the state he ruled.

The critical fact about the Maharajah was that he was a Hindu. Of course, he was not alone in this; nearly all the others were as well. But it was the question of religion that was the fundamental one. There were four states that did not join the new Indian Union immediately because of it. One was the tiny state of Travancore, which held out only for a few days before joining. More important was Junagadh, a small seaport state on the coast of Kathiawar, which had a Hindu population and a Muslim Nawab. It opted for union with Pakistan but after a few weeks Indian troops occupied the state and a plebiscite voted for union with India. Much more important was Hyderabad, a large inland state in the Deccan with a population that was 85 per cent Hindu, but with a government that had been Muslim for hundreds of years. India felt that it could not permit so large and so powerful an enclave. The Nizam dallied with shifts and evasions, refusing tempting terms of entry negotiated for him by the British, and, seeing the growing hostility of India, finally allowed an extremist organization, the Razakars, to seize control. This provided India with an excuse for 'police action' in 1948, as a result of which Hyderabad was forced to join the Indian Union. Pakistan protested, but to no avail.

However the gravest and most permanent problem occurred in Kashmir. This was a very large and beautiful inland state in the north-west, beloved of honeymooners on account of its limpid lakes and cool alpine meadows, its magical charms celebrated in many popular melodies. It was a state on the borders of Pakistan and India, and was important to both of them. Politically, however, it was a ramshackle state. Though its Maharajah was Hindu, its population was 60 per cent Muslim: to the east there was a Hindu majority centred on Jammu; in the Vale of Kashmir itself the population was well over 90 per cent Muslim; while in the North and West there were mountain regions partly controlled by hill chieftains who were Muslim, and partly Buddhist-Tibetan in character.

Sir Hari Singh hesitated for a long time over what he ought to do. He had no wish to link himself with Pakistan, but neither did he want to be ordered about by the Indian Union. The Indian Independence Act, passed in July 1947, went into operation in early August. The Maharajah seems to have wished for independence and freedom of action, and to have seen Kashmir in a balancing role, a sort of neutral 'Switzerland of Asia'. Hence he played for time and did not join either of his two great neighbours. But events did not wait upon his decision. The remote northern third of the country, around Gilgit, declared itself to be Azad ('Free') Kashmir and joined its powerful Muslim neighbour. Simultaneously Muslim farmworkers rebelled against their Hindu landlords, and found themselves supported in October by an army of Pathan irregulars, who burst in from Pakistan's North-West Frontier Province and advanced on Srinagar, looting, raping and murdering as they went. As this ragtag army neared the capital the Maharajah in panic acceded to India, and in the nick of time the Indian government sent in airborne troops to retrieve the situation. From this time, the Indian government stood on the legal ground of accession, branding Pakistan as the aggressor since the Pathans came from its territory, while Pakistan insisted on the sovereignty of the people and called for a plebiscite. A brief war flared up between the two dominions, settled by a UN truce in January 1949, with Nehru agreeing (in principle) to a plebiscite and accepting a 'line of control' across the divided country and the presence of an international peacekeeping force, both of which have been there ever since. Though Nehru was quick to accept that Kashmir's future would be decided by its inhabitants, he and his successors unfortunately were never able to accept any proposals for carrying out the plebiscite proposals. He installed the pro-Indian Sheikh Abdullah as head of state, and he agreed to hold elections to the Kashmiri assembly in 1951, but before the elections the Sheikh banned all opposition parties, with the result that the voters boycotted the polls, and seventy-three of Abdullah's candidates were returned unopposed out of a total of seventy-five.

India and Pakistan again went to war over Kashmir in 1965–66, and for a third time in 1971, at the time of the secession of East Pakistan to form Bangladesh. In 1972 the two states agreed to the terms of the Simla Agreement, whereby both consented to negotiate over the future of Kashmir; no progress, however, was forthcoming, and the problem continued to fester. In 2002, the two sides were confronting each other again along the tortuous frontier across Kashmir, the threat of conflict aggravated by the likelihood of a resort to the nuclear weapons with which both were provided. Even after a disastrous earthquake in the Pakistani-controlled area of Kashmir in 2005, when hundreds of thousands died, there was still no settlement. The Indians made much of their claim at this time that there was wide backing in Pakistan for extremist Muslim groups such as the one that carried out a bombing outrage against the Indian Parliament in December 2001, or for the al-Qaeda movement that had recently been defeated in Afghanistan. But the real reason for their mistrust was Pakistani intractability over the Kashmir question. As a result India remained uneasily conscious of the uncomfortable statistic that there were more Muslims living in India than there were in Pakistan, which explained their unwillingness to grant even the token autonomy requested of them in 2000 by the normally quiescent Kashmir Assembly.

Sir Hari Singh himself, after his removal from power in Srinagar, went into exile in Delhi, and squandered his last years before his death in 1961 indulging his passion for tobacco, drink, fast cars and racehorses. But in delaying his decision and then making his unfortunate choice in 1947, Sir Hari Singh created one of the gravest problems of contemporary India.

Did the leader of the Liberal Party employ a contract killer?

The indictment and trial of Jeremy Thorpe, leader of the British Liberal Party until 1976, on a charge of conspiracy to the murder of Norman Scott, his homosexual lover, proved to be the salacious highlight of 1979, the year in which the trial took place. The burden of the charge was that Thorpe had incited three men – who stood with him in the dock – to kill Scott, who had become an embarrassment to him and a threat to the future of the whole of British Liberalism. The affair caused a scandalized protest at the time by the press and by the public, though strangely it produced little lasting political damage for the party he headed, since it reduced Liberal representation in the British House of Commons only from the thirteen or fourteen seats the party had held in the 1970s to eleven it won in the election of 1979. Nevertheless, the case was the ruin of Jeremy Thorpe himself.

Born in 1929, Thorpe was the son of a Conservative MP, and was educated at Eton and Oxford. At Oxford he became President of the university debating society, the Oxford Union, and was called to the bar in 1954. He then went into politics and joined the Liberal Party. Though he failed at the first attempt, he was elected for North Devon by the narrow margin of 362 votes in 1959, and achieved the leadership of the Liberal Party in 1967 at the age of only thirty-eight, when he replaced Jo Grimond as party leader, and revitalized the flagging efforts of the party to recover its former eminence. He staged a mini-revival of Liberal fortunes in the 1970s, making a great impression in the Commons with his wit and oratory. There was only one fly in the ointment: a routine security check into his background revealed that he had homosexual tendencies. Homosexuality still aroused powerful public repugnance at this time, and homosexual activity, even in private and between consenting adults, still constituted a criminal offence. Hence it was essential that anything of this kind should be kept quiet.

It was in 1960, on a visit to a riding stable in Oxfordshire, that Jeremy Thorpe met the man who was to bring about his downfall. Norman Josiffe, later known as Scott, was eleven years Thorpe's junior, a child of a broken marriage and with recurrent emotional problems. He did not always succeed in staying on the right side of the law, and when Thorpe met him, was serving probation after a conviction for larceny. Thorpe offered him help, and a year later, after a failed suicide attempt, Scott arranged to meet Thorpe at the House of Commons. The two met regularly after that, chiefly in Thorpe's mother's house in Oxted, Surrey. Scott said that to allay Thorpe's mother's suspicions on his first visit he was asked to masquerade as a TV employee, but that even at this first meeting, Thorpe made his intentions clear, appearing in Scott's bedroom in a dressing gown during the evening and later sodomizing him. Scott claimed he hated the sex act, and submitted to it only as means of getting employment on the staff of Len Smith, a Liberal Party central official. Thorpe got him a flat near the House of Commons and even took him on a visit to Devon. But their relations were tempestuous. Before long, Scott was in trouble with the police again, accused of minor theft, and Thorpe arranged that the police should interview him at the House of Commons, where he represented himself as Scott's guardian. Scott went to work on a farm in Somerset; Thorpe wrote to him, and the two were once more reconciled. Later, however, Thorpe received a bill from his tailor for silk pyjamas that Scott had ordered on Thorpe's account (a bill he refused to pay). Then Scott moved to Ireland, where he was once more working with horses, and before long was asking Thorpe for money for a trip to Switzerland to take up a new job. Thorpe agreed readily enough, if only to be rid of him, but Scott did not like his new life and soon came home, losing his luggage on the journey. Thorpe made the mistake of enlisting the help of a colleague, the Liberal MP Peter Bessel, who, though a fellow MP and apparently respectable, turned out to be a dangerous acquaintance. Bessel was a self-confessed liar and a crooked businessman who eventually fled Britain with huge debts and went to live in the USA. Furthermore it was he who was the chief prosecution witness in Thorpe's trial in 1979. Bessel was asked by Thorpe to deal with the matter of the lost luggage and later with Scott himself, who by this time was becoming, by reason of his continuing demands, an embarrassment and a problem.

There was even an element of attempted blackmail in the relationship between them, and when Thorpe became party leader in January 1967 he decided he had to put a stop to it.

Scott was by this time blackmailing Thorpe quite openly. He got £2500 from him for the return of certain compromising letters, and with the money retired to a cottage on Exmoor, where he took to drinking heavily and to experimenting with drugs. Thorpe suggested to Bessel that Scott had to be silenced – and even killed if necessary. The two engaged the help of Andrew ('Gino') Newton, a former airline pilot, who posed as one 'Peter Keene' to put the frighteners on Scott. Newton contacted Scott and told him that a hit man had been hired in Canada to kill him, and persuaded him to agree to a meeting to discuss the matter in Combe Martin in October 1975. Scott took the precaution of taking with him to the meeting his Great Dane, Rinka. The meeting started amiably enough in Newton's car, but then he took out a Mauser handgun, and began to threaten him. He shot the dog through the head and killed it, brandishing the weapon as if he meant to use it on Scott himself. Then he made off in his car. Scott was terrified, and went to the police for their protection. Newton made only perfunctory efforts to avoid detection and was shortly afterwards arrested, when he told the police that Scott had been blackmailing him and that he shot the dog to scare him. He received a two-year sentence for threatening behaviour, of which he served slightly more than one. Less than a year later, Scott was in trouble again, this time accused of defrauding the DHSS. This time he did what he had been threatening to do for a long time – he made a comprehensive statement to the police about his relations with Jeremy Thorpe, who soon afterwards was forced into the open and had to resign as Liberal leader.

Newton sold his story to the press, and the sensational news about the Scott affair broke in an article in the *London Evening News* early in 1979. Bessel adjusted his loyalties at once. He abandoned his support of Thorpe, declared he would have no more to do with him, and put the record straight in a statement to the police shortly afterwards. Meantime the press had found the connection between Thorpe and three obscure South Wales businessmen, who had hired Newton to frighten Scott into ceasing his pursuit of Thorpe. The four of them were together charged with conspiracy to murder at the Old Bailey in May 1979.

The most important and damning witness for the prosecution was Peter Bessel. He told how Thorpe had first suggested killing Scott off in 1968, and that they had discussed ways of disposing of his body. When Bessel pointed out the dangers of a contract killing, Thorpe was alleged to have replied: 'It's no worse than shooting a sick dog.' Bessel even suggested that the money he had used as an inducement to Andrew Newton had been embezzled from Liberal Party funds. However George Carman, QC, for the defence, in his cross-examination uncovered the uncomfortable fact that Bessel had taken the precaution beforehand of selling his story to the papers: if Thorpe was convicted he would be paid £50,000, but only £25,000 if he was found not guilty. Bessel's admission reflected badly on the reliability of his evidence and disposed the jury to think that he had a vested interest in a conviction. Scott created an even worse impression in the dock. He was alternately ingratiating and evasive, and under cross-examination was obliged to confess that many of the details of the affair with Thorpe, such as their first encounter at Thorpe's mother's house, were either exaggerated or entirely fictitious. In his summing-up the judge called Scott a fraud, a whinger and a parasite. Largely on the strength of the judge's words the jury brought in a not guilty verdict and all four were acquitted of the charge of attempted murder.

Though the judge was accused later of undue partiality towards the defendants, there were few who really believed that Thorpe and his associates were guilty of conspiracy to murder. What was evident afterwards was that while it was Scott who was torn apart in court, it was Thorpe who received the heaviest punishment – a scandalous dismissal from public life.

Thereafter the arguments over Thorpe's guilt in the Scott affair refused to be put to rest. Though he had been completely exonerated in court, Thorpe continued to be subjected to a good deal of innuendo and open criticism. The impartiality of the judge in the case, Mr Justice Cantley, was also made the subject of adverse comment. As a result in 1996 Channel 4 television produced a heavily critical programme dealing with the conduct and the outcome of the case, and ITV returned to the attack in 2002, this time enlisting contributions from the egregious Norman Scott himself, still anxious to restore his reputation as the injured party in the relationship, and to portray himself as Thorpe's victim. By this time, Thorpe was in his seventies and had been for many years a victim of Parkinson's disease. He maintained a dignified silence throughout his two 'retrials', but many in his immediate circle of friends and former colleagues suggested that it was time that the matter was allowed to drop.

Jonathan Aitken and the simple sword of truth

It is not entirely surprising that a Member of Parliament and a Cabinet minister, whether or not he was a well-heeled and public-school educated individual like Jonathan Aitken, should be caught out in barefaced lies. It was, however, rather more scandalous that he should persist in his dishonesty, and – ignoring the well-known adage that 'when you are in a hole, you should stop digging' – even seek to brazen it out by means of increasingly implausible explanations, until eventually his excuses ran out and he was publicly humiliated and sent to prison for his shortcomings. Aitken's only redeeming feature appears to have been that he eventually saw the light, and even underwent a kind of moral regeneration through his adoption of the Christian faith.

Aitken entered Parliament as a Tory MP in 1974 and was rich, intelligent, hospitable and charming to his many friends and colleagues. He was generally popular and gracious, even to his political opponents. He had many things going for him: he was the son of a Tory MP, his grandfather was a peer and his great uncle was Max Aitken, Lord Beaverbrook, the press magnate and proprietor of the *Daily Express*. Young Aitken was seen by many as a rising star. He was already rich, and increasingly influential after he was appointed managing director of Slater Walker, Middle East. He got to know Mohammed bin Fahd, son of the Saudi king, and his powerful business manager Said Ayas. His Middle East connections were so well-spread that he was even suspected of being involved in the espionage business. His commercial connections were even more extensive. He founded a merchant bank, Aitken-Hume, purchased a health hydro in Berkshire, and, using Saudi funds, bought a controlling share in TVam, using a front company in the Caribbean as a tax haven.

But there were already more dubious sides to Aitken's character. In 1970, while seeking a parliamentary seat in Thirsk and Malton, he was shown a classified report by his constituency chairman that Britain was aiding the rebels in the Nigerian civil war, and sent a report on it to the *Sunday Telegraph*, as a result of which he was charged with breaching the Official Secrets Act, and only escaped by denouncing his colleague and giving up his candidacy. In 1979 he incurred the lasting hostility of the Prime Minister, Margaret Thatcher, by dumping her daughter Carol as his fiancée, and marrying Lolicia Azucki, a wealthy Yugoslav-born Swiss economist. By 1988, he became a highly-paid non-executive director of BMARC, an arms manufacturing company, and became involved in the international arms trade as an agent for the Saudis. The retirement of Mrs Thatcher in 1990 enabled him to quit the back benches, and he became John Major's Minister of Defence for Procurement in 1992. In this capacity his official duties coincided neatly with his private interests. He joined the Cabinet in 1994 as Chief Secretary, and it was universally assumed that he had fulfilled the necessary rules by giving up his private interests in favour of his job. Some, however, at the time suggested that this was simply untrue. The *Sunday Times*, for example, declared that Aitken, acting as 'Saudi Ambassador to Europe', had brokered a £5 billion arms deal with his Saudi associates (which was said to entitle him to a personal 'commission' of £750m).

So far, Aitken had enjoyed an impressive run of good fortune in his meteoric rise to prominence, but had begun to think his luck was somehow fireproof. The end, when it came, was humiliating and complete, but sprang from quite trivial causes.

At the end of 1994, one of Aitken's most persistent critics, Peter Preston, a member of the Press Complaints Commission and editor of the *Guardian*, published evidence that he had stayed in his acquaintance Mohammed al Fayed's hotel, the Paris Ritz, as the guest of Said Ayas, with whom it was said he had discussed a lucrative arms procurement deal involving the sale of large numbers of Tornado aircraft to the Saudis. At the conclusion of the two day visit Said Ayas had paid the Minister's bill for about £1000, a copy of which the *Guardian* published on its front page. At first Aitken said that the Ritz had made a mistake, and that his wife had sorted it out by a payment into Ayas's account (though she herself had not actually used the hotel room). Then later he produced a more convoluted explanation for the problem: he had arrived late from a ministerial meeting in Poland to meet his wife and daughter en route to Switzerland, where she was being taken to her new school, but they had missed each other, and it was only after several days that he had met his wife briefly in the lobby there, before he went on to Switzerland himself to visit his daughter, and had left his wife enough cash to settle his hotel bill. Later he assured the Cabinet Secretary, Sir Robin Butler, who was investigating the matter, of his innocence and was able to corroborate this by the fortunate recollection of the hotel's cashier, who said he remembered receiving a cash sum (though for a smaller amount) paid by 'a brunette lady of European aspect', confidently identified by Aitken as his wife.

There the matter might have rested, but for the emergence of Mohammed al Fayed on the scene. He was engaged in an entirely different tussle with the British government over its failure to give him naturalisation, and now accused four British ministers of taking cash in return for raising questions in Parliament. Al Fayed's purpose in the 'cash for questions' scandal was to show that, in spite of all their claims of moral integrity, members of the government behaved more reprehensibly than he did. Aitken's behaviour was more grist to al Fayed's mill.

The *Guardian* also jumped on the bandwagon, seizing the moment to point out that the sum paid by the 'brunette lady' to the hotel's cashier and the sum credited to Said Ayas were in fact quite different, and that Aitken had deliberately concealed this difference. In the chamber, Aitken waxed eloquent over 'the hysterical atmosphere of sleaze journalism' and Parliament erupted when it became known that the *Guardian* editor, the courageous enemy of government 'sleaze', had in fact used House of Commons notepaper to help secure his copy of the Ritz bill. The Speaker was incensed. Preston was summoned to appear before the Commons, was roundly abused,[1] and eventually forced to resign both from his editorship and from the Press Complaints Commission.

Once again, Aitken had apparently survived the storm. But it was not long before he was in trouble again. This time it was the *Independent* that led the onslaught, claiming that BMARC (of which Aitken was a

---

1 The Tory MP for Thanet North, Roger Gale, led the attack by calling Preston a 'whore from Hell'.

director – though a non-executive director) was engaged in selling their armaments to Singapore, whence they were being sold on to Iran. The company denied any knowledge of this, and Aitken used the privileges of office to denounce the *Independent* in Parliament, once again pleading innocence in the whole affair. Almost immediately afterwards the attack on him was renewed, this time by Granada TV's documentary programme, *World in Action*, which accused him of involvement in the international arms traffic, an accusation he angrily refuted with words that were to be long remembered:

> If it falls to me to cut out the cancer of bent and twisted journalism in our country with the simple sword of truth and the trusty shield of fair play, then so be it – I am ready for the fight.

In a Cabinet reshuffle in July 1995, Aitken resigned from the Front Bench[2] and retired for about a year into relative obscurity. Before the end of the year he had issued writs for libel and 'aggravated damages' against both the *Guardian* and Granada TV. 1996 saw him exonerated from blame for misconduct in his ministerial dealings by a parliamentary enquiry, and after the general election of May 1997 (in which the Conservatives lost power to Tony Blair's New Labour Party) the much-heralded libel suit came to court.

The case started well for the plaintiff, with Aitken performing confidently, but then his luck began to run out, and he found himself struggling. The more he struggled, the deeper he found himself embedded in the mire. His lies collapsed about his ears like a house of cards: he admitted he had lied to Sir Robin Butler about the disputed cash payment; he admitted he had spoken with the Saudis while in Paris; he dug himself in deeper about whom he was supposed to have been with in Paris, and when; he elaborated his story of cash payments by his wife, alleging that she was dyslexic and preferred to use cash rather than credit cards; he even brought his mother-in-law into the story and said it was she who had shared a hotel room with his wife. Finally, both American Express and British Airways were subpoenaed to produce dockets that proved that neither his wife nor his daughter had

---

2 In order '... to spend more time with his solicitors', as one press reporter neatly put it.

been anywhere near Paris at the time in question. Overnight, his case collapsed.

Aitken's lawyers withdrew his allegations against the defendants, and offered instead to pay their costs in full. His wife divorced him, and he vanished – some said in Ayas's private jet – on holiday to New York and California. He disappeared completely from public life. Facing bankruptcy and further ruin, he constructed an elaborate fantasy that he and his associates had been secret 'couriers' working for MI6. As a result, in June 1999, at the insistence of the press, he was charged with perjury and perverting the course of justice, and sentenced to jail for eighteen months.

He served seven months in Belmarsh Prison (the same jail in which Jeffrey Archer served time) before being released in January 2000 under a home detention order and with an electronic tagging device to enforce his curfew. Prison was a totally new experience for him. At first he was physically bullied and mocked and derided as a 'toff'. Later he was better accepted. He came to recognise that his tormentors, though apparently violent and tough, were vulnerable and mostly illiterate.[3] He wrote letters for his fellow inmates, and it was said the quality of the prisoners' letters sent out from Belmarsh was greatly improved.

While in prison his misery turned him to God. He confessed he had been 'puffed up with pride' and that he had treated God 'rather like I used to treat my bank manager'. He said he understood why medieval monks liked cells so much – he found a prison cell a great place to pray in (even if he did not get a cell all to himself). In Belmarsh he started a Bible study and prayer group which attracted about a dozen prisoners, who came at first to mock, but later stayed to worship, and on his release he was enrolled as a mature student at Wycliffe Hall, an Evangelical School of Theology at Oxford, where he continued his studies. At the same time, on completion of his degree course, he never felt he was good enough to contemplate ordination in the Church; rather, he did a lot of prison visiting and gave his life over to the ministry, 'in the broadest sense of the word'.

---

3 His fellow convicts came to know him as 'the geezer with wonderful joined-up writing'. He himself delighted in colourful rhyming 'prison-speak', and liked to refer to his 'teeth' as his 'Hampstead Heath'.

Was Prime Minister Blair naïve or dishonest over his war against Iraq?

The problem created by the Anglo-American invasion of Iraq in 2003, and the consequences of this effort at a 'regime change' there, have created more international controversy than its originators intended, and at the same time a good deal of questioning of the two governments' integrity in undertaking the campaign. Suggestions of ulterior motives have not been slow to emerge, and with them the implication that the whole affair was scandalously conceived and conducted.

When Britain and the USA invaded Iraq in March 2003 Prime Minister Blair secured the support of a large majority in the House of Commons by insisting that the war was to enforce the Resolutions of the United Nations, and to remove Iraq's threat both to its neighbours and to the world in general. There were protests from a small minority of the Labour members, and the Liberal Democrats refused to support the government on the grounds that the war lacked a mandate from the United Nations. But within weeks of the invasion the good faith of the government was called into question. It was alleged that the government had secured the vote for war by 'sexing up' (i.e. exaggerating the importance of) the intelligence dossier of September 2002 which provided the main evidence against Iraq. The inquiry by Lord Hutton found the government innocent, and laid the blame for the unfounded allegation firmly at the door of the media, in particular the BBC. Lord Hutton had not considered it his brief to enquire into the accuracy of the intelligence information, only whether the government had distorted it. It was Lord Butler's inquiry reporting in July 2004 which tackled that second question, criticising the unreliability of the intelligence, but absolving both the intelligence services and the government of any responsibility for its inaccuracy and misuse. Both inquiries and reports left unanswered the major questions: if the government was unaware of the unreliability of the intelligence, then the Joint Intelligence Committee should have made it aware, so the government was incompetent in not probing the JIC more searchingly. And if the government was aware of its unreliability then the government was dishonest in its use of the evidence.

By almost universal consent Saddam Hussein would be ranked high on the list of the most vile and revolting dictators. On coming to power he disposed of many of his opponents by judicial murder, and did not hesitate to subject rivals within the Ba'ath party to the same treatment. He was not unique in suppressing dissident nationalities, but his use of cyanide and mustard gas against the Kurds in Helabjeh in 1988 was only surpassed in depravity by Hitler; others, like Stalin and Pol Pot, may have exceeded him in numbers killed, but he had the edge over them in method. His unprovoked attack on Kuwait in 1990 brought universal condemnation, even from Arab neighbours professing friendship, and the public executions in Kuwait City were broadcast to the world on television and aroused widespread horror. Coalition forces with United Nations' backing liberated Kuwait in 1991. Saddam was forced to agree to 'no-fly' zones over Northern Iraq, policed by American and British planes, and he was to give up biological weapons and abandon his attempts to become a nuclear power. Nor was he to manufacture or stockpile long-range missiles. Inspection teams were to have free access to all of Iraq, and to seek out and destroy any weapons or raw materials that contravened these terms. United Nations' sanctions were imposed to bring Saddam to heel, and to prevent him interfering with the free access of the weapons inspection teams. Saddam co-operated only desultorily; sometimes he was positively obstructive. Eventually the arms inspectors were expelled altogether. The sanctions hit hard, and although Iraqi oil could be exported in exchange for medical supplies and other limited essentials, the quality of life in Iraq sharply declined and corruption at the top ensured that Iraqi hospitals were desperately short of essential medical supplies. Meanwhile the weapons' inspection teams found no great quantity of any of the banned weapons and materials, and it was widely assumed that Saddam had hidden them well. Nevertheless there was no specific intelligence to this effect.

The al-Qaeda attack on the New York Trade Centre on September 11 2001 precipitated President Bush's crusade against international terrorism. He was angry with Saddam for his half-crazed plotting to assassinate former President Bush (senior), who had been President at the time of 'Operation Desert Storm' in 1991. Such schemes were not unique to rogue states; the CIA had long plotted the extermination of Fidel Castro. But in his 'axis of evil' speech President Bush seemed to be implying a link between terrorists such as al-Qaeda and Saddam Hussein; it was not stated explicitly, but many were convinced by it. Why Saddam, leader of a secular Iraq, should want to encourage a militant Islamic fundamentalism that would undermine his own regime was never explained.

Saddam's expulsion of the United Nations' weapons inspectors in 1998 had convinced the world that Saddam had something to hide. Saddam's denials that Iraq possessed weapons of mass destruction were treated with contempt and disbelief, and although the weapons inspectors were eventually allowed back into Iraq, their failure to find such weapons was generally attributed both to the skill of the Iraqis in concealing them, and to the difficulties under which the inspectors worked. On 24 September 2002 Britain's Joint Intelligence Committee (JIC) submitted a report to the Cabinet in which generalisations were made about Iraq's aims and capabilities, and in which it was specifically stated that Iraq was ready and able to use weapons of mass destruction within forty-five minutes of the decision taken to use them. On the day of publication Tony Blair told MPs that the contribution of the intelligence agencies was *extensive, detailed and authoritative,* an assertion which Lord Butler's Report was later to question. This September JIC dossier was to form the intelligence basis upon which Britain was to go to war six months later. In the meantime the weapons inspectors, finding nothing but convinced there was something to find, became exasperated by Iraq's attitude which varied from lukewarm co-operation to deliberate obstruction. The chief inspector, Dr Hans Blix, asked for more time. But even the United Nations Security Council felt that too much extra time would merely encourage Saddam to continue to prevaricate. In Resolution No. 1441, agreed by the Security Council in November 2002, it

> recognises the threat that Iraq's non-compliance with Council resolutions and the proliferation of weapons of mass destruction and long-range missiles poses to international peace

and proceeded to threaten *serious consequences* if its resolutions continued to be ignored. Whatever was meant by *serious consequences*, on the basis of this resolution the USA and Britain threatened Saddam with war if he did not at once produce for inspection and disposal the said weapons. For four months there was much sabre-rattling as Britain and the USA attempted to garner support for their intended war. With the failure of Germany and France to support them it was impossible to obtain a Security Council resolution for war, and this failure made the war illegal to those individuals and the several countries which would not support it. Unable to win the support of the United Nations, Britain and the USA decided to act on their own. Blair's decision to give Bush (junior) unqualified support for the war has been attributed to various motives. 'Greed for oil' has been among the more fanciful. But far more probable was Blair's desire to stand shoulder to shoulder with Britain's most powerful ally, and to share in the international kudos accruing from a joint stand, far better than playing second fiddle to Germany and France from within the EU. Both Labour and Conservative politicians have long shared the misapprehension that, despite the loss of Empire, Britain still has a great role to play on the international stage. Blair's righteous conviction that UN resolutions must not be defied with impunity seems a rather hollow explanation of his stand in view of Israel's notorious defiance of UN resolutions and the UN's own reluctance to enforce them. But he probably had a genuine belief – derived from faulty intelligence information – that Saddam constituted a threat not only to the stability of the Middle East but also to the wider world. Whatever his motives it was difficult for Blair to avoid being depicted in parts of the media as 'President Bush's poodle'. The vote in the British House of Commons for war was boosted by Conservative support. The Conservative leader Iain Duncan Smith had a private interview with Tony Blair at 10 Downing Street which appeared to convince him of the necessity and justice of the war. Many people felt that Blair had made Duncan Smith privy to secret intelligence information not contained in the September dossier and which it would not be prudent to reveal to the public. The Liberal Democrats, however, and a number of Labour MPs refused to support the war so Conservative support was vital. The war began in March 2003 and military operations were over by May.

The invading armies faced little resistance and found no weapons of mass destruction. It was widely rumoured that two Iraqi ships had left

Basra two or three days before the invasion laden to the gunwales with heavy but concealed cargoes bound probably for Pakistan. Did they contain the banned weaponry? We shall never know: the story of the ships passed into mythology, and they certainly never made an Asian port. So since the Iraqis had not deployed their WMDs (weapons of mass destruction) within the forty-five minutes mentioned in the JIC dossier, and indeed had not deployed them at all, voices began to be raised about the origin and accuracy of the forty-five minute claim. At the end of May, Andrew Gilligan, a BBC defence reporter, began alleging that the September dossier had been 'sexed up' in order to convince doubting politicians and a doubting public of the justification for war. Gilligan repeated his allegation in June, this time asserting that the Prime Minister's press secretary, Alastair Campbell had been responsible for inserting the forty-five minute claim. Gilligan repeated before the foreign affairs select committee this assertion which Campbell, appearing before the same committee a week later, vigorously denied. Gilligan refused to reveal his source but hinted that it came from high up in the intelligence services. But the media were given enough clues by the Ministry of Defence to identify Dr David Kelly, a former weapons inspector, as the source from whom Gilligan obtained his material. Since Dr Kelly was not in the intelligence services but a minor official in the Defence Ministry without an office or even a desk of his own, it was presumed that a higher source must have been involved. The foreign affairs select committee of the House of Commons summoned Dr Kelly before it and subjected him to a gruelling cross-examination. Labour MPs in particular gave Dr Kelly a roasting; they must have felt that to protect Blair they must humiliate Kelly. On the day of his last appearance before the committee, Dr Kelly committed suicide.

Dr Kelly's death was an embarrassment to the government, which a few days later set up an inquiry under Lord Hutton, a former Lord of Appeal, to look into the circumstances of his death. In the meantime the BBC and Alastair Campbell engaged in a war of words, and Campbell, now the subject of intense press hostility, resigned while still protesting his innocence of Gilligan's charges. Lord Hutton reported at the end of January 2004. Lord Hutton agreed that some minor changes were made to the intelligence dossier at Alastair Campbell's suggestion, nevertheless Campbell was absolved of the charge of adding the forty-five minute reference; this, Hutton said, was inserted before Campbell had made any changes to the dossier. Lord Hutton did not blame any individual for Dr Kelly's death, but he did criticise the BBC for its attack on the *integrity of the government and the Joint Intelligence Committee,* and for its uncritical backing of Gilligan. On the issue of Dr Kelly, Hutton had no doubt that he had expressed reservations to Gilligan about the content of the September dossier and that Gilligan had put his own slant on his conversations with Kelly. It is most likely that Kelly queried some of the dossier's general conclusions. It was unlikely he did more, since he had no access to information that would have allowed him to challenge any specific evidence it contained. On the day the Hutton Report was issued, the BBC chairman, Gavyn Davies, resigned, and on the following day Greg Dyke, the BBC director general, followed suit. Gilligan managed to hang on for only a few more days. As Hutton absolved the government of responsibility for the forty-five minute reference it must have been inserted while the dossier was still in the hands of the Joint Intelligence Committee and before it was submitted to the Cabinet. Lord Hutton declared that his terms of reference related specifically to the circumstances of Dr Kelly's death and the allegations against the government made by Gilligan and the BBC. It was not his brief to cover the issue of the reliability of the September dossier or how the government built up the case for war.

So the government faced increasing media and political clamour for a separate investigation into the reliability of the intelligence information contained in the dossier. Iraq is a large country and the WMDs could well be waiting to be discovered. But by the summer of 2004 even those politicians in Britain and America who had favoured the war most strongly were now not expecting any WMDs to be found and were saying so publicly. It was with considerable reluctance that the British government established a new inquiry headed by Lord Butler, a respected establishment figure and former Cabinet Secretary. He was to judge the reliability of the evidence contained in the September dossier, but as an establishment figure he was not expected (by the media at any rate) to be too censorious of those in high places. He reported surprisingly quickly in late July 2004. The Butler Report was highly critical of the methods of MI6. It had had no agents in Iraq, yet it relied on information from sources hostile to Saddam, and this information had not been cross-checked for accuracy or reliability. In the original dossier the JIC had expressed doubts about the reliability of the evidence upon which the judgments of the dossier was based, but when the dossier reached the Cabinet the 'caveats' had been removed. Blair was to claim that the removal of the 'caveats' did not materially alter the judgments of the JIC's report (that Saddam was a bad lot?), and anyway the 'caveats' had been removed in the preparation stage before the government became involved. As for the forty-five minute claim, this referred not to long-range but to short-range missiles, and this was not made clear at the time either to Parliament or the public. So who neglected to clarify the forty-five minute claim? Butler does not say; presumably he could not find out. And did the dossier lose its 'caveats' in order to please the politicians? The culpability can rest only lightly on the shoulders of the JIC, since Butler specifically recommended that the promotion of John Scarlett, chairman of the JIC, to be Head of MI6 should still go ahead. Is this suggesting that although the 'caveats' were presumably removed by the JIC, Scarlett himself was not responsible? Or if he was, do Butler and Scarlett share Blair's view that the removal of the 'caveats' was insignificant? There seems to have been some crucial failure of duty in all this; Butler accepted Blair's good faith, and in so doing seems to suggest that on the crucial issue of whether or not to go to war he was served by incompetents.

The complicity of the Attorney-General, Lord Goldsmith (himself a Blair appointee), whose advice was sought on the matter of the legality of the war, has also been blamed for Britain's error in going to war 'on a faulty prospectus'. In fact, being a lawyer, he was careful to offer advice – opaque, and in any case later completely revised – to the Prime Minister, advice which finished by suggesting that the legality of the war did not finally depend on the passing of a second UN resolution in favour of it. He also asserted that the 'serious consequences' threatened by the Security Council in Resolution 1441 could be interpreted as including those consequences that followed from British and American 'police action'. If his advice was as reliable as Blair said he believed, the doctrine it enshrined certainly rewrote the meaning of Article 51 of the UN Charter, which clearly limited 'the inherent right of self-defence' to the occurrence of 'an armed attack against a member of the United Nations' – and, even then, only 'until the Security Council has taken the measures necessary to maintain international peace and security.' No amount of judicial word-play could ever have suggested that Saddam Hussein had attacked (or indeed could attack) Britain and the United States; or that the

Security Council was willing to undertake armed action against his 'acts of aggression'. Prime Minister Blair scarcely needed legal advice to tell him something so obvious.

So Britain seems to have been bounced into war on faulty judicial advice and inaccurate intelligence information. To what extent was the government aware of this, and how far was it prepared to gloss over the shaky intelligence in order to please Bush? Butler said that intelligence played only a *limited* role in determining the legality of the war. But its legality was not at the time satisfactorily determined; indeed, Prime Minister Blair did not reveal the nature of the Attorney General's advice until the eve of the 2005 General Election. And, in spite of what Lord Goldsmith said, Security Council Resolution 1441 could *not* be extended to provide an adequate pretext for war.

And then there is the question of 'sexing up'. Hutton absolves the government of this charge. But if removing the 'caveats' is not 'sexing up', it is difficult to know what is, even if those who removed them failed to appreciate the significance of their removal. Dr Kelly's death was a regrettable side effect of a conscientious man's efforts to provide the press with the truth, even if Gilligan's attempt to blame Blair for the 'sexing up' was his own gloss on Dr Kelly's information. Who, and for what reasons, omitted the 'caveats'? It seems to have been the JIC, and if so why did it not report the doubts concerning those aspects of the dossier to the Cabinet? And since it seems that the Conservatives were persuaded to vote for the government on the basis of evidence that was faulty, their new leader Michael Howard's statement that had he known he would not have supported the government, hardly deserved the fury of some Labour MPs, at least one of whom described Howard's statement as 'cynical political opportunism'. The weakness of Howard's assault on the Prime Minister in the Butler debate seems to reinforce the air of mystery that hangs over Ian Duncan Smith's pre-war visit to Downing Street.

Saddam Hussein will have had cause, in his prison cell, to regret how ineffective allied intelligence was. His probable game of bluff – denial of the existence of WMDs to be disbelieved in Iraq to bolster the regime, and believed by the UN, in order to stave off a war he had no resources to fight – backfired in a way he could not have anticipated. Better intelligence would have meant no war. If, after all, Blair was involved in sharpening up the September dossier by omitting the 'caveats' and then using it to obtain a favourable parliamentary vote for war – an accusation he continues to deny – then the whole episode is, indeed, a scandal. If, on the other hand, government and opposition alike were misled by doctored intelligence information, doctored by person or persons unknown within the JIC, and if the government relied on faulty, and reluctantly divulged, judicial advice from its own Attorney General, then the whole episode betrays more naivety, more contempt for international law and for the British democratic process, and more incompetence than the Prime Minister would ever be prepared to admit. And this, if anything, is even more of a scandal!

ROYAL SCANDALS

Was Essex responsible for his own ruin?

Elizabeth I's treatment of the Earl of Essex has often been considered as vindictive. The last years of her reign lack the glorious quality of her first thirty years, and her handling of Essex is often seen as an indication of how her judgment had withered with age.

It was perhaps unwise of Elizabeth to make such an inexperienced and headstrong young man into a favourite, and then treat him more like a son than a subject. She refused his first request to join one of Drake's expeditions, but Essex defied her and went anyway. Elizabeth's capricious Tudor nature showed itself in her petulant quarrelling with her new favourite, and then her efforts to make up, fortified by a bribe of some new high office. She slapped his face in public, and comforted him in private later. And then against his wishes she sent him on an impossible task in Ireland and abused him for his failure, and for his return without permission. When Elizabeth added her criticism of his conduct to those of his many enemies Essex, in despair, attempted a disastrous coup. This Elizabeth chose to regard as treason, and she had fewer misgivings about signing Essex's death warrant than she had for those of Mary Queen of Scots or the Duke of Norfolk. The story of Essex returning Elizabeth's ring, which she had told him to do if ever he desperately needed her help, is certainly apocryphal, but it illustrates later opinion that Elizabeth's treatment of Essex was scandalous.

But was Elizabeth wholly to blame for Essex's tragic fate? Of course, as Wentworth was later to remark in similar circumstances to those of Essex, 'Put not your trust in princes'. Tudor despots were notoriously fickle. Henry VIII was champion here, but his successors Edward,

Mary and Elizabeth had made passable attempts to follow his lead. Essex was young and at first innocent in the ways of the world, but he allowed Elizabeth's attention to go to his head, and believed that her devotion to him gave him the right to do as he pleased. Here he was grievously mistaken.

From the first Essex had enemies. The Cecil faction, at whose head stood the powerful Lord Burghley, Elizabeth's chief minister, regarded Essex as a bumptious young upstart with nothing to recommend him but his youth and good looks. They were jealous of his influence with the queen and did their utmost to undermine it. Older favourites including Sir Walter Raleigh and Sir Charles Blount naturally backed the Cecils. These men could do little against Essex while he enjoyed the queen's adulation, but they resisted vigorously Essex's attempts to promote his friends – most of whom had little to recommend them anyway. When Essex fell from grace it was natural that his enemies should seek to destroy him rather than merely to tame him.

Elizabeth first noticed Essex as early as 1587 when he was nineteen years old. She showered him with lucrative offices, but it was not until the death of the Earl of Leicester in 1588 that Essex became established as the favourite. The gap in their ages gave Elizabeth the encouragement to treat him as the son she might have had, but it gave him the confident belief that he was not answerable to her for his actions. Anything reprehensible could soon be smoothed over with charm and flattery, and he assumed that as her vicarious son, he would be treated by her with the utmost indulgence. For most of the time it worked. When, in 1589, Essex defied her, and joined Drake's expedition to Corunna and Portugal, Elizabeth's concern for his safety was agonising, but Essex behaved with great valour and returned to court firmly re-established in Elizabeth's affections. He had defied the queen with impunity; there was no reason, it seemed to Essex, why he could not get away with it again. Nevertheless he should have realised the limitations of his influence over the queen; when in 1590 Secretary Walsingham died, Essex was unable to prevent the promotion of Robert Cecil, Burghley's son, even though Cecil did not receive the actual Secretaryship. Essex's battle against the Cecils rankled with them, even though Essex did not bear a grudge. And while Essex had long forgotten the hue and cry over Robert Cecil's promotion, the Cecils' hatred of Essex festered even more. At this time Essex married the widow of Sir Philip Sidney. In view of the ambivalent nature of his relationship with Elizabeth, this was bound to put extra strain on relations between the two.

However for the next five years Essex was unassailable, even though the Cecils criticised him both in private and in public. In 1596, when the attack on Cadiz was being planned, Robert Cecil reproached Essex for his lack of devotion to the Almighty and his greater concern for military glory. Even so, Essex was still given command of the expedition's army, while Lord Howard of Effingham commanded the fleet. Essex was undoubtedly the hero of this campaign, but during his ten weeks' absence the Cecils went to great lengths to undermine Essex's credibility with the queen, and to stress the enormous cost of the expedition for so little return. Essex maintained that had it not been for the obstruction of the Cecils, he might even have captured the Spanish treasure ships which had safely eluded the British and taken to Madrid over £2 million. Essex accused Burghley of being a miscreant and a coward, and for a time Burghley was excluded from the court. This triumph only served to convince Essex even further of his invincibility and of the queen's absolute confidence in him. Essex was, indeed, put in full charge of the expedition of 1597, with Howard of Effingham as a subordinate. The expedition failed to achieve its aims and the English coast was even threatened by a Spanish fleet. On his return, Essex was so dismayed by public criticism and the queen's reproaches that he retired in a sulk, and refused to put in an attendance either at court or in parliament. The queen, who could not bear to be parted from him, won him round by creating him hereditary earl-marshal.

A new quarrel soon broke out between Essex and the Cecils over peace negotiations with Spain. The Cecils wanted Spain's peace proposals to be taken seriously; Essex, despite the recent failures and enormous expense, was all for continuing the war. Burghley accused Essex of thinking of nothing but blood and slaughter, and quoted the Old Testament to him to the effect that *bloodthirsty men shall not live out half their days*. The quarrel intensified over the question of Ireland. The people of Ireland, who had clung contumaciously to their Catholic religion, had found a leader in the Earl of Tyrone. He had soon roused much of Ireland in rebellion, and had expelled the English garrisons from most of the country. Clearly the English cause in Ireland needed a man of great military skill, a diplomat of genius and tact, and one in whom the queen and her government had utmost confidence. But the rival groups did not see it that way. The Cecils wanted to hand this poisoned chalice to someone from among Essex's closest friends and supporters; Essex wanted it to be given to an influential supporter of the Cecils. Discussions at court became heated. The queen reprimanded Essex in public, and Essex was so mortified that he turned his back on the queen while she was berating him. Elizabeth was so furious with Essex that she slapped his face, and he reacted angrily swearing that he would not have put up with such treatment, even from Henry VIII himself. Whereupon he stormed from the court. Of course, Elizabeth, as queen, had the right to slap any face she chose, but Essex, as a subject, had no right to insult the queen. Reconciliation had to wait for three months – much longer than usual. And the queen never fully forgave him.

Burghley's death in August 1598, while Essex was still absent from court, did little to strengthen Essex's position. Robert Cecil succeeded his father, and the Cecils' animosity towards Essex continued unabated. In order to remove him from court and bring about his political ruin Cecil strongly promoted Essex as the man to deal with Ireland, where the situation had deteriorated even further. Essex was most reluctant, but the queen bribed him with money, and with greater power in Ireland than that enjoyed by any previous governor, so Essex reluctantly consented to take on the task. It was an impossible one. From the first the queen interfered with Essex's authority, refusing to sanction the appointment of his friend the Earl of Southampton as general of the horse. She then accused him of wasting time and money, and of wanting to prolong the war. His army was plagued by desertion and sickness, but when he tried to buy time by signing a six week armistice with Tyrone he received angry despatches from the queen accusing him of exceeding his instructions. Essex, in anger, and without Elizabeth's permission, abandoned his post and hastened to London. He attempted to win the queen over with some argument and liberal use of the old charm, but after a few hours' reflection the queen placed him under house arrest. Her changed attitude towards him could not have been clearer; in the eight months during which his freedom was restricted, he was allowed neither the company of his wife, nor the attendance of his physician, even when he fell seriously ill. Essex should have recognised that although he was being harshly judged for his conduct in Ireland and his ill-timed return, there was little that he could do about it. A wiser man might have taken his release in August 1600 as a signal to retire to the country, lie low, and wait for better times, but Essex showed that he had learnt little over the years. When the queen refused to renew his lucrative wine monopoly, on the grounds that the best way to tame a horse was to deprive it of provender, Essex was furious and reckless. Prompted by Cuffe, his secretary, Essex now proposed to use force to deprive the queen of the counsellors hostile to him. He convinced himself that armed rebellion against the counsellors could not be construed as armed rebellion against the queen. Here his opinion was very much a minority one. No Tudor despot would countenance armed rebellion, whatever the circumstances and whatever its aims. Essex's naivety remains beyond belief.

Essex now opened up his house to all who had any quarrel with the ministers. These included Catholic priests, laying Essex open to the charge of wanting to restore the Roman Catholic faith; after all Essex's father-in-law was a Roman Catholic. He then wrote to James of Scotland telling him that the Cecils were proposing to support the claims of the Infanta of Spain to the succession. This correspondence soon became known to the government who demanded that Essex appear before the Privy Council to explain his conduct. Fearing for his life, Essex decided to rouse the citizens of London on his behalf. Nothing frightened Tudor monarchs more than the possibility of a hostile London. If Essex could use his popularity with the Londoners to carry all before him, ministers and the queen herself would be mere puppets in his hands. Essex had now passed the point of no return; success would give him absolute power, failure would mean total ruin. There was little enough prospect of success, but at this crucial time Essex hesitated, parleyed with some of the ministers, and then locked them up. Then, riding furiously through a deserted city, he attempted to rouse support, crying *'For the Queen, my mistress. A plot is laid for my life.'* But among the citizens, not one would declare for Essex. He eventually made his way back to his house where he was surrounded, and at length, after a busy day, surrendered at ten o'clock at night on February 8, 1601.

His trial opened on February 19. The charge against him was treason; to the queen and her ministers, a lesser charge was unthinkable. Essex defended himself with spirit. But it was very difficult for him to prove that his actions were against his political enemies and not the queen. Had he not consorted with Roman Catholics? Had he not spread seditious lies about the succession to James of Scotland? Had he not attempted to rouse the citizens of London in armed rebellion? And all this in time of war! Essex faced the considerable oratory of the prosecution in the persons of Sir Edward Coke and Francis Bacon. He had to be his own advocate – prisoners in treason trials were allowed no assistance from lawyers – and Essex conducted his defence with great skill. But his attempt to prove that the ministers favoured the succession of the Infanta backfired on him, and he was left to assert, not prove, his innocent intentions. Inevitably on the following day he was found guilty and sentenced to death. This time the queen did not delay; the warrant was signed and the execution was fixed for 25 February. Such was the heinous nature of his attempted rebellion, that had there been a ring and a royal promise, Elizabeth would not have been able to honour it. Essex's execution took place in private in an inner courtyard of the Tower of London. It was alleged that the government dared not allow a public execution for fear of what Essex might say and whom he might impugn. More likely it did not want any expression of public sympathy if the Londoners were let in, and public executions are more nerve-wracking for the victim.

At his own execution some seventeen years later Sir Walter Raleigh attempted to distance himself from responsibility for Essex's fate. Up to a point he was right. Essex was a considerable man of letters and possessed of a lively intelligence, but he had no gift for politics. Nothing could be less adroit than his dealings with the queen. Nothing could be more foolish than his final escapade. Essex's enemies exploited his weaknesses, but Essex played into their hands. Elizabeth may have been a little over-indulgent, but throughout their relationship she was consistent in denying him a political position of strength. The more Essex pushed, the more she denied him. Essex became more and more irresponsible, the queen more adamant. When it came to a choice between her personal relationships and the interests of the country, the queen, as always, placed the interests of the country first. There was some logic in her treatment of Essex, even though it may not have seemed so to those contemporaries for whom Essex epitomised the last of the great Tudor adventurers. So Essex had largely himself to blame for the premature cutting short of so promising a career, and the triumph of the Cecils, as Elizabeth recognised, was better security for the safety and future of England than the romantic and unachievable aspirations of her one-time favourite.

Was there a baby in
the warming pan?

One of the most hotly-contested controversies of the late seventeenth century related to the legitimacy of one of the last of the Stuart line, James III, or, as he is better known, the 'Old Pretender', who attempted to recover the British throne in 1715 from George I of the House of Hanover. The rumour was circulated that the baby which was supposed to have been born in June 1688 by Queen Mary Beatrice of Modena, wife of James II, had in fact been brought into the birthing chamber in a warming pan, and passed off as her own; though the baby was in fact of humble birth, and a mere miller's son. Is there any doubt about the true explanation of this long-standing mystery?

There can be no questioning the electric atmosphere of the time, charged with passionate prejudices between Catholic and Protestant and kept at boiling point by professional agitators such as Titus Oates (see chapter on *How Did Titus Oates Try to Save England from the Popish Plot?*), because both the two main religious communities in England felt they had reason for extreme concern.

For their part, the Protestants in 1687–8 believed that there was no action too base and no deception too villainous for James to resort to for the purpose of enslaving his people to the Papacy. His policy in the two Declarations of Indulgence in suspending all penal laws against Catholics and annulling all religious 'tests' debarring them from office, his efforts to secure the election of a favourable parliament by persuading corporations and the county authorities to readmit Catholics to the franchise, his attempts to 'pack' the Court of Ecclesiastical High Commission and the academic staffs of the Universities with Catholic sympathisers, and his prosecution on charges of seditious libel of seven well-respected bishops who had criticised him, were all part of this design to restore England to Rome, by force if necessary; whilst the birth of his son was seen as a means of perpetuating his dynasty, superseding his two Protestant daughters, Mary and Anne, so that the counter-revolution he was planning would continue after his death.

The Catholics, on the other hand, believed that the Protestants' reaction against the king's policies was as hysterical as it was unnecessary, and their fears quite groundless. Though the king was sometimes scornful to his critics and was peremptory in his manner, his policies were aimed at producing a harmonious, multi-sectarian society that would include other faiths, such as the Dissenters on the left of the Anglican Church, as well as the Catholics on the right. Although the intransigence of his parliament had forced him into a temporary dependence on French finances, he was anxious for independence for himself and freedom of action for the country, and did not intend to remain a pensionary of Louis XIV for a moment longer than necessary. Furthermore, the notion that he would disinherit his two daughters, whom he dearly loved, in order to foist a bastard baby on the nation was totally out of keeping with his character and quite inconceivable as a solution to his succession problems. Which of the two sides of the argument can we believe?

James had undoubtedly had a chequered background. In 1659, while still Duke of York, he had married Anne Hyde, daughter of Edward Hyde (later made Earl of Clarendon and chief minister to his brother Charles II), and was subject to some criticism, not least from Charles, because Anne was only a commoner. She it was who gave him his two daughters Mary, in 1662, and Anne, in 1665. Three years before her death in 1671 the Duke and Duchess were admitted to the Catholic Church, though their conversion remained a secret until 1672. The two children remained within the Protestant persuasion. In 1673 James, now forty years old, remarried, this time to Maria Beatrice d'Este, fifteen-year-old daughter of the Duke of Modena. At this time Mary was eleven and Anne nine, so that their stepmother easily became their playmate. Lady Mary of York, later to become Princess Mary, was a modest and rather uncommunicative young woman of earnest religious convictions who in 1677 married her first cousin, William of Orange, son of the Stadtholder of Holland, William II; her younger sister, Lady (later Princess) Anne was more flighty and irresponsible and distressingly prone to gossip. When she was still young she was reputedly seduced by one of the courtiers, Lord Mulgrave, but partly redeemed herself by marrying the somewhat stolid Prince George of Denmark in 1683, a man scarcely more educated than herself. James succeeded to the throne on the death of his brother in 1685, and the two girls became first and second in the line of succession to the throne. Mary became Queen of England when her father was deposed in the 'Glorious' Revolution of 1688, William her husband becoming joint sovereign with her in that year; though she died without surviving children in 1694 at the early age of thirty-two. Anne became Queen in her turn when William III died in 1701, and had seventeen pregnancies in union with her husband. However, nearly all her children were stillborn or died in early infancy, and only one, the young Duke of Gloucester, lived to be eleven, when he predeceased her. The death of legitimate Stuart heirs before her death in 1714 meant that in 1701 a special Act of Settlement was passed which vested the succession in the distantly-related House of Hanover, whose George Louis, Duke and Elector of Hanover, King George I of Britain, was the grandson of a daughter of James I. This Act also had the effect of debarring Roman Catholics in future from inheriting the throne (a provision never afterwards repealed).

Many of these problems might conceivably have been avoided if Queen Mary Beatrice had presented her husband with a prince of undisputed legitimacy in the year of the revolution, 1688. But doubts, real and imagined, lingered. James had made a special detour to visit St Winifred's Well at Holywell near Flint during his tour of the western counties in the autumn of 1687 in order to pray her to grant him a son; and Protestants thought, when the queen's pregnancy was announced in December, that the prompt granting of the royal wish owed less to divine intervention than to a royal plot to extract the king from his predicament by foisting a new male baby on the nation to ensure the permanence of his reforms. They felt that the cheery optimism of the Catholics, and James's serene assurance that the baby would be a boy – and would survive – were pretty clear indications that the pregnancy was a hoax. This scepticism was reinforced partly by the modesty of the queen, who, though she was daily getting bigger, demurely declined to have her belly inspected, even by her relatives; and partly by the errors of her medical advisers, who asserted that the child was not due until August, when in fact it was born, as she herself believed it would be, on 10 June. Mary, of course, was away, living with her husband in their new palace in Guelderland, and Anne, though specifically urged in letters from her sister to be present at the birth, chose this moment to make a visit to Bath for several weeks, so that she was not at hand when the prince was born. Her absence was partly due to the doctors' erroneous predictions of the birth date, but chiefly due to her unwillingness to give unimpeachable witness to the child's delivery. Hence Anne was able to say, when she wrote to her infuriated sister that 'Tis possible this may be her child; but whereas one may believe it, a thousand do not.' Mary might have been tempted to retort that, if she had been present, Anne would have known the truth with absolute certainty.

Not that there was much doubt what the truth was. On 9 June, which was a Saturday, Queen Mary Beatrice decided to leave Whitehall Palace, which was noisy and dusty and in course of refurbishment, and her bedroom too small and too exposed to the heat of the sun in her confinement. She would dearly have liked to go to Windsor for her lying-in, but this was too far for the necessary witnesses to the royal birth, so in the end she settled for St James's. This was a large and rambling place, full of poky little rooms and winding corridors – just the place, as Anne observed in her malicious letter to Mary, 'to act such a cheat in'. The queen's labour started the following morning, and James hastened to her side, to join Mrs Dawson, her (Protestant) bed-chamber woman, and the midwife, Judith Wilkes. Mary Beatrice was not *in* bed, which had not been aired, and Mrs Dawson persuaded her to go back to the great bed, sending for a warming pan full of hot coals to warm *that* one. This was the only warming pan that appeared in the scenario, and this could not by any stretch of the imagination have concealed a baby. It was not long before the witnesses to a royal birth, prescribed by long tradition, made their appearance. The twenty or so members of the Privy Council and a sizeable number of other aristocrats and courtiers crowded in, some, like the Lord Chancellor, standing on the step of the bed to get a better view, others, like Godolphin, ostentatiously turning their Protestant backs so that they could not later be called upon as witnesses. There were another twenty or more female witnesses, some of them aristocrats and others less noble ladies of the court, who watched minutely all the gynaecological details of the event, notwithstanding all the limited efforts to screen the queen to preserve her modesty. The bedroom was not a large one, and, with upwards of forty people crammed into it, was pretty hot and crowded. The queen's labour lasted for about two hours before the baby was born. The midwife then passed the infant to his nurse, and James asked anxiously, 'What is it?', to which she responded, 'All that Your Majesty desires.' The queen moaned, 'I don't hear the child cry', whereupon he did, very lustily. Several witnesses averred that they saw the birth, and afterwards testified to the same effect, saying they had been there when the umbilical cord was cut. The baby was normal, not a great deal distressed though a little black in the face. The king displayed the infant to his Privy Councillors, asking them to concur that a prince had been borne to him; then the baby was taken away to be cleaned up and dressed, and brought back by the nurse a few minutes later to the cry of: 'Make room for the Prince of Wales!'. Delightedly, James knighted the physician on the spot and gave the midwife 500 guineas 'for her breakfast'.

Thus there were no grounds for the later very positive assertion that some deception had taken place, or for the strongly held opinion of many Protestants (some of whom had actually been present and played a part in the birthing ceremony) that the pregnancy had been a hoax and that the child was not really James's own. But the Protestants believed it fervently because they thought it was in their interests that they should. It was the birth of the little Prince James that persuaded a group of influential Protestant noblemen to appeal for Dutch support against the Catholic monarchy; and which further decided William of Orange to invade England at the head of 15,000 of his troops, each man of them politely spoken and well-behaved, to overthrow the king and put his own wife in James's place. The hoax was not that an illegitimate baby was foisted on to an indignant nation, but that a powerful Protestant clique pretended that it was. The true facts show that the baby was legitimate, but shamefully deprived of his throne by a combination of domestic insurgency and foreign intervention. Though James II's foolishness and obstinacy contributed in no little way to the final catastrophe, the 'Glorious' Revolution was really no more than a sordid little conspiracy.

Did George III give up his true love?

Most wealthy young English aristocrats were sent by their parents on the 'Grand Tour', when they spent a year in Europe getting through vast amounts of money and gaining valuable experiences. Thus they set out as innocents and returned worldly wise. George, Prince of Wales (later George III), did not have this valuable form of education. Since his father died in 1751 he had been brought up by his mother Augusta, dowager Princess of Wales, virtually in seclusion. In his court appearances, hovering tongue-tied and somewhat embarrassed behind his grandfather's throne, he appeared gawky and immature. It was at one of these that he met the beautiful Lady Sarah Lennox, and fell madly in love – or so he believed. But the pair never married. Did George sacrifice connubial happiness out of a sense of duty?

Lady Sarah Lennox was the fourth of the five surviving daughters of the second Duke of Richmond. The eldest, Caroline, was twenty-two years her senior, and had caused a scandal in 1744 by marrying the politician Henry Fox in defiance of her parents' wishes. Although the subsequent estrangement had been patched up, Richmond showed that he had still not totally forgiven Caroline when in his will he left the care of his younger children, not to the eldest Caroline, but to the second, Emily. She had married the Earl of Kildare, and taken up residence with him in Ireland, so when the death of the duchess (1751) closely followed that of the duke (1750) the three younger girls were packed off to Ireland. Sarah was six years old. The new duke and his younger brother remained in England for their education and became strongly attached to their brother-in-law, Fox. The Richmond-Fox alliance was to become a very powerful political force when political parties meant a great deal less than political connections. By the time Sarah arrived in London in

November 1759, and had taken up residence with her sister Caroline, Henry Fox was at the peak of his political career.

Although Sarah was only fourteen, she had come to London for the season and her purpose, and that of Emily who sent her, was to make a suitable marriage. Time was on her side, but if, after two or three seasons she was still unattached, young men might jib at courting a young lady who had been on the market for so long. Her assets were her Richmond name, her Fox connections, her physical attraction (some said she was pretty, others described her as beautiful), and a dowry of £10,000. Sarah was presented at court at the end of November, and disregarded the stiff formality of the court by reminding George II of how forward she had been with him when a child of six. Prince George, although smitten, did not approach Sarah directly, but told Caroline of his admiration. Young George had enough sense to realise that if he pursued Sarah successfully he would be in danger of losing the friendship of his tutor and confidant the Earl of Bute. The Fox faction was ranged alongside Bute's political enemies. From the first, therefore, while no one else took George's infatuation seriously, Bute did. He pestered George to admit his feelings for Sarah, but George admitted nothing, and continued to see Sarah frequently.

A rumour began to circulate that Sarah was to be married to the nineteen-year-old Duke of Marlborough, a very suitable match. George was distraught. He retired to his chamber where he remained in his own words for several hours 'in the depths of despair.' Jealousy of Marlborough now impelled George to confide in Bute. He was naïve enough to think that Bute would approve of the marriage and still find ways to retain George's friendship. Bute was horrified and told George so. He pointed out the long tradition of British kings and heirs to the throne seeking brides overseas; it was after all, only thirteen years since the Jacobites had been overthrown at Culloden, and marriage to a daughter of the aristocracy would encourage political jealousies and undermine the monarchy. It would also, of course, undermine Bute's position. George's infatuation was not so powerful that he was blinded to his duty, and he authorised Bute to search the continent for a suitable wife. It was traditional for the British aristocracy and monarchy to marry for convenience and cohabit for love. George seemed to think his promise to Bute allowed him to indulge his attachment to Sarah, and he continued to see her frequently until the end of the season in May, when husband-hunting temporarily ended, and the eligibles and the matched left London for the country. Sarah and Caroline joined in this exodus.

They returned to London in October, only for the usual round of parties and balls to be thrown into disarray by the old King's death on 25 October. Sarah declared that she was 'absolutely in love' with the new King. But this was less a declaration of attachment than delight at the prospect of coronation festivities and all that these involved. George, on the other hand, despite his promise to Bute, talked in March 1761 of taking an English wife, while in the same month he promoted Bute to the Secretaryship of the Northern Department with a seat in the Cabinet. Meanwhile in the same month Sarah had, on a visit to Somerset, fallen off a horse and broken her leg. Fox, hopeful of promoting his sister-in-law's marriage, stepped into the breach and having given a graphic account of this disaster to George, was convinced from his pained reaction that he really was in love. Fox preferred money to honours, but with Sarah as queen, he could not fail to achieve at least an earldom. It is sometimes alleged that had Sarah not broken her leg, she would have become queen, but this is unlikely. George had already committed himself to a marriage of convenience. By the time Sarah returned to court in May the bride had already been chosen, Charlotte of Mecklenburg-Strelitz. She lacked Sarah's looks and charm, but she was to make George a dependable companion and a fertile mother for his numerous children.

George believed that now the bride was chosen he could freely indulge his fancy, but he was affected by conscience, and at the end of June hinted to Sarah that all was over. Early in July Fox told Sarah that the king's betrothal had been announced to the Privy Council. Sarah was not devastated, but she felt humiliated and let down. She wrote to a close friend that 'I did not love him, and only liked him'. There is no reason to disbelieve this frank admission. Sarah was later to embellish the story of her relationship with George to make George's commitment seem greater than it actually was. Few men would give up love to keep a friend, but a monarch might give up his beloved if duty demanded. If George had really loved Sarah he would surely have put up a much tougher fight for her, even if in the end he would be bound to give way to Bute's arguments. George did not refer to Sarah for many years, but when he was ill in 1789 he declared to one of his ministers that he had renounced the woman he loved in order to marry another. Many of

George's other declarations at this time were unfairly dismissed by his contemporaries as the ravings of a madman; this one was more likely an idealised memory of happier times. In 1761 he was young, inexperienced, and most likely in love with the idea of being in love. What he felt for Sarah was probably infatuation; he was dazzled by her rather than won by her. In 1805 he awarded her a pension of £800 a year, with sympathy, as he put it, from 'one blind person to another'. There is no reason to assume that this was prompted by guilty conscience, but merely the response of one old friend to another old friend in adversity.

How were diamonds *not* a queen's best friend?

One of the grubby but complicated affairs which afflicted the royal court of France in the years before the Revolution was the notorious diamond necklace scandal, which reflected badly on the person of Queen Marie Antoinette, but even continued to discredit her memory years after her death. The queen was supposed to have cheated Charles Auguste Boehmer, the court jeweller, out of an extremely valuable diamond necklace, or at least to have ordered such a necklace and, having obtained it, then refused to pay for it. In point of fact, though neither the French court nor the public at large could bring themselves to believe it, she was innocent on both counts.

It was in 1785 that Boehmer offered the queen an elaborate and rather flashy diamond necklace, containing nearly 650 South African diamonds and weighing 2800 carats. Marie Antoinette found it over-designed and somewhat vulgar, and was not keen. She responded by saying that the case it was housed in was rich enough for her, and politely turned aside all Boehmer's entreaties, refusing to listen to the representations made to her by a string of courtiers he had engaged to plead with her. Boehmer later reduced his asking price from 2 million *livres* to 1.8 million, and even offered to arrange for its purchase by easy instalments on a credit agreement. The jeweller suggested that the purchase might be regarded by the royal family as a useful endowment for the young Dauphin, an idea that quite appealed to the king until the queen advised against it. She remained firm, saying the family had little need of diamonds and that the money would be better spent publicly on the French navy. It was all the more surprising, therefore, that in July 1785 the queen received an enigmatic little letter from Boehmer, saying how happy he was with 'the latest arrangements' and adding 'his real satisfaction' that 'the most beautiful set of diamonds in the world will be at the service of the best of queens.' Marie Antoinette puzzled over it briefly, wondering whether perhaps Boehmer was again touting for custom. She came to the conclusion that the message meant his workshop had produced some other piece of jewellery he wished to sell to her. Her first Lady of the Bedchamber, Mme Campan, was no wiser, so the queen twisted the message into a spill and burned it at the candle on her dressing table.

The contents of the note had in fact been dictated to Boehmer by the Cardinal Louis de Rohan, churchman and a prince of the distinguished House of Rohan, who was labouring under two mistaken impressions: that the queen wanted to acquire the necklace but lacked the necessary funds to pay for it, and that if he got it for her he would gain the queen's favour. His error soon became apparent: the queen never put the necklace on, and no signs of her favour were ever conferred on him. The plot thickened when, in early August, Boehmer went to see Mme Campan at her own country house and asked for the queen's reply to his letter. Mme Campan told him there was no reply, and that the queen had burned his note. Boehmer was astonished. He retorted that such a thing was impossible, and added: 'The queen must know she owes me money!'. Now it was Mme Campan's turn to be astonished. The Court Jeweller told her that it was the cardinal who had actually purchased the necklace on her behalf, and that he actually had the queen's instructions in writing for the purchase; indeed, he had already received the first 30,000 *livres* from the queen through Cardinal Rohan as her intermediary. Mme Campan told him this could not be the case: the queen had not seen the cardinal since they had met in Vienna eight years earlier, and it was quite impossible that she should have made such a request privately of him and then have forgotten about it afterwards. Indeed, instead of wanting the diamonds she had persistently refused them, and had never had them in her possession. Mme Campan remained puzzled, but instead of raising the matter directly with the Queen, she finally decided to leave its solution to Breteuil, the Minister of the Royal Household. She did not know that Breteuil, who was on bad terms with the cardinal, would use this opportunity to do all he could to bring about his disgrace.

Thus it was that a confrontation between the queen and the cardinal took place on the occasion when he was already robed to conduct Mass on the Feast of the Assumption (15 August), and was summoned by Louis XVI to appear before the Cabinet. Tackled directly by the king with the charge of obtaining the diamonds by subterfuge from Boehmer, Rohan said he understood they were delivered to the queen, and that he had the queen's instructions in writing for doing her this service, instructions delivered to him by the Comtesse de Lamotte Valois, who he understood to have been one of her close confidantes. Marie Antoinette demanded to know how he could have believed that she would demand this of him, since she had not spoken to him for so many years, and assured him that in any case she would not have made use of Mme Lamotte, who was an individual of low rank and not *persona grata* in court. The king asked to see the letters, read them, and then pointed out rather haughtily that they were not in the queen's handwriting, and in any case were signed 'Marie Antoinette de France' and not in the correct style, of which he, as a royal prince himself, should have been well aware. The cardinal, his face almost as red as his pontifical robes, muttered uneasily that it was clear he must have been duped.

For a time, both the king and Marie Antoinette believed that Rohan had forged the letters himself, until it became clear that if this were the case, the cardinal would have managed the deception more skilfully. In fact, he was taken in simply because of his aspirations: he *wanted* the letters to be genuine, and so he believed they *were*. He was not a simpleton, and he was not unduly credulous; but he allowed himself to be blinded by his ambition into thinking that, however unlikely it seemed, he had suddenly gained promotion into the queen's favour. However, he was firmly caught in the trap. Louis offered him the alternative of pleading for his mercy, or standing trial before the Parlement de Paris. He, being a proud man, chose the Parlement in order to have the opportunity to justify himself, and Breteuil gleefully arrested him for trial.

The true circumstances of the affair were involved and rather sordid. Cardinal Rohan had had some sort of liaison early in the 1780s with the young, social-climbing Jeanne de Lamotte, so that she became aware early on of his obsession with gaining the queen's favour. She herself, though, had been brought up in the most abject poverty, and had Valois blood in her veins, her father being illegitimately descended from Henri II. Thus, when she married Nicolas de Lamotte, the two added a quite unilateral 'Comte' and 'Comtesse' to their names, and tacked on 'Valois' for good measure. She then hung round the court at Versailles in the hope that she would attract a pension by right of her Valois blood; but she never managed to get an introduction to the queen, and was resentful of her exclusion from the circle of the royal acquaintance. In 1785 she and her husband hatched a plot to revenge themselves on the queen, rob the cardinal (and the royal jeweller) of a vast sum of money, and make off with the coveted necklace at the same time. She arranged with her lover Rétaux de Villette, who was an accomplished forger, and currently living with them *à trois* in the Lamotte household, to forge the queen's instructions to the cardinal to obtain the necklace, agreeing to arrangements for paying in instalments. Boehmer jumped at the chance to dispose of it, and even agreed to reduce the price further, to 1.6 million *livres*. Then Lamotte hired the services of one Nicole d'Oliva, one of the 'young ladies' of the Palais Royale who bore an uncanny resemblance to Marie Antoinette, to dress up in a floaty white muslin frock similar to the ones she favoured, and to meet with the cardinal in the grounds of Versailles, in a corner known from its statuary by the name 'Grove of Venus', by moonlight and veiled, to give him promises of royal favour if he did what she was asking of him. The impersonation worked. Rohan was irrecoverably ensnared, and the hapless jeweller parted with his gems.

Lamotte rushed the necklace to London where he roughly prised out the stones and sold them as loose diamonds to a London firm of jewellers, who, immediately suspicious that they might have been stolen, prudently checked with the police before they bought them at a knockdown figure. The bulk of them were later sold to the Duke of Norfolk, and some may have passed to the Duchess of Sutherland and made into a necklace (though expert comparison with the original necklace casts some doubt on this, chiefly on account of the size and cut of the stones). The firm of Boehmer, which had long used the letters of supposed patronage by the queen to reassure their numerous insistent creditors, went bankrupt and was sold up. The case their heirs brought against the House of Rohan dragged on until 1867, and the sums remaining were not paid off much before 1900.

Jeanne de Lamotte was arrested and locked up; the forger Villette was brought back from Geneva where he had fled; even the unfortunate Nicole d'Oliva (who imagined she was being hired for an amorous tryst and not for such a 'sting') was arrested; only the Comte remained at liberty in London. Cardinal Rohan appeared with the other conspirators before the Paris Parlement in May 1786. Nicole escaped with a reprimand for her part in the escapade; Villette was banished and his goods declared forfeit; whilst ferocious sentences of flogging, branding and life imprisonment were pronounced on the two Lamottes (in his case *in absentia*). She was stripped naked and whipped by the public executioner, branded with a 'V' (*Voleuse*) as a thief, and imprisoned in the Salpêtrière for life. Only Rohan was acquitted, but even he had to make a humiliating public apology, seek the king's pardon, surrender all his offices, make a sizeable donation to the poor, and suffer banishment from the royal court for life.

Nevertheless the blemish on the queen's character, however innocently produced, was never removed. Her efforts to hush up the secret moonlight assignation with Rohan in the 'Grove of Venus' failed when Parlement refused to be muzzled, and many people thought that the queen's efforts to have this part of Rohan's evidence struck from the record could only mean there was a great deal more that she *had* been successful in suppressing. It would be true to say, however innocent she was, that the diamond necklace scandal was, as she herself bitterly predicted, an affair that she never managed to live down.

Queen Caroline:
heroine or whore?

Queen Caroline, the wife of George IV, was one of the most unpleasant and disreputable queens that England has ever had, and yet, in spite of all her shortcomings, she proved to be one of the most popular. Her career was one endless scandal from start to finish. The nation was amused and shocked at her antics, and her husband was continuously embarrassed by her. It was only because he was even more detested than she was that she remained in such high esteem.

Born in 1762, George Augustus Frederick, Prince of Wales and 'Prinny' to his intimates, was the son of George III, and later, when his father became incapable of further rule, his Prince Regent for the last ten years of his life. His father, determined that he should grow up into the ideal Platonic monarch, had him educated from his youth away from the court and well out of the public eye. But he failed – the youthful prince became a rebel, a spendthrift and a waster. He was only sixteen when he had his first affair, with the actress Mary ('Perdita') Robinson, whom he first met when he saw her in Shakespeare's *Winter's Tale*. They remained together for a short time until he fell in love with another, when his letters to her had to be bought back for £5000. Over the next seven years he worked his way through a dozen other mistresses, who all cost him and his father a small fortune to silence. In other ways, too, he ran up vast debts. He became a member of a hard-drinking, hard-gambling set that included Charles James Fox, one of the King's main political opponents, and the playwright Richard Sheridan. When he was twenty-three, he encountered an attractive young widow, Maria Fitzherbert, six years his senior, who became perhaps the only true love of his life. He was desperate to marry her, and she fled to France to escape his attentions. The marriage, however, was politically impossible, since she was a Roman Catholic, and marriages between members of the royal family and Catholics were forbidden as part of the Protestant settlement under the Act of 1701 (see *Was there a baby in the warming pan?*). The bar was further strengthened by George III's own Royal Marriages Act of 1772, forbidding any member of the royal family under twenty-five to marry without the consent of the king and the Privy Council. Nevertheless the Prince defied his father and married Mrs Fitzherbert secretly. Fidelity, however, was not amongst his virtues, and it was not long before he took another mistress, the Countess of Jersey.

By the time he was thirty he was an embarrassment to his father and intensely unpopular with the British public. George III tried desperately to curb his excesses, but the prince, who had spent vast sums on building his own home at Carlton House in London, lived a very debauched life, eating and drinking to excess, becoming grossly fat and increasingly given to violence. His debts amounted to nearly £650,000 (well over £10,000,000 in today's money), and Pitt's government showed no enthusiasm for taking them on. Eventually the king and Parliament persuaded him to marry properly and in due course furnish the country with an heir to the throne, and he agreed, on condition that Parliament paid his debts. Lady Jersey may have helped to persuade him to the king's choice, Caroline of Brunswick, since she was likely to be less of a rival to the prince's affections than the more beautiful Louise of Mecklenburg-Strelitz, who provided the alternative. So Caroline came to London to meet him.

Caroline was short, ugly, almost as fat as the prince himself, and like him was given to violent tantrums. By reason of her sketchy and infrequent toilet she suffered badly from body odour. The prince must have been unaware of her reputation when they met, for, in spite of all her shortcomings, she had already had at least one affair during her youth. Prince George was so shattered by her appearance when first introduced to her three days before their wedding in April 1795 that he called for a large brandy, and continued to anaesthetise himself with a succession of bottles of the same thereafter. He was drunk throughout the wedding service and spent most of his wedding night in a stupor before the fire. On the honeymoon – with Lady Jersey in attendance – he appears, however, to have done his conjugal duty, and nine months later to the day she produced his only offspring, Charlotte Augusta. But otherwise

George and Caroline avoided each other as much as possible, and were officially separated soon after the birth of the little princess. He wrote to her almost apologetically, 'our inclinations are not in our power', and thereafter had very little to do with her. Caroline was denied any part in the child's upbringing and went off to found an orphanage in Kent in 1797, whilst George reverted to Mrs Fitzherbert, who still regarded herself as his legal wife.

Rejected by her husband, Caroline later retired to a house in Blackheath, where she led a life that got her the reputation of being 'a downright whore'. She was reputed to divert herself with a series of obscene clockwork toys which made explicit gestures when they were wound up, and she was further alleged to be in the habit of dancing whilst wearing inadequate clothing, her vigorous actions exposing a good deal of her person as she did so. She was in dispute with him in 1804 over the custody of the princess, with the result that the child was given into the care of her grandfather, George III himself. Irritated by this, the prince began a series of criticisms of her conduct, alleging that one of the 'orphans' in her charge, the four-year-old William Austin, was in fact her own illegitimate son. This led to a 'delicate investigation' by a Royal Commission in 1806, which eventually cleared her name, at the same time finding Lady Douglas, who had been instrumental in spreading the rumour, guilty of perjury. However, years later, Caroline confessed that the child was indeed the natural son of Prince Louis Ferdinand of Prussia, who had earlier been her lover. In 1814, Caroline was finally forced into exile from England. On the continent, however, she had a high old time. In Geneva, at a ball staged in her honour, she shocked the assembled company when she danced in just her skirts, her garments low on her hips and exposing her navel, and her ample figure naked from there up. Later she became the mistress of King Joachim, brother of the Emperor Napoleon and King of Naples. Finally she fell in with Bartolomeo Bergami, a swarthy, swashbuckling hero who had formerly been a quartermaster in a regiment of hussars. She found him all man and completely satisfactory. The two travelled widely and notoriously together to many of the capitals of Europe, including Munich, Athens and Constantinople, before finally settling in her villa in Pesaro.

The Prince Regent, meanwhile, was beset with difficulties. Princess Charlotte, who married in 1816, died in childbirth in November 1817, leaving him without an heir. Caroline, even if she were willing, could not provide him with another, being by this time in her fifties; in any case it was now his chief aim to rid himself of her forever. Then, in 1820, George III, by this time hopelessly demented, also died, and the Prince Regent in turn became King. Caroline determined to take her place as queen. He offered her £50,000 a year to stay away, but she brushed this offer aside and returned in June, taking up residence at Brandenburg House in Hammersmith. George brought in a special bill, the Pains and Penalties Bill, demanding an enquiry into her conduct. In August she was summoned before the House of Lords in what came to be regarded as her trial, though she never spoke a word in her own defence. The Lords were determined to dissolve the marriage on account of her 'unbecoming and degrading intimacy' with Bergami, 'a foreigner of low station'. Because of the contempt in which her husband was held, Queen Caroline unexpectedly found herself the centre of the popular adulation of the London mob: they saluted her every public appearance, crowds of them followed and cheered her coach in the streets, and the House of Lords had to protect itself by the erection of a double timber fence against popular indignation. On one occasion, it is said, the mob halted the Duke of Wellington's coach on his way to the House of Lords, insisting that he give three cheers for Queen Caroline. Overcoming his natural unwillingness he rose to his feet and said: 'Gentlemen, since you would have it so, three cheers for Queen Caroline (raising his hat), and may all your wives be like her.' The Bill passed through all its parliamentary stages in fifty-two days, but passed the last one by a majority of only nine; hence the Lords capitulated, and dropped it amid wild rejoicing.

George IV's coronation was planned for 29 April 1821 with great pomp and expense, and Queen Caroline, with full public approval, was determined to have her share in it. She wrote to the Prime Minister, Lord Liverpool, to enquire what sort of dress to wear for the occasion; he replied tersely that 'she could form no part of that ceremony'. Nevertheless she turned up at the Abbey in a plain white muslin slip and demanded to be admitted, shouting: 'The queen – open!' and when pages opened the doors: 'I am the Queen of England!'. Officials roared: 'Close the door!' and the doors were slammed in her face. Then she drove back amid commiserating crowds to Brandenburg House, where she sat down and wrote a note to the king demanding her own coronation 'next Monday'.

But it never happened. Caroline died less than three weeks later, it was said 'of an inflammation of the bowel', but so suddenly that it was rumoured she had been poisoned. When her coffin was on its way to the ship that was to carry it back to Brunswick, there were riots in front of Kensington church, stones were thrown, and two men were shot dead by the Life Guards.

By the end of the twentieth century, the daring – even the glamour – of this strange lady has faded, and the successive scandals of her behaviour are now quite forgotten; all that remains is a grotesque and rather pathetic Regency character who was unfortunate enough to be paired in marriage with George IV.

Did Queen Victoria have an affair with John Brown?

The accusation that no less a person than Queen Victoria, the person whose public reputation during and after her own lifetime was revered by her whole generation, was guilty of a scandalous affair with one of her own domestic staff, was something which threatened the very foundations of the British monarchy. Even now it is sometimes used to cast aspersions on Queen Victoria as an individual and the monarchy as an institution.

The suspicion that the personal relationships between John Brown, the manservant, and Queen Victoria on the death of the Prince Consort were of a scandalous nature was assiduously hushed up. Their 'affair' was said to have lasted for over twenty years after her husband's death in 1861, though the polite conventions of the time meant that it was never publicly reported or commented on in the press. Even so, the suggestion of their intimacy left something of a shadow on the royal reputation.

John Brown was a Scotsman and came into contact with the royal family at Balmoral, their house in the Scottish Highlands. He had earlier served her beloved husband, Prince Albert, as a *ghillie*, i.e. his attendant and guide on hunting and fishing trips, and before he died Albert recommended him to the queen as a thoroughly trustworthy servant. A recommendation of this sort, especially from one whose advice Victoria so much revered, was enough to get Brown a position in the royal household, where he remained until he died in March 1883. There must have been a degree of intimacy between them dictated by their close proximity to each other, and illustrated by the numerous small items she gave him during his lifetime, cufflinks, brooches etc., none of them of any great value, but reflecting Victoria's regard for him and her conservative good taste in personal jewellery.

Victoria was far from popular in the years after the Prince Consort's death, at least partly on account of the way she withdrew herself from public life, living in mourning and seclusion in one royal residence after another. Her critics attributed her isolation to the masterful influence over her of John Brown. They even suggested he had an amorous relationship with the queen, whom they unkindly dubbed 'Mrs Brown'.

There seems to have been no truth in the allegation, but it is a fact that on his death John Brown's diary, in which the details of his service and his thoughts were recorded, unaccountably disappeared, suggesting that someone at court thought that his unexpurgated comments might be explosive enough to warrant suppression.

In fact Brown turned out to be all that the queen wanted him to be. She was a lonely woman, surrounded by a sycophantic court, and Brown's solid and reliable forthrightness, often bordering on impertinence, came like a breath of fresh air. She saw in him, perhaps, an expression of the loyalty of her people, and a humble substitute for the helping character of Albert, on whom she so much relied. He was always at hand to seize a pair of runaway horses, or – as he did in 1872 – a would-be assassin with a pistol. He drove away importunate newspaper reporters with a flea in their ear, and was always ready to offer blunt common-sense advice instead of courtly flattery if the queen asked for it – and sometimes when she did not. He served her not only at Balmoral, but in her other houses, too, and frequently exchanged sharp words not only with the queen's private secretary, but even with Prince Edward, later Edward VII, of whom Brown seems to have held no very high opinion. Victoria liked him because he was honest and direct, and not afraid of showing his feelings. He wept readily at misfortune, and the Queen noted more than once in her diary, 'good Brown was quite overwhelmed.' He also liked a regular tipple of whisky, though he was seldom drunk. He had, in short, a number of simple human qualities, joined with shortcomings, and this was probably the reason that Victoria was attached to him.

Edward VII's destruction of all papers, monuments, etc. relating to Brown immediately on his own mother's death in 1901 not only reflected Edward and Brown's antipathy towards each other, but at the time and afterwards was seen as a justification for the unsubstantiated rumours which fuelled the 'Mrs Brown' legend.

New light was cast on Brown's supposedly 'missing' diary at the very end of the twentieth century by the discovery in the attic of one of his grandchildren of a number of the mouldering pages whose loss in 1883 had given rise to so much surprise. Even then they were not released for study or for publication – on the rather curious grounds that publication might give some disquiet to the then Queen Mother, Elizabeth, formerly Bowes-Lyon, wife of George VI. Herself a minor scion of the Scottish aristocracy, it is difficult to see what feelings other than those of hilarity the disclosure could have provoked. Whether this limp excuse provides evidence of Victoria's improper intimacy with John Brown, or whether there was an even subtler plot to conceal the fact that the diaries were entirely innocent, it is quite impossible to say. What is certain is that the death of the Queen Mother at the ripe old age of 101 at Easter 2002 removed the last scintilla of justification for suppressing the diaries any longer.

Since then, the missing diaries have never been published, and Queen Victoria still continues to enjoy the benefit of the doubt. So it is still only gossip to suppose that there was anything indelicate in their relationship.

RELIGIOUS SCANDALS

Was Sir Thomas More
a rebel or a saint?

In July 1535, Sir Thomas More, writer, savant, scholar and respected former servant of Henry VIII, was beheaded for high treason, and his head displayed for a month on London Bridge before it was removed by his eldest daughter Margaret to be preserved in spices. Opinions on Sir Thomas remain deeply divided: whether he was a determined rebel who obstinately refused due allegiance to his king, or whether he was a saint and a hero who died for his Christian conscience. Modern opinion tends towards the latter view. In 1935 he was canonized by the Catholic Church, and in 1960 the views of his biographer William Roper, his son-in-law and one of his many family admirers, were enshrined in the play A Man for All Seasons *written by Robert Bolt, and played to great public acclaim in late 2005 by the TV actor Martin Shaw. A modern view might appear less hagiographic, but it cannot avoid the conclusion that More, whatever his own shortcomings, was the sacrificial victim of scandalous and rather sordid contemporary political expediency.*

Born in 1477, More went to school in London and became a page in the household of Cardinal John Morton, Archbishop of Canterbury, in 1490. His patron gave him a place at Canterbury College, Oxford, but he did not take a degree; instead, following in his father's footsteps, he returned to London to study law in New Inn and Lincoln's Inn, and soon built up a flourishing legal practice. He was one of the foremost humanists of the age, counting amongst his friends William Lily and John Colet. He valued especially the warm friendship of Erasmus, and the two kept up a correspondence which lasted most of his life.

In 1509 More was elected to Parliament for the City of London, and in 1516 entered the Royal Council. A gifted linguist, he spoke French, Latin and Greek fluently, and soon came to serve Henry VIII in the field of diplomacy, both at home and in Europe. In October 1527 More came back from a diplomatic mission to France to find a tense situation in the royal Court, where Henry, after twenty years of marriage with Catherine of Aragon without male issue, was contemplating putting her aside and taking in her place Anne Boleyn, with whom he was already madly in love. The Court was split into two groups: the Boleyn faction, inclined towards Lutheranism and political change, and headed by Sir Thomas Boleyn, Anne's father; and the Conservative faction, stout defenders of traditional views and strong adherents of the Spanish marriage, prominent amongst whom was Princess Mary, Catherine's daughter. More inclined towards the latter group. Henry had been consulting with scholars to sound out divorce proposals. The advice he most wanted to hear came from the Oxford theologian, Robert Wakefield. He told the king that according to the Book of Leviticus, Henry had sinned in marrying his brother Arthur's widow. Such a marriage was not only against the law of the Church, it was also against the law of nature. It was doomed to be childless. More, himself an austere character, was sceptical of all this: he pointed out that the royal marriage was not 'childless', since the king had a daughter by Catherine, but Wakefield's reply was that the author of Leviticus was referring to *male* children, and it was a *prince* of the House of Tudor that Henry wished for above all. Wakefield hinted at what the king wanted to hear, that the Pope, in sanctioning Henry's marriage to his brother's widow, had perhaps exceeded his authority. Such a suggestion was anathema to More.

Why, then, did More agree to Henry's proposal on the fall of Wolsey in October 1529 to become Lord Chancellor in his stead? It was not that he misunderstood the situation or underestimated its seriousness. Indeed at his home up-river in Chelsea, where he lived with about twenty of his household and a staff of about sixty servants, More gave long and careful consideration to it, talking it through with Margaret, his favourite daughter by his first wife Jane. He was an ambitious man, and beneath his surface humanist affability there was a streak of steeliness and author-itarianism. He thought that if he went along with Henry he might be able to moderate his thinking, or if the king's infatuation with Anne Boleyn faded as quickly as it had arisen, a break with the Papacy might be averted. His voluminous writings at this time (about 1½ million words) make his conservative leanings quite plain. He condemned Tyndale's English translation of the Bible as heretical – he had no wish for people to read the scriptures for themselves – and arrested and questioned under duress numerous individuals suspected of Protestant beliefs. He arranged to have Tyndale watched and betrayed by a professional spy in his refuge in the Lowlands, and used the most violent language in denouncing him; when he returned to England he set in motion the wheels that would eventually lead to his execution by burning. At the same time he imposed a strict censorship on the circulation of Tyndale's translations, and others of his printed works; it was even made a crime to read the English Bible. More went further. Suspected heretics were whipped; six others were burnt as heretics. Erasmus did not agree with him on this: he took the view that it was the heresy that ought to be punished, not the heretic.

Henry VIII, however, did not relent in his drive towards the Boleyn marriage. Thomas Cromwell, who had been solicitor to, and a loyal servant of, Wolsey, was now in the ascendant and a prominent member of the Boleyn faction, eventually becoming Secretary to the King. He masterminded the passage through Parliament of a series of laws culminating in the Act of Supremacy in 1534, which made Henry head of the English Church. He went on, ignoring More's warnings against making the king too powerful, to dissolve the English monasteries, stoking further the king's wealth and ambitions. More had already seen the danger to which he had exposed himself, and decided to leave office. In May 1532 he resigned the Chancellorship the day after the promulgation of the Submission of the Clergy, a document by which the Convocation of Canterbury had surrendered the church's right to legislate for itself. Retiring into private life, but not into obscurity, More produced from Chelsea two further books: one a denunciation of heresy, the other a defence of church independence from the royal interference. Though he had been invited, More did not attend Anne Boleyn's coronation; and in April 1534 refused to swear the oath of loyalty under the Act of Succession to the heirs of Henry and Anne. Henry was furious with his conduct and demanded that he be brought into line.

More was therefore arrested, questioned by the royal commissioners headed by Thomas Cromwell, and detained in the Tower of London. Correctly anticipating further action against him, More reassigned the ownership of his property to Margaret and other members of his family. In October he was attainted by Act of Parliament, along with Bishop John Fisher. Now in much more rigorous confinement he began his last work, on the theme of Christ's sufferings (though nowhere did he draw any comparisons between his own ordeal and that of Christ). Here he was visited both by Cromwell and by his old associate, Sir Richard Rich, both of whom tried to persuade him to take the oath. In confidence he declared to Rich his belief that it was *ultra vires* for Parliament to declare Henry the Head of the English Church. In July 1535, four days after Fisher was executed, he was tried in Westminster Hall under the provisions of the new Treason Act. He argued his case skilfully. Three of the four indictments were quashed, but the fourth one related to the matter he had discussed with Rich in the Tower. Here he could not escape condemnation. His accusers called Rich to the stand, where he repeated in public the confidences More thought he had made to him off the record. His impugning of parliamentary authority proved to be the clinching argument against him, and he was convicted of treason. He was allowed to bid farewell to the members of his family – for Margaret he set out in full his justifications for his conduct – but five days later he was executed. He was, however, spared the pain and indignity of the usual penalty (hanging, drawing and quartering); because of the special regard in which the king was supposed to have held him he was permitted to have his head struck off by an axe.

Henry's deed scandalized England. There were many in the country who secretly sympathized with More's opinion, though few with the courage to say so openly. Cromwell himself found out the dangers of an over-mighty sovereign five years later, when he followed More to the block. Indeed, in his later years, Henry VIII became a ruthless and unpredictable monster. He gained little but strife from his creation of the Church of England, whilst his pillaging of the monasteries brought him little but cost him much. Finally it is richly ironic that all Henry's ruthless efforts to strengthen his dynasty ultimately failed: his only son was a weakling who failed to reach manhood, and in fact he was succeeded by two of his daughters, Mary and Elizabeth, until finally the throne passed into the line of the house of Stuart.

How innocent was Lady Jane Grey?

Queen Mary Tudor's reputation among historians has generally stood fairly low, not least because of her treatment of the hapless Lady Jane Grey. Sentenced to death for treason, Lady Jane was kept by Mary on tenterhooks for three months before finally being beheaded within the precincts of the Tower. Was this simply a case of an innocent woman being hounded to death by a cruel and merciless sovereign?

Henry VIII had, wittingly or not, set England upon the road to a rejection of Roman Catholicism and the adoption of Protestantism. In his final years the Howard faction attempted a vigorous defence of the old faith, and at Henry's death in 1547 the issue was still in the balance. His nine-year-old son and successor, Edward VI, soon showed that he was susceptible to reforming influences. He sent his more cautious and compromising Seymour uncles to their deaths without scruple, and came under the influence of the Earl of Warwick, whom he soon promoted to be Duke of Northumberland. Northumberland threw in his lot with the more radical reformers, not so much out of religious conviction but because by doing so he was able to ingratiate himself ever more firmly into the king's favour and thus strengthen his hold on power. By 1552 the new English Prayer Book, compiled by Archbishop Cranmer, was required to be used in all churches, papal supremacy was denied, marriage of clergy was encouraged, and the physical change of the bread and wine into the body and blood of Christ in the Mass was denounced as Catholic superstition.

The triumph of Northumberland and the Protestant party seemed complete. Yet Protestantism's hold on England was tenuous. Protestant preachers flooded into south-east England and the new faith gained a strong foothold in London and some of the south eastern counties. But in most of the country the inhabitants were indifferent to the changes, acquiesced in whatever new religious law was promulgated, made peace with their consciences, and prayed for better times. So Northumberland was aware that the fate of Protestantism was bound up closely with the policies and predilections of the monarch. When Edward became seriously ill at the beginning of 1553 Northumberland realised that the accession of Edward's fanatically Catholic sister Mary would place English Protestantism in jeopardy. Yet he was cautious. Despite the need for haste he moved only slowly and stealthily towards his objectives. Eventually he came up with the idea of disinheriting both Mary and her sister Elizabeth (whose own religious inclinations were uncertain) on the grounds that they had both been bastardised by Parliament. He conveniently ignored the claims of the eleven-year-old Mary Queen of Scots whose descent from Henry VII's eldest daughter placed her next in succession. Instead he turned to the Suffolk line. Henry VIII's younger sister Mary had married Charles Brandon, Duke of Suffolk. Of their two daughters, the elder, Frances, was mother to Lady Jane Grey. Thus Lady Jane was second cousin to Mary and Elizabeth and fourth in line to the succession. In May 1553 Northumberland secured Frances's consent for the marriage of her daughter, Lady Jane Grey, to his fourth son, Lord Guildford Dudley. Lady Jane was young and as her father-in-law he felt certain he could manage her and exercise power from behind the scenes. Once the marriage had taken place Northumberland made great efforts to conceal how seriously ill the king was, while at the same time persuading the king that the reformed religion would be in grave danger should he be succeeded by either of his sisters, and urging him to will the succession to Lady Jane. It is probable that Lady Jane was unaware of Northumberland's plans for her; politics were for men. Yet she was a young lady of considerable ability. Her tutor, Roger Ascham, one of the great teachers of the day, affirmed that at fifteen she could read Plato in the original Greek. Moreover she had become deeply committed to the reformed religion. And possibly out of duty or physical attraction she seems to have speedily become devoted to her young husband. So unaware of how ill Edward was, and largely ignorant of her father-in-law's intrigues, Lady Jane looked forward to a life of domestic and marital bliss at Sion House, supported by her deep religious faith, and enriched by books and learning. She was soon to have her dreams of the simple life rudely shattered.

On 21 June, Edward's new will was approved by the Privy Council. Edward died fifteen days later, on 6 July. For two days Northumberland kept the death secret while he tried to secure the persons of Edward's two sisters, Mary and Elizabeth. Both were warned by informed well-wishers in high places not to come to London to visit their dying (already dead) brother. Mary set off and turned back; Elizabeth, feigning illness, did not move at all. Meanwhile, after Northumberland had met a deputation of Londoners, shown them Edward's will, and secured their allegiance to Jane, he moved to Sion House and on 8 July tendered homage to Jane as Queen. None of the contemporary accounts dispute that Jane met this homage without joy or even equanimity. It is reported that she burst into floods of tears, and she remained tearful when she was proclaimed in London two days later. She took up royal residence in the Tower where it was hoped she would be safe from attack from without and secure from intrigue from within. Mary's response to these events was to promise to make no religious changes (a promise easy to make and easy to break with heretics) and began gathering an army. Those who had a conscience about supporting Jane and who disliked Northumberland's naked ambition were won over by Mary's promises and the undoubted legality of her cause. Protestants and Catholics alike flocked to her standard which she raised on 12 July in Norfolk. Northumberland proposed to put Jane's father, the Duke of Suffolk, in charge of Queen Jane's forces. But Northumberland trusted neither the counsellors in London, nor his commanders in the field. He reluctantly agreed to take command himself reminding his men of their oath to Jane who 'by your and our enticement is rather of force placed on the throne than by her own seeking and request'. This smacks of the truth; Northumberland was far too selfish to protect his daughter-in-law's future by promulgating a fiction, but he is saying in effect that the coup was not her idea and that it was in reality his own devious work. It was all to no avail; there was little general support for Jane. On 18 July the counsellors, including Cranmer, surreptitiously sneaked out of the Tower and immediately declared for Mary. Lady Jane's weak-kneed father, the Duke of Suffolk, let Mary's supporters into the Tower and Lady Jane publicly expressed her joy at no longer being queen, an office which had been such a burden to her during her nine days' tenure.

Northumberland, realising that all was lost, proclaimed Mary in Cambridge on July 20, one day after she had been similarly proclaimed in London. Mary's supporters soon rounded up Northumberland and his main associates. When the crunch came his determination crumbled away: as well as being wily and ambitious, he showed himself to be pretty much a coward. Lady Jane, meanwhile, remained in the Tower under arrest. Not a drop of blood had been shed either for Mary or for Jane, and such had been the mood of the country that Northumberland's ill-conceived plottings and manoeuvrings had had no chance of success. Northumberland paid for his insatiable ambition at the hands of the headsman on Tower Hill on August 22. His revolt lacked the true courage and principle of one acting for his country and his conscience; his motives were the grubbier and pettier aims of a man seeking power for himself and his family. His actions, too, in abjuring his Protestant faith for himself and abandoning it for the country merely to save his skin confirmed Mary in her contempt for Protestantism, and led her later to underestimate the intensity of religion of Protestant zealots. She did not immediately proceed against Lady Jane and her husband; she was far too busy reversing the recent religious changes, depriving married bishops and arresting Protestant divines. Eventually on 13 November Lady Jane, her husband Lord Guildford Dudley and his brother, together with Archbishop Cranmer were condemned for treason. Cranmer was pardoned of his treason soon after but was returned to the Tower on the newer and more sinister charge of heresy.

Mary's intentions towards Lady Jane and her husband were less patent; she certainly had no intention of bringing them at once to the block. It is not inconceivable that Mary shrank from shedding the blood of so young a couple. After all, their involvement in Northumberland's intrigues had been passive rather than active. And Northumberland's incompetence meant that Mary's position had never been seriously threatened. Just before Christmas Lady Jane was given freedom within the precincts of the Tower, and the other prisoners, including her husband, were treated less rigorously. Mary's motives here have been disputed. She certainly was not the cold heartless woman depicted by her enemies. She was loyal and generous to her servants; she was capable of strong emotions as shown in her fleeting passion for the handsome Edward Courtenay (who naturally preferred her much younger sister Elizabeth) and her obsession with her more ravaged husband, Philip of Spain. But she was fanatical in her religion, and in the early months of her reign was only held back from burning heretics by her advisers, who strongly recommended caution. Later Cranmer was allowed to return to his house and library at Oxford with the intention of undermining his commitment to the reformed religion. It nearly worked. Was Mary on this earlier occasion hoping to weaken Lady Jane's resolve by giving her a glimpse of the freedom that might be hers, before sending in learned priests to argue Lady Jane out of her faith and into Catholicism?

We shall never know: there is a strong possibility that Mary might have spared and released Jane and Guildford Dudley, provided they did not flaunt their Protestant religion. But a new situation had arisen. In January 1554 Mary contracted to marry her cousin Philip of Spain. Catholics and Protestants alike reacted with alarm. To Protestants Philip was synonymous with the worst horrors of the Inquisition, to most others it seemed that England was about to become a mere province of the Spanish Empire. By late January the formerly loyal and Catholic Sir Thomas Wyatt was in rebellion in Kent. At the beginning of February London was his for the taking, but he wrecked his chances by unnecessary indecision and delays. His primary aim was to prevent the Spanish marriage, but secondary to it was the release of Lady Jane from the Tower. On February 6 Wyatt was forced to surrender. Within five days Mary had signed Lady Jane's death warrant. She had not allowed herself much time for agonizing. Her advisers had pointed out to her how dangerous the Wyatt insurrection was, how close it had come to success, and how Lady Jane would be the rallying cry of any future rebellion. Nor did Mary wish to jeopardise her Spanish marriage by showing weakness toward those who might wittingly or unwittingly pose a threat to her throne. Even so it seemed that Mary did not take much convincing, but neither would her father or grandfather in similar circumstances.

But it was not in her dying but in the manner of it that Lady Jane was to arouse public sympathy and to excoriate Mary. The queen was anxious for Jane's soul, and she sent the learned and devout Dean of St Paul's to torment Jane in her final hours. She resisted his blandishments and referred constantly to the English prayer book she carried. She refused a final meeting with her husband, who was executed publicly on Tower Hill where he said prayers, shed tears and *died quietly*. This aroused some public sympathy and had been anticipated by Mary who had ordered

Jane's execution to take place within the privacy of the Tower. But as Jane was being led to execution a bier was carried past her containing the headless body of her husband. In reply to her agitated questioning it was confirmed to her that it was indeed the body of her husband under the white sheet. The officers of the Tower, not Mary, were responsible for this blunder. On the scaffold Jane spoke briefly to the few bystanders, explaining that she justly deserved this punishment for allowing herself to have become, although unwilling, the instrument of the ambition of others, and hoped that her fate might serve as a memorable example to others. She was *in countenance nothing cast down, neither her eyes anything moistened with tears, although her gentlewomen, Elizabeth Tilney and Mistress Helen, wonderfully wept.* She put on her own blindfold and then, unable to find the block, was heard to whisper as she groped forward, 'Oh, what shall I do? Where is it? Where is it?'. When her head fell, no one witnessing the scene was dry-eyed.

To many this was a young, beautiful and innocent girl who had been cat's paw of the ruthless scheming Duke of Northumberland and who had died steadfast in the Protestant faith, victim of the vindictiveness of Queen Mary. The queen might have done better to have allowed Jane to rot in the Tower had she not been so paranoid about the possibility of another insurrection, and, more particularly, so anxious to convince her husband-to-be that England was fully loyal and ripe for conversion. Her reservations about killing Jane evaporated with the Wyatt rebellion. Jane's manner of death made her a saint for the Protestant faith rather than the just recipient of death for treason. Jane's involvement in treason was tenuous, and both she and her father-in-law took pains to say so. It seems most likely that Jane's involvement in treason was reluctant, and that she was outsmarted and out-manoeuvred by people who were older, more cunning and less idealistic than she was.

How great a danger was the Babington Plot?

In the middle of war no news is more alarming than that of treachery within. The English government, in the summer of 1586, announced the chance discovery of a plot to release Mary Queen of Scots and to 'despatch' Elizabeth, both aims to be supported by a Catholic rebellion and a foreign invasion. At the centre of this dastardly plot were its instigator, Sir Anthony Babington, and his chief confidante, Mary Queen of Scots herself.

Such was the universal horror when the plot became public that Mary was brought to trial and condemned as a traitor. Elizabeth showed considerable reluctance to sanction Mary's execution, but she was subjected to intense pressure by her ministers, and on 8 February 1587, Mary was executed in the great hall of Fotheringay Castle. How fortunate that the government stumbled by accident on this plot, for the outcome, had the plot remained undiscovered, might well have been the overthrow of Elizabeth and the subjection of England to foreign domination. Or so it might seem, but in fact the main function of the plot was not to overthrow Elizabeth, but to destroy Mary.

In 1568 Mary Queen of Scots had escaped into England, where she sought the protection and assistance of Queen Elizabeth. She needed both: protection against the Scots who wanted to put Mary on trial for the murder of her husband Lord Darnley, and the assistance of an English army to overthrow her enemies and help restore Catholicism in Scotland. Neither of these seemed very attractive to Elizabeth who wanted to be responsible neither for Mary's death nor for her triumph. Nor did she care for the other alternative, which would mean allowing Mary to escape to France where her relatives would restore her to the

Scottish throne, and French armies would be poised to invade England from the North, endangering both Elizabeth's throne and England's religion. Elizabeth played for time, summoning a Court of Inquiry to look into Mary's guilt or innocence, and feeding it with unreliable witnesses and shaky evidence. It is not surprising that the court was unable to arrive at a firm conclusion. Negotiations then dragged on for months with the Scots demanding Mary's head, and Elizabeth denying that she had offered to help Mary and that protection was all she could rightfully expect until her innocence was fully established.

All changed in 1570. The Northern rebels fought their last gasp at the New Year – some of them had taken up Mary's cause. In February the Papal Bull *Regnans in Excelsis* excommunicated Elizabeth, deprived her of the English throne, absolved her subjects from loyalty to her, and, in effect, threw the throne of England open to Catholic claimants, of whom Mary was the most important. Elizabeth's Catholic subjects were put in an impossible position: if they remained loyal to Elizabeth they were defying their Church, while if they obeyed their Church they were disloyal to Elizabeth. It is therefore not surprising that from 1570 the air was thick with plots: to rescue Mary, to depose Elizabeth, to restore the Catholic church in England, to restore it in Scotland, to establish Mary as Elizabeth's successor and to support a foreign invasion whether French or Spanish. The plots usually had multiple objectives, and Mary, through her various contacts with the outside world, was aware of most of them and involved in some of them. The government, too, was aware of many of them. Sir Francis Walsingham had entered Queen Elizabeth's service in 1568. Already he was building up an efficient network of spies and double agents both at home and abroad, and he was not particularly scrupulous as to method. His forte was the rack, and he found it just as easy to incriminate the innocent as to investigate the guilty. As early as 1572 two mainly unconnected events, the Ridolfi Plot, an international conspiracy for the seizure and possible assassination of Elizabeth to which Mary had given her approval, and the massacre of 30,000 French Protestants on St Bartholemew's Day, to which Mary was not privy, caused alarm in both high and low places. Parliament demanded that Mary share the fate of the Duke of Norfolk, executed despite the reluctance of his involvement with Ridolfi. And the Protestant masses, believing Elizabeth to be in great danger, echoed the views of their betters with demonstrations and petitions. Elizabeth baulked at executing a Queen and cousin, and the moment passed. But from here on Mary was more closely confined and more closely watched, and Walsingham's spies kept a sharp lookout for anything that might incriminate Mary. From Mary's point of view she was prepared to support anything that would result in her release from confinement, even if it coincidentally would be uncomfortable for Elizabeth and English Protestants. From 1569 to 1585 Mary's jailers were the Earl of Shrewsbury and his formidable wife Bess. Mary spent most of that time at Sheffield Manor. Mary used her ingenuity, her friends, and her money to keep abreast of the news, and to correspond with the outside world without Shrewsbury's knowledge. But Walsingham was not so ignorant and he was aware of the general nature, and often the specific content, of many of her letters.

For a long time it seemed that the greatest danger to Elizabeth came from Mary's plotting with her French relatives, the Guises. But in 1583 the government discovered a plot whose instigator, Francis Throckmorton, was in close league with Spain. His confession, full and explicit as one might expect from one subjected to the full rigours of the rack, alarmed the government, and led to the expulsion of the Spanish ambassador, Mendoza, in January 1584. Since Mary had been closely involved in this plot while at the same time negotiating with Elizabeth for release and joint mother-and-son rule in Scotland (with the future James VI), Elizabeth decided that any further attempt to compromise with so dangerous a woman was doomed to failure. In June 1584 the Privy Council promulgated the Bond of Association which received parliamentary sanction early in the following year. It pledged all who signed it to pursue to the death any person in whose name any attempt was made on Elizabeth's life. This could point only at Mary.

In 1585 the international situation deteriorated sharply. Now that Spain, rather than France, was the enemy, Elizabeth at last responded to the appeals of the Netherlands Protestants for assistance in their revolt against Spain. The Earl of Leicester was sent with an expedition to aid the rebels, which meant that England and Spain were at last and in effect at war. Mary seemed now a greater danger to Elizabeth than ever before. In January 1585 she had been moved back to Tutbury in Staffordshire (which she hated the most of all her various prisons) where she was placed under the charge of Sir Amyas Paulet, a man of Puritan sympathies and unlikely to bend the rules for his prisoner as Shrewsbury had done. Under his strict regime no strangers were allowed into the castle, soldiers accompanied servants in and out of the gates, and the letters Mary was allowed to send through the French ambassador – after inspection by Walsingham's agents – were stopped in September. At Christmas she was moved to Chartley in Derbyshire, and virtually cut off from the outside world.

By now Cecil and Elizabeth's other ministers were determined on Mary's destruction. In a way they were victims of their own propaganda. Mary was by no means such a danger to England as they made out, or they themselves believed. Mary was, of course, always a focus for English Catholic dissidents, but she posed no threat to the Protestant establishment in Scotland or to her son James VI: the vast majority of Scots regarded her crimes as unforgivable and her religion as abhorrent. France was too busy with internal problems to make a serious attempt to release her and restore her to the Scottish throne, and would regard with alarm any Spanish attempt to do so. Nor was Philip of Spain aiming to overthrow England for Mary's benefit. He may have allowed Mendoza to raise Mary's hopes, but Mary's advancement would be for the benefit of France and Mary's French relations the Guises, and Philip would prefer to replace Elizabeth with a puppet friendly to Spain. Nevertheless Elizabeth's ministers put pressure on her to put Mary on trial for her involvement with treason and plots. They could have secured her legal conviction under the Bond of Association, but realised that Elizabeth would not act unless very clear evidence of Mary's treason was forthcoming. And there was no evidence to collect. The government had made it virtually impossible for Mary to commit treasonable indiscretions by its effectiveness in isolating her.

So when, in December 1585, Gilbert Gifford was arrested and interrogated by Walsingham, a great opportunity to incriminate Mary presented itself. Gifford was ostensibly a devout Roman Catholic, was trusted in Rome, and had been privy to the secrets of the recent plots on Mary's behalf. Walsingham put pressure on Gifford to become a double agent. He was sent to the French Embassy to persuade them to hand over Thomas Morgan's letters to Mary which had been held up by the increased security surrounding her. Despite French suspicions (Gifford actually shared lodgings in London with one of Walsingham's agents) the letters were entrusted to him, and he assured the French that he had a foolproof method of getting letters in and out of Chartley without detection. In fact the move to Chartley had necessitated a change of brewer, and both the French Ambassador and Mary were led to believe that beer and wines were now being supplied to Mary by a man loyal to her cause. The brewer cynically accepted payment from both Mary and Walsingham, and then had the audacity to complain that he was not being paid enough, but he was playing a very risky game. Letters were to be inserted, wrapped in waterproof, into the bungs of the casks, full on arrival at Chartley, empty on leaving. But the letters were not for Mary's eyes alone. The letters were opened by Walsingham's agents and scrupulously copied before being passed on to their intended recipients. Walsingham's aim was to trap Mary into committing herself on paper. It might take time, but he was prepared to wait. At first the delayed correspondence and Mary's replies to it yielded little that Walsingham did not already know, and little that could be used in evidence against Mary. So Walsingham instructed Gifford to set in motion a spurious plot for the assassination of Elizabeth. This was joined by Gifford's known associates, including a former Catholic priest, John Ballard; but in the spring of 1586 a number of other Roman Catholics joined the plot, among them Sir Anthony Babington. Since the Catholic Babington had travelled much abroad and had mixed with Catholic exiles in Rome, he had been entrusted with details of the many foreign and Catholic plots against Elizabeth. On his return to England he received Scottish letters for Mary at his house for passing on to the brewer, and acquainted himself with Ballard. The Ballard intrigues then became subsumed in the overall plans of Babington, and the government's attempts to fabricate a fictitious plot were now converted into a real one. From the government's point of view the key questions were whether Mary would enter into the new conspiracy and how far she would commit herself. Since Babington was passing on her Scottish letters, and since Thomas Morgan had written from Paris recommending Babington, Mary had no reason to be suspicious, and entered wholeheartedly into the scheme.

Babington was over-confident and reckless. In mid-July he committed all the details of his plans to paper, and sent them to Mary, asking for her complete approval. Despite the misgivings of some of her advisers, and after a three day delay, Mary wrote back on July 17 a detailed letter in which she gave her assent and support to all of Babington's proposals, which specifically included the 'design' of assassinating Elizabeth. Mary did not mention assassination, but frequently talked of her approval of the 'design'; Mary had now committed her treason to paper. The letter was carefully copied, as usual, by Thomas Phelippes, one of Walsingham's secretaries, but on this occasion Walsingham added a false postscript in which Mary was purported to ask for the names of the six leading conspirators. Within two weeks of Babington's reply on 3 August all the major conspirators, including Babington, had been arrested.

Cecil and his fellow ministers did not intend to allow their principal prey, Mary, any chance of escape. Mary was subjected to official arrest on 11 August, and her secretaries were arrested and taken away. Their evidence, some of it incriminating, was extracted under duress, and Mary's demands to have them appear at her trial so that she could cross-examine them were refused. It was difficult for her secretaries to deny the evidence of the letters, which they themselves had taken part in writing. But their interrogators were careful to show them only copies, and the forged postscript to the letter of July 17 was carefully omitted. Babington and his fellow conspirators were executed before Mary's trial so that their evidence and statements, too, could not be challenged. Walsingham even had some of the witnesses gratuitously tortured for evidence that the government already possessed. And at the trial Mary, despite her royal status, was denied the assistance of legal counsel. She defended herself well, but the incriminating letters forced her into dishonest denials, and anyway the result of the trial was a foregone conclusion whether she chose to defend herself or not.

So the Babington Plot was not a conspiracy uncovered by the diligence of the government, and which placed England in grave peril. It was a plot fostered in part by the government's secret service and agents provocateurs and used as a method to entrap a desperate and rather foolish woman. It certainly did not place England in any real peril, but gave Elizabeth the apparent justification for eliminating her troublesome royal prisoner. It also sheds a rather disturbing light on the murkier side of the activities and methods of the Tudor state. Such methods were still being used in 1605 in a rather different context.

Were there witches in Salem?

The end of the seventeenth century produced one of the most curious episodes in the history of the North American colonies of England: the prosecution and trial in 1692 in Essex County, Massachusetts, of women alleged to be witches, for being possessed by the devil and for practising necromantic ceremonies in the village communities there.

The affair started when two young girls in Salem, the eleven-year-old niece and the nine-year-old daughter of a local minister, the Reverend Samuel Parris, were taken suddenly ill with an ailment for which no physician could suggest a remedy. Their behaviour was strange and frightening, their suffering genuine but their behaviour unpredictable. Eventually they claimed to have been bewitched by the devil after playing at voodoo with a West Indian slave, Tituba. Other older girls developed, or imagined they developed, the same symptoms, and blamed them on anyone who seemed a suitable person to be called a 'witch', or on anyone who threatened their new and exciting status as informers against the devil. Tituba and three older women were accused of witchcraft and forced into signing confessions. Hysteria took hold of the small town. Local magistrates and the Court of the Commonwealth took up the cause, and the Witch Hunt and the Witch Trials became the outlet for superstition, local hate and local vendettas. A large number of people were arrested and tried by special courts convened by the Governor, Sir William Phips. The charges brought were so broad and vague that those accused scarcely knew how to defend themselves, whilst others dare not doubt nor question the accusers for fear of being thought to be witches themselves or else in league with them. The accusations spread like wildfire, and the number of trials mounted. Even domestic animals were not free of charges of working witchcraft. Altogether nineteen persons – and two dogs – were executed (eighteen were hanged on Witches' Hill; one, eighty-year-old Giles Corey, was stoned to death) and many others narrowly acquitted before the hysteria began to abate. One of the judges, Samuel Sewall (1652–1730), later admitted he had been intimidated by popular pressure into making erroneous decisions, though none of his judgments was ever reversed. Other Puritan leaders, such as Increase Mather (1639–1723) and his son Cotton Mather (1663–1728), suspected of whipping up the panic as a device to bolster their waning influence, were perhaps unjustly criticized: the father, one of the founders of Congregationalism in Massachusetts, doubted the veracity of much of the testimony at the trials and according to his book, *Cases of Conscience,* published in 1693, intervened personally to stop a number of the executions, whilst the son, not unsympathetic to enlightened ideas and later one of the founders of Yale University, also opposed the imposition of the death penalty subsequent to the trials.

How can this scandalous treatment of harmless individuals be excused or understood? A modern scientific explanation has put down the bewitchment of the original two girls (though perhaps not the others) to the 'witches' cake' which Tituba is supposed to have baked for them before they had conversed with the Devil. History records a number of individuals in the past who have experienced hallucinations and have done so because the bread (or the 'witch cake') they have eaten has been made from flour contaminated by a parasitic fungus that resulted in *ergotism,* a condition in which the body responds in much the same way as these girls did. But perhaps the explanation is purely psychological, and arose from environmental influences. To the modern mind, there is no doubt that the wild and desolate conditions prevailing in the New England colonies accentuated the stresses experienced by the settlers, while the linked psychological factors such as sexual repression in a backward society, mass hypnosis, a lust for power, a craving for attention by the young females and fear of opposition on the part of bystanders all had their own contribution to make. It was however perhaps the Puritan character of colonial society which provided the main explanation for these extraordinary events.

The Puritans have been refugees from the church establishment in England since the days of the *Mayflower* Compact in 1610. With the official doctrine of the Anglican Church as expressed in the Thirty-Nine Articles they had no quarrel; but they were repelled by the corruption and incompetence of the clerical hierarchy and wished to 'purify' it. They aimed to do away with all clergy above the rank of parish priests, to abolish the Book of Common Prayer, and re-organize themselves either on the Presbyterian principle, through a hierarchy of councils, or on the Congregational principle, on the basis of a free federation of independent parishes. Furthermore they were disgusted and repelled by the frivolity and extravagance of society in Stuart England, the gaming, stage plays, the dancing and semi-pagan practices that disfigured everyday life, and wished to return to the simple and original style of living as expressed in the New Testament. Idleness, dishonesty, excess and modernity to the Puritans were deeply sinful; society had to get back to the 'purity' of life as it had been practised of old. Magic and witchcraft were amongst the traditional ways that the Puritans, perhaps mistakenly, identified with this old faith. In the dark and primitive life of the New England colonies in the seventeenth century, a belief in witchcraft was not difficult to conjure up.

Witchcraft, however, was by no means confined to New England alone. It was equally ingrained in Britain and in Europe. While the total number of executions for witchcraft in the New England colonies in the whole of the seventeenth century amounted to thirty-four, the number in England, and especially in Scotland, was more than a hundred times greater. Perhaps the best way of looking at the Salem Witchcraft Trials is to regard them as part of the battle between the old and the new in Massachusetts. The seventeenth century in the colony witnessed the weakening of the traditional bonds: science turned against religion, scepticism against superstition and reason against authority. As the colonists asked disrespectful questions of their traditional rulers, the Puritans, sensing the ebbing of their strength, attempted to tighten their grip over colonial lives. The confrontation is illustrated by Cotton Mather himself, who, though sympathetic to scientific and philosophical ideas, produced at the time of the Salem Trials a book entitled *Memorable Providences Relating to Witchcrafts and Possessions,* in which he flatly asserted: 'God tells us that there are Devils and Witches'. But, far from strengthening his position, this book marked the beginning of the end for New England theocracy. Accusations of the practice of witchcraft, and belief in witchcraft itself, declined sharply after the trials. Roger Williams had already broken away from the Puritan stranglehold, and had been expelled to his settlements on Narragansett Bay, which federated as Rhode Island in 1644. Here he allowed full freedom of conscience to settlers to worship God in any way they chose. By now the colonists were liberating themselves as much from superstition as from tyranny.

Could the Gordon Riots have been prevented?

The English were renowned in the eighteenth century for rioting; in London there was a major riot almost every year. But even the hardened eighteenth-century public were shocked by the Gordon riots of June 1780 which were the worst of the century, resulting in more than 200 deaths and several hundreds more injuries. For nearly a week London was in the hands of the mob and corpses littered the streets. The government at first seemed paralysed, and the mayhem was not halted until Alderman Wilkes (once a mob hero when he confronted the government over the Middlesex Election in 1769) confronted the mob with Captain Holroyd's militia in defence of the Bank of England. Could the death and destruction have been prevented?

Roman Catholics in Britain suffered a number of political disabilities, many of which had fallen into abeyance, although remaining on the Statute Book. In 1774 the Quebec Act virtually removed all political disabilities from Canadian Catholics, and progressive politicians argued that it was illogical, therefore, to retain them in Britain. There was a practical reason too; recruitment for the armed forces in wartime was proving difficult and made more so by the oaths on a Protestant bible required of Roman Catholic recruits. Sir George Savile's Catholic Relief Act of 1778 replaced the oaths by affirmations, and it was proposed to extend the Act to Scotland in the following year. Immediately there was a great outcry in Scotland. Presbyterian Protestant organisations sprang up, steeped in the old prejudices and obsessively intolerant. Riots and widespread disturbances in Edinburgh and elsewhere led the government of Lord North to decide that it was not appropriate to extend the Act to Scotland, and the proposed legislation was abandoned in the spring of 1779.

Immediately Protestant England rallied to demand that the new Act applying to England be repealed. Corresponding Societies (which exchanged information, ideas and plans by letter) and Protestant Associations sprang up – there were 85 throughout the country – all committed to promoting Protestant prejudice, and stirring up religious intolerance. These groups found a leader in Lord George Gordon, third son of the Duke of Gordon. A young man of twenty-nine, he had left the navy eight years earlier because he had failed to rise above the rank of Lieutenant. This lack of promotion, at what he thought was such a mature age, he believed to be a personal slight inflicted on him by Lord North, whom he therefore hated. At the age of twenty-three he became MP for one of the family rotten boroughs at Ludgershall. In the House of Commons he soon became known for his slovenly dress and his increasing mental instability. What drove him to take the lead in the Protestant Associations was a new slight planned for him by the government. Needing the Ludgershall seat for its own purposes it began negotiations with Gordon's eldest brother to make him Lord Admiral of Scotland in return for the youngest brother giving up the parliamentary seat. This would have the added benefit of removing a mental case from the House of Commons.

But the government plan was thrown into disarray by the rapid turn of events. Unable to find opposition MPs who shared his religious bigotry (they mostly wanted political reform and religious freedom), Gordon turned to the idea of using the Associations to organise a huge anti-Catholic petition which he would present to Parliament. He boasted of 150,000 signatures or marks (of the illiterate), and a huge procession to Westminster. His threats were greeted in the House of Commons with ribald laughter; no one took him seriously. Ominously his main supporter in the House was Alderman Bull who represented the City. He was more in touch with popular feeling than the rest of the House, and he knew how easily radical London wards could raise mobs whose cause local aldermen would refuse to support at their peril. Gordon's mobs prepared and polished up their 'No Popery' banners, their discontents heightened by North's trade concessions to the Catholic Irish, while the American War had intensified trade stagnation.

On Friday 2 June a huge procession wound its way to Westminster. Its size was variously estimated by contemporaries as between 60,000 and 100,000. There were many 'No Popery' banners, and many of the crowd were wearing blue cockades reminiscent of the riots in support of Wilkes twelve years earlier. So great was the crush that Lords and MPs had difficulty in reaching Parliament. Some had their wigs knocked off. The Bishop of Lichfield had his gown torn from his back, other Lords including the Archbishop of York and the Duke of Northumberland were roughly handled, and the Bishop of Lincoln, after the mob had wrecked his carriage, was so frightened that he fled into a neighbouring house, climbed through a garret window and escaped over the rooftops. Meanwhile Gordon was rushing to and fro, consulting with the crowds outside and threatening the MPs inside. The House of Lords summoned the local magistrates, demanding to know why such a large crowd had been allowed to assemble. The magistrates' excuse was that they had very few constables to deal with the situation. There had been some improvement recently in the quality of the constables, largely as a result of the work of the blind magistrate, Sir John Fielding, brother of the novelist Henry Fielding of *Tom Jones* fame. The constables used to be so poorly paid that they could only be recruited from the retired, the unemployed, or the unemployable. Fielding's constables were usually able-bodied but there were too few of them. The alternative was to send in the local militia officered by the gentry who played at dressing up as soldiers but whose rank and file were recruited by compulsory ballot, and were too poor to buy substitutes to take their place. Their enthusiasm for dispersing a mob might well be uncertain. Alternatively the army itself might be called in, but in wartime there were very few troops available in London for civilian policing. There was also the widespread, but mistaken, belief that the army could only be called in after the Riot Act had been read, and no magistrate was going to risk his own life, limb or property by reading the Act ordering the crowd to disperse. When one of the Middlesex magistrates arrived in late evening with a few troops, and promised not to use them if the crowd would disperse, the mob gave him three cheers and began to wend their way home. The reading of the Riot Act had not been necessary. So far, apart from a few toppled wigs, the crowd had been reasonably well-behaved and good-humoured. But as it dispersed some of them attacked the chapels of the Bavarian and Sardinian ambassadors, destroyed their contents and set fire to the buildings.

The next day, Saturday, was quiet, and the danger appeared to have passed. But late that evening, after men had received their weekly wages, and fortified themselves in the local inns, a mob gathered in Moorfields and attacked Catholics there. On Sunday morning troops were sent to

Moorfields, but had strict orders from the government not to open fire. The local magistrates had either joined the mob, or were too frightened to do anything to restrain it; they hastily disappeared from the scene whenever the troops asked for their support in attempting to seize the ringleaders. Lord George Gordon had by now lost control of events and decided to lie low. The Lord Mayor, Kennet, who had once been a waiter but was now a respectable wine merchant, refused to take any action and refused to allow others to do so. Demands in Parliament for strong action were resisted by such eminent politicians as Charles James Fox, so immediate and decisive action was talked out. Not surprisingly things went from bad to worse. Parts of Smithfield and Wapping were set alight, Catholic houses were destroyed, and houses of Protestant sympathisers were attacked.

Early on 5 June Sir George Savile's house was attacked, stripped of its contents and burned to the ground; he was anathema to the rioters as being the author of the Catholic Relief Act. By the evening of the 5th, London was in the hands of the mobs who were breaking open prisons, and releasing more villains to join the lawlessness. When parliament tried to meet on the 6th, Lord Sandwich was attacked, dragged out of his carriage and severely injured. One of the magistrates, Justice Hyde, rode to his rescue with a small party of light horse. He attempted to disperse the mob by sending his light horse among them, but they were not allowed even to draw their sabres. As the crowd began to give way one of the leaders cried out, 'To Hyde's house, a-hoy', and the excited fanatics rushed off to nearby St Martin's Street and wrecked the magistrate's house, setting it alight. That evening they repaired to Newgate prison, which had recently been rebuilt at a cost of £140,000, and proceeded to burn it down, releasing its 300 inmates. Sir John Fielding's house was ransacked. On the 7th all the shops and most of the houses were shut up, and those which did not have a 'No Popery' banner prominently displayed were in danger of destruction. Crowds of those made homeless by the disturbances flooded the London parks to seek what shelter they could.

So far damage was colossal, but loss of life minimal. But when the mob destroyed the Holborn distillery and neat spirits ran down the gutters, many of the mob drank themselves into insensibility and perished in the fires that followed. Five more prisons were destroyed and innumerable private houses, not only Catholic ones. The Common Council of the City proposed to restore order by petitioning the

Commons against Roman Catholic relief. The Privy Council, however, issued a proclamation authorising the use of troops regardless of the attitude of the city authorities. Some of the more respectable citizens had already formed themselves into armed associations to work with the militia and regular troops. Alderman Wilkes, after some brief initial hesitation, demanded urgent action to restore order. The first use of firearms occurred on the evening of the 7th, when troops used their muskets to attack rioters who had seized the toll gate on Blackfriars Bridge. Several were killed, and others, who had jumped into the river Thames in their panic, were drowned. Those who tried to storm the Bank of England were driven back by Captain Holroyd and his militia who had on that day marched twenty-five miles to reach London, and had placed themselves at the disposal of Alderman Wilkes.

Lord Mayor Kennet still despaired of success. Although the militia and troops had shown what needed to be done, there were still not enough of them. On 8 June the governor of the New Gaol could only avert an attack by releasing his prisoners, and as late as the 9th, Kennet was trying to appease the mob by urging the military to release their prisoners. It took three more days for order to be completely restored. Gordon had been captured and conveyed to the Tower, and other ringleaders were rounded up for trial. The official figures of 210 dead and 248 wounded were an underestimate; some of those who died in the fires were burnt to ashes, many of the wounded retired to the safety of their houses to dress their wounds. In the retribution that followed fifty-nine were sentenced to death, but thirty-eight of these were reprieved and transported. Gordon was acquitted of treason on account of insanity; he afterwards converted to Judaism, and died in a French prison in 1793. He had insulted Marie Antoinette in 1788, but the egalitarian French revolutionaries had not seen fit to release him.

So could the Gordon Riots have been prevented? The government had had some warning of the extent of popular bigotry by the riots in Scotland in 1778, and it was unwise to treat the Protestant Associations and Lord George Gordon's activities with such disdain. The opposition to Lord North was more concerned to embarrass the government than to safeguard the capital, so Parliament, at first at least, remained paralysed. The failure to use force was compounded by the belief that troops could not be used without the Riot Act being read, yet every citizen had the right of arrest once a felony had been committed. The London magistracy, with notable exceptions, was timid to the point of cowardice and Lord Mayor Kennet was still objecting to the use of force when the main danger had passed. Some of this lack of co-operation between city and government came from the mistaken belief that the city, as it had done under Wilkes's leadership, must stand up to government, but all it achieved in this instance was widespread destruction of property and loss of life. It is true that there were few troops available at the start of the disorders, but had the few been effectively deployed within the first two or three days of the riots, the disorder could have been suppressed; the rioters showed little boldness when confronted by muskets. When the authorities eventually acted with vigour the mobs melted away. Many lives and much property could have been saved by prompt action. Both government and local authorities in eighteenth-century England regarded riots as endemic and inevitable; the Gordon riots, and later the French Revolutionaries, swept away such complacency, and ensured that in future civil disturbance, no matter how minor, was taken seriously.

Did Captain Boycott
deserve to be boycotted?

It was the notorious Captain Boycott who gave his name to the custom of the 'boycott', a practice developed by the Irish Land League to punish landlords with whom they quarrelled, and which bestowed on Boycott unenviable immortality. But whether or not Boycott deserved the humiliating treatment meted out to him, or whether he was scandalously victimized by his angry tenants, remains to this day very much an open question.

Ireland, since the Plantation of Ulster at the beginning of the seventeenth century, had been in effect an English colony, with much of its land owned by Protestant landlords. Many of these landlords were absentees, living in England in considerable luxury on their rents, their interest in their peasantry limited to how much money they could squeeze out of them. If they had any desire to improve their farms, this desire was dictated purely by commercial considerations. Their economic exploitation of the Irish peasantry went hand-in-hand with their inflexible religious bigotry: they were convinced that their Irish labourers were violent, drunken, quarrelsome, (and of course) Catholic whingers who would do anything rather than a good day's work. As a result, Ireland seethed with discontent.

In 1880, Charles Stuart Parnell, the Protestant leader of the Irish nationalists, speaking for the 23,000 tenants evicted by grasping landlords during the previous three years, organized the Land League in order to conduct propaganda meetings up and down Ireland to denounce their actions. 'What are you to do,' asked Parnell, 'to a tenant who bids for a farm from which his neighbour has been evicted?'. 'Kill him! Shoot him!', responded his audience. Parnell held up his hand and went on: 'You must show him on the roadside when you meet him, you must show him in the street of the town, you must show him at the fair and in the market place, and even in the house of worship, by isolating him from his kind as if he were a leper of old. You must show him your detestation of the crime he has committed.' It is to be noted that what Parnell – much to his credit – suggested was social ostracisation, rather than the physical violence which many of the nationalist peasantry favoured and often practised.

It was Charles Cunningham Boycott who first received the treatment. A former soldier from Norfolk, he was currently farm manager and agent of Lord Erne, a large landowner in County Mayo on the shore of Lough Mask in western Ireland. He kept the roads in a good state of repair; he encouraged the farmers to improve their lands by building barns and cowsheds with timber provided by Lord Erne; and he prided himself on increasing rents only by half of any augmented value of the holding, and of allowing reductions of rent (usually two shillings in the pound) in times of agricultural depression. It is true that he had carried out evictions of defaulting tenants, but only because of persistent non-payment of rent. It was said by those who knew him that he was by no means an unjust or an unfair man. He was sober, hard-working and innocent of most of the shortcomings that bailiffs often possessed. But he was a terse, peremptory, rather pompous man, dedicated to discipline and efficiency and unwilling to explain himself. His military rank, which he still insisted on employing, commemorated only a brief and long-past army career. He was a stickler over the trivial fines he imposed for mislaid tools, straying stock and even on parents for their trespassing children. His attitude was harsh and unfriendly and won him a reputation as a martinet.

All the same, it was unfortunate, and somewhat unjust, that it was he who was selected as a victim. The people of the area agreed to 'send him to Coventry.' No one would speak to him, or buy from him, or have any social or commercial dealings with him; he could not buy what he wanted, or hire labourers. Indeed, feelings ran so high that the locals attacked his farm buildings and animals, and his crops were gathered in only by a specially recruited force of Orangemen working under the protection of 1000 troops. On 13 December 1880, the *Daily Mail* coined the word 'boycott' to describe this new weapon of the Land League, and it entered into general usage thereafter. But there were many others who deserved this treatment much more than Boycott. It was simply his misfortune to be picked on by the Land League, and so become its first and perhaps its most famous victim.

The 'abode of love':
a refuge or a racket?

Among one of the many obscure and controversial religious sects of Victorian times there was one – the Agapemonites – that proved to be heretical, scandalous and richly comic all at the same time. The sect was founded in 1846 by a thirty-five-year-old Anglican curate called Henry James Prince, a graduate of Lampeter who set up a small religious community at Spaxton, near Bridgwater in Somerset, to pray, study and work for the further glory of the Lord. The community was housed under one roof in a building known as the Agapemone, which gave its name to the growing sect. The word itself was Greek and meant 'abode of love'. A large country house formed the nucleus of the community; a church was built nearby, the two being connected by a conservatory full of palms and ferns. The members, men and women, were bound together by 'spiritual marriages', though it was questioned whether these in fact were always entirely spiritual. The Agapemone was built with a legacy received from Prince's wife, Martha, and soon began to prosper. Those who joined it gave their lives to the community, and made over all their sometimes quite substantial worldly possessions to common ownership under the leadership of the Reverend Prince, the man they called their Lord. In short, the Agapemonites were the nineteenth-century equivalent of the Moonies.

Observers were not slow to note the high proportion of wealthy people who patronized the sect, and the high proportion of females among them. Then tongues began to wag. It was rumoured that among the freedoms practised in the commune was free love, and as a result a number of unmarried ladies indicated their wish to withdraw from it. They were even able, through an action in Chancery, to recover some of their money which the House had sequestered. None the less, the sect prospered, and large numbers joined, so that funds were plentiful and life in the commune was pleasant and comfortable. Reverend Prince, convinced that a Second Coming was at hand, was treated by sect members as if he were a latter-day John the Baptist. Unlike the Baptist, however, he lived in luxury, travelled widely in his own coach-and-six, held meetings, celebrated his own form of religious service, and in 1896, on the fiftieth anniversary of the sect's foundation, when he was already eighty-five, commissioned the building of a large church in Clapton in South London with an adjoining mansion dedicated to the service of the order. Unfortunately, three years afterwards, Prince died. Since he was considered immortal by many members of the sect, the death came as a great shock and surprise to them: how was it possible that their herald of the Day of Judgment could die, when he had given them his promise that both they and he would live forever after the Second Coming?

Hence many were not surprised when, in his sermon at a Sunday evening service in 1902, the Rev. Smyth Pigott stepped in to fill the breach. A tall, imposing man with fiery eyes and a booming voice, he had been carrying out the duties of his predecessor in the sect since Prince's death. Now he announced his new status, claiming to be the 'Lord Jesus Christ arisen'. Though the rest of the world – even that part of it in the immediate vicinity of South London – had failed to notice the Apocalypse, the Agapemonite congregation of Clapton took it comfortably in their stride, and welcomed their new Saviour. The London populace, when they heard of it, were not nearly so tolerant. Their curiosity prompted them to attend the following Sunday's service, when they flocked round the church, climbed the railings, broke a good many of its windows, pelted the Reverend with stones, and rioted noisily. A local paper later noted that but for the intervention of the police the new Christ the Redeemer would probably have been thrown into the pond on Clapton Common.

Dismayed by their ingratitude and their scepticism, Smyth-Pigott retired to the community in Somerset with his wife, Kathie, and the person he used as his handmaiden in his church work, Ruth Preece. She was his especial 'spiritual bride', and indeed in due course she bore him two sons whom, in celebration of the occasion, he christened Power and Glory. South Londoners were grateful for his absence and put him from their minds; not so the Bishop of Bath and Wells, who charged him with scandalous and immoral behaviour and defrocked him in Wells Cathedral in 1909. Thereafter numbers began to wane. His spiritual bride bore him yet another child, but at the time of his death at the age of seventy-eight in 1927 less than a hundred sect members were left, nearly all of them women. In 1956, with the death of 'Sister Ruth', as she called herself, the Agapemonites were reduced to a mere fourteen females and finally broke up. The church in Clapton was sold off to another fringe sect, and the 'abode of love' in Spaxton was sold for conversion into council flats.

WAR SCANDALS

Did Captain Jenkins lose his ear?

The celebrated occasion took place on March 17, 1738. Before the House of Commons appeared a certain Captain Robert Jenkins, formerly of the ship Rebecca, *and he gave his halting evidence while brandishing a bottle containing, in saline, a rather indeterminate piece of gristle. This he claimed was his ear, sliced off by Spanish garda costas (coastguards), retrieved by him from where it lay on the deck, and subsequently preserved in brine. The Spanish conduct, if truly reported, was an appalling peacetime atrocity. The House of Commons clamoured for revenge, and war eventually ensued. But was it actually an ear in the bottle, or was it, as some of the government asserted, a sow's ear? And did Jenkins actually lose an ear, or did he lose it in a brawl or even in the pillory? Perhaps under the black patch Jenkins wore there lurked the real ear, still firmly attached to his body. The war that began in October of the following year was named after Jenkins's brutal loss, but was the well-preserved relic the main cause of hostilities?*

Spain, like all other colonial powers, very jealously reserved the right to trade with her own colonies to her own nationals. But Spain could not provide her colonies with all that they needed. The limited quantities of domestic manufactures that Spain shipped to her colonies were woefully inadequate to meet demand. Nor could Spain provide what the colonies particularly required, a regular supply of slaves. So in 1713 the Treaty of Utrecht revived and extended the *Asiento* agreement, whereby Britain supplied the Spanish colonies with 4,800 slaves a year, and was allowed to send one ship a year of 500 tons (later 650) to the annual fair at Porto Bello (on the Darien Isthmus) where it could legitimately sell its cargo of English goods, such as domestic utensils, cutlery, pottery, cloth, fish and timber. The British government awarded this Spanish concession to the South Sea Company, which expected to return considerable profit from it. But it was to be disappointed. The Spaniards did everything they could in the form of regulation and red tape to obstruct the fulfilment of the *Asiento*. Between 1713 and 1738 only seven ships reached the fairs. Two were held up in other Caribbean ports by Spanish officials for three years and never reached Porto Bello at all. Others were subjected to protracted measuring and disputed estimates of tonnage.

In such circumstances the South Sea Company became less fussy about sticking to the strict terms of the *Asiento,* and in consequence was unwilling to publish its accounts in detail. The pent-up demand in the Spanish Caribbean led to large numbers of interlopers both defying Spanish restrictions and breaking the South Sea Company's monopoly. The *garda costas* claimed that the only way to curb the contraband traffic was to search all British merchant ships that ventured into Caribbean waters. Any British ship found there was assumed to be smuggling, even if it was plying legitimate trade with the British colonies. As the illegal traffic spiralled out of control the methods of the *garda costas* became more desperate. They boarded ships on the high seas, they resorted to arms at the slightest pretext, they confiscated cargoes and naval instruments, and they dragged British seamen before Spanish colonial judges who would convict on the slightest evidence. Even possession of Spanish 'pieces of eight', a currency widely used not only in the Spanish but also in the British and French colonies, would be regarded as evidence of illegal trading.

In such circumstances the ill-treatment of Captain Jenkins was not unique. By his account the assault on him took place in the spring of 1731, his ship was completely pillaged, he had been tied to the mast and his ear cut off, and then the ship had been turned adrift. He had complained to the local Spanish authorities at the time, but had secured no redress. He had not pursued the matter with the British government, presumably because Prime Minister Robert Walpole's peace policy would inhibit too strong a protest. Jenkins's story was challenged. Horace Walpole thought that Jenkins was the tool of the opposition who were clamouring for war, and that Jenkins had not lost an ear at all. So later did Edmund Burke. But Jenkins's story, in its main essentials, is supported by Admiralty records. Rear-Admiral Stewart, in his protest to the Governor of Havana about various *garda costa* outrages, specifically refers to Jenkins:

> About April 20th last (n.s.) … after using the captain in a most barbarous, inhuman manner, taking all his money, cutting off one of his ears.

An Admiralty list of vessels taken or plundered refers to

> The *Rebecca*, Robert Jenkins, Jamaica to London, boarded and plundered near Havana, 20th April 1731.

A report of 1742 records the capture of Fondino, who 'took Jenkins when his ears was cut off'; it exaggerated the number of ears removed, but otherwise is further corroboration. So Jenkins did lose an ear at the hands of the *garda costas*. It does not really matter whether he had actually been able to retrieve it at the time, and managed to preserve it for seven years in a bottle of saline. This could have been a touch added for dramatic effect. Walpole was losing ground, and the opposition led by the Prince of Wales and the Elder Pitt saw its chance. It was rumoured that the Family compact between Spain and France in 1733 was about to be consolidated into an alliance that would threaten Britain and particularly damage British trade. The opposition rehearsed the various outrages committed by Spain against Britain in the West Indies, and Jenkins's fortuitous presence in England in March 1738 offered it a heaven-sent opportunity. The ear-patch and the bottle were dramatic enough, but the trump card was in the questioning. Merchant seamen were in general much more uncultured than naval officers, and Jenkins's answers to the questions put to him by members were mostly monosyllabic. But he had been well coached. When asked what he did when his ear was cut off – a rather superfluous question, since he was tied to a mast at the time – he replied, 'In my hour of outrage and impotence I commended my soul to God and my cause to my country.' This was a finely honed phrase and could well have been put together by Pitt himself. Its effect on the House of Commons was electric. The House clamoured for war.

But it did not get it. Walpole put all his effort into coming to an accommodation with Spain. The old grievances were rehearsed and the outrages listed. Spain, in return, complained of breaches of the *Asiento* and the excessive trading secrecy of the South Sea Company. Eventually, in January 1739, agreement was reached by the Convention of Pardo. The Spanish government conceded damages of £200,000, which, offset by £105,000 which Britain agreed was owed to Spain for various excesses, including the sinking of the Spanish fleet at Cape Passaro in 1718, left a mere £95,000 owing to Britain. And even that was further whittled down by a Spanish claim for £68,000 worth of arrears owed to Spain by the South Sea Company. But at least Spain was now admitting in monetary terms culpability for some of the outrages such as that suffered by Captain Jenkins. Walpole believed peace had been achieved and he ordered Admiral Haddock to remove the British fleet from the Mediterranean. Pitt protested vigorously against the convention of Pardo, but it was Walpole's ally Newcastle, fearing the indignation of the London merchants, who caused a change in policy. If the merchants abandoned the government, electoral majorities might tumble and merchant money might find its way to finance opposition candidates. Newcastle persuaded Walpole to take a firmer line. Haddock was sent back to the Mediterranean and Admiral Vernon, a bitter critic of the Convention of Pardo, was sent to the West Indies. Spain complained that it still had not had access to the South Seas Company's accounts, and the terms of the Convention of Pardo remained unfulfilled. War was not declared until 19 October 1739, by which time Captain Jenkins had sunk back into semi-obscurity. Walpole blamed the war on Newcastle, 'It is your war, and I wish you well of it', and upon popular clamour, 'They are ringing the bells now, soon they will be wringing their hands.' Popular opinion was soon to name the war after Jenkins, and the name has stuck ever since, but there were far more cogent reasons for the war than a scrap of gristle in a bottle.

There is no doubt that Jenkins's ear was sliced off, but whether he had the presence of mind to retrieve it, and what was contained in the famous bottle can only be conjectured. His immortal words were a rousing call to patriotism, but they were almost certainly not his. The war that bears his name did not immediately result from his celebrated appearance before the House of Commons, but from long-standing grievances over trade, and fears over the balance of power. But he had his moment of greatness, and history has paid him the compliment of remembering him, even if doubts remain about the detailed accuracy of his account, the depth of his intellect, and his influence on the course of events.

Who was responsible for the fate of Admiral Byng?

Contrary to the oft-quoted opinion of Voltaire the English did not, in the eighteenth century, 'kill an admiral from time to time to encourage the others'. But they did kill Admiral Byng. On March 14, 1757, Admiral John Byng was brought up to the quarterdeck of The Monarque, *a ship he had once commanded. He tried to refuse a blindfold, but changed his mind when it was pointed out to him that if he stared at the firing party it might unnerve them and cause them to miss their aim. He knelt on cushions, prayed silently for a few moments, and then dropped his handkerchief – the signal for the firing party of marines to despatch him. No one who witnessed the execution doubted Byng's courage in his final moments. But did he, even by eighteenth-century standards, deserve his fate?*

Undeclared war between Britain and France had continued throughout the early 1750s in Canada, India, the Caribbean and on the high seas. The British government, led by the Duke of Newcastle, in its vain hope of preserving peace, neglected to prepare for war. As early as December 1755 the government had been warned that the French were planning to attack Minorca, Britain's island base in the Mediterranean. In February 1756 the British government received specific evidence of the French intent, but nothing was done to counter the French threat for a full month. Moreover the government had been fooled by supposed French preparations for the invasion of England. It therefore concentrated on home defence, and had little to spare for the Mediterranean. Even so it did not want disaster in any sphere of operations, and in looking for a suitable commander for the Mediterranean it wanted an experienced officer who would obey Admiralty regulations, would not take unnecessary risks, and who would do his political masters' bidding.

It has often been said that Admiral Byng was the wrong man for the job, but to Newcastle at the time Byng seemed ideal. Byng had served on the court martial of Admiral Thomas Matthews, when Matthews was cashiered for endangering his fleet at the battle of Toulon, 1744, and failing to adhere to the Admiralty's strict Rules of Engagement. Unsupported by the treacherous vice-Admiral Richard Lestock, whose inactivity at Toulon almost led to disaster, Matthews had done his best in an impossible situation and had been unjustly punished for it. Byng was all too well aware of the fate of admirals who fell foul of the Admiralty on a technical breach of the rules. So the politicians knew perfectly well what they were doing when they appointed him.

It has often been held against Byng that he owed his naval rank to the influence of his father George Byng, later Lord Torrington. His father had had a distinguished naval career and no doubt encouraged his son to follow in his footsteps. But John Byng progressed the hard way, working his way up from midshipman, and his father died in 1733, before John's career had fully made its mark. There was nothing unusual in the eighteenth-century navy for fathers and sons to be admirals. It made for continuity. And nepotism was not then regarded with the same disfavour as it is today. But there was a political dimension to Byng's appointment. The government of the Duke of Newcastle had an impregnable majority but was under constant attack from William Pitt, whose appeal to patriotism was distasteful to the ministers, but glorious to the rest of the nation. Newcastle's prime concerns were to stay in office not to prosecute the war, and to keep Pitt out of office, since Pitt had offended George II and the House of Hanover by his persistent complaints that George preferred the interests of the Electorate of Hanover to the interests of the Kingdom of Great Britain. When the battle of Minorca took place and the decision to try Byng by court martial was taken, Newcastle was still supreme. But when the court martial's verdict was delivered, Newcastle had taken William Pitt into a shaky coalition. Pitt's reputation did not hinge on destroying Byng's reputation, but Newcastle's did.

It is often asserted that from the moment of Byng's appointment he showed little enthusiasm for the task. But in such circumstances would any other admiral have shown greater enthusiasm? Admiral Anson could spare little for Byng as he had been ordered to concentrate on home defence. Byng was even forbidden to recruit merchant seamen from the seaports as these were needed to bolster the Home Fleet. Most of his twelve ships were unfit to put to sea, and four of them were seriously undermanned. His numbers were supplemented by pressed men from Ireland, and by men who were too ill to sail. He was 400 short of complement, and 400 of those he had were too ill to be of any use; soldiers he was carrying to reinforce the Minorca garrison had to be coerced into acting as deckhands.

Under pressure from Anson and the politicians Byng sailed on 7 April. If he was gloomy about the undertaking, who can blame him? But at least he had been promised supplies and reinforcements when he reached Gibraltar. There he was able to increase his fleet marginally to thirteen, but Thomas Fowke, the governor of Gibraltar, adamantly refused to give Byng more than token support, so afraid was he of an imminent Spanish attack on Gibraltar itself. By now it was known that the Duc de Richelieu had landed 16,000 troops on Minorca and that he had penned the 2000 defenders under General Blakeney into St Philip's fortress in Port Mahon. Supporting Richelieu were twelve French men-of-war commanded by the French admiral de la Galissonière. Byng was relieved to find, when he eventually arrived off Minorca on 19 May, that Port Mahon was still holding out. His task was obviously to destroy or drive away the French fleet, leaving Richelieu stranded and without support on Minorca. So while Byng endeavoured to close with the French, the French despite their superior gunnery adopted evasive action. Byng's efforts to close in meant that the Rules of Engagement were not strictly adhered to; if they had been, the French would have got clean away. Throughout Byng showed great personal courage, but his instructions to his captains needed greater clarity, particularly as they involved bending the Admiralty's rules. Even when one of his ships got between the French and the shore, such was the confusion that Byng was unable to take advantage of it. As dusk fell, no significant damage had been inflicted on the French, and the English fleet had suffered greater damage and casualties.

At this juncture Byng had various options. He could try to renew the fight the next day, or he could attempt to cut the French supplies. But Byng was worried that if he was worsted in another encounter, England would lose control of the Mediterranean and Gibraltar would be next to fall. So he called a Council of War. This has often been seen as a sign of Byng's weakness, the implication being that, as he did not know what to do next, he was asking his captains for their opinion. But the questions Byng put to his captains suggest that Byng knew perfectly well what he was going to do, but thought it prudent to have the full backing of his captains in doing so. He asked them whether they thought there was any chance of relieving Minorca, and whether a further engagement with the French might endanger Gibraltar. To these questions, Byng's captains replied that there was no chance of relieving Minorca and that further action would indeed endanger Gibraltar. Thereupon Byng gave orders for the fleet to sail back to Gibraltar, and the despairing Minorca garrison had no choice but to surrender.

When news of the fall of Minorca reached England there was patriotic outrage and shame, especially when de la Galissonière's prompt despatch to Paris was known in London before Byng's own despatches arrived. The French admiral heaped coals on fire by pointing out that French losses at Minorca were minimal. The Duke of Newcastle was alarmed that Minorca's loss would be laid at his own door. If he was to avoid political disaster he must blame someone else for the naval disaster. Byng was the obvious scapegoat. Thus Newcastle could be heard muttering as he flitted between Whitehall and Parliament, 'He shall be tried immediately, he shall be hanged directly'. Byng was ordered to return to England, and was clapped in irons as soon as he landed. Anson was instructed to arrange a court martial. It was not difficult to find suitable charges. Byng was not accused of cowardice, but of failing to do his utmost to destroy the enemy (thus negligence) and for technical breaches of the Rules of Engagement. The officers trying Byng were well aware that they might themselves be in a similar position one day, but in the face of the evidence they had no choice but to find him guilty. They had no option about the sentence either. Since 1749 the death sentence had become mandatory for such offences; they did, however, unanimously recommend him to mercy. But now politics took a hand and many voices were raised in support of Byng. But if extenuating circumstances justified a reprieve, and if Byng were not to take the whole blame for what happened, then some of the blame must attach to the government, and in particular Newcastle himself. He attempted to divert the flak by persuading the Admiralty to refer the court martial's verdict to a committee of judges. They had to decide on points of law, and these, on the evidence, could only be decided against Byng. By now Newcastle had decided to muzzle Pitt by taking him into the government. Newcastle took care to deny Pitt any real power, but now that Pitt was in the government he could see the king on a regular basis. He subjected the king to argument and pressure for Byng's reprieve, but the more he pushed, the less inclined was George to listen. He disliked Pitt anyway, and resented Pitt's efforts on Byng's behalf. So George became more adamant that Byng must die. When Pitt claimed that the House of Commons was inclined to mercy it provoked George's famous reply, 'You have taught me to look for the sense of my subjects elsewhere than in the House of Commons'. Representations from Pitt were bad enough, but George and Parliament were bombarded with petitions for clemency; one was even sent by de la Galissonière (well, he would, wouldn't he? He would not like to see his victory over the British diminished because of the British admiral's culpable incompetence).

Amid the entire furore, Byng behaved with commendable stoicism and courage; he was well aware that efforts to bring him a reprieve were bound to fail. When a friend asked how tall he was, Byng replied that he knew the measurement was needed to determine the length of his coffin, and that his friend need not fear to ask him directly. So Byng went to his death. Was anything gained by it?

In the short term it looked as if Byng's death had got Newcastle off the hook. He, the king and the Duke of Cumberland even managed to remove Pitt from the government in April. But Newcastle's triumph was short-lived. War disasters led to infighting among Newcastle's supporters, and his position weakened. It was necessary, at the end of June, to recall Pitt, and this time he came in on his own terms. Whereas from December 1756 Pitt had served in Newcastle's ministry in a subordinate and muzzled capacity, from the end of June 1757 Newcastle served in Pitt's ministry in a subordinate capacity. Pitt let Newcastle manage patronage, while Newcastle let Pitt manage the war. So the sacrifice of Byng had not saved Newcastle's government, except for a few months. Worse still, the execution of Byng deprived naval commanders of freedom of action in battle. From 1757 Rules of Engagement were occasionally unintentionally contravened, but not until Admiral Jervis broke the Spanish line at Cape St Vincent in 1797 were the Rules effectively buried. The death of Byng was therefore a disaster for Newcastle's reputation, a tragedy for Britain, and an embarrassment for the navy; not least it enabled Voltaire to hold England up to ridicule. But it did enable Byng to be remembered, not so much as the admiral who lost Minorca, but as the admiral who was the victim of a terrible injustice.

The case of Helen Duncan:
another casualty of war?

The trial at the Old Bailey, the conviction and the subsequent imprisonment of Mrs Helen Duncan under the Witchcraft Act of 1735 caused a wartime scandal that provided a cause célèbre just before the D-Day invasions of the continent in 1944. Was she really guilty, as charged, of 'conjuring up the spirits of the dead', contrary to Section 5 of that ancient Act?

Born in Scotland towards the end of the nineteenth century, Helen Duncan was credited at an early age with the gift of 'second sight', i.e. a capacity for clairvoyance that enabled her to perceive things through her extrasensory skills, and to make uncannily accurate predictions about the future. Her childhood nickname was 'Hellish Nell' – not, as might be imagined, because of her supernatural powers, but merely because she was something of a tomboy. In her middle years, married to a mild husband who acted as her impresario, she made quite a handsome income as 'Madame Duncan' by practising as a spiritualistic medium, performing séances at which there appeared the spirits of those dead who spoke through a spirit medium, or 'guide', to relatives present at the séance. One such 'spirit guide' she claimed was a lanky Scotsman called Albert, who spoke in a curious combination of clipped BBC English and Australian; another, more jolly, a little girl called Peggy who frisked about singing songs. These occurrences took place at what was rather grandly called the 'Master Temple Psychic Centre', but which in reality was a rather dingy room over a chemist's shop in back-street Portsmouth. Before these sessions she submitted to rigorous physical examinations by female persons in which she was stripped naked and was personally minutely searched before resuming her clothing and proceeding with the séance. Those who carried out this intimate search were absolutely certain there was no trickery. When the séance began, the lights were lowered until the only illumination came from a five-watt electric bulb painted red. Then, somehow, ectoplasm with a rather disgusting smell appeared from her, and from this filmy material spirits appeared to be created, visible to all those present.

Not all her audience, however, were so easily satisfied. Many, including the well-known psychic investigator Henry Price, accused Mrs Duncan of trickery: indeed, some of them tried to take photographs to expose her, and on one occasion actually rushed behind the stage and found her on her hands and knees manipulating her tricks. Her own maid said that masks and a dummy were kept in the bathroom, and that 'Peggy' was merely a cleverly manipulated stockinette vest. Other hostile witnesses maintained that the so-called ectoplasm was nothing more than a vast quantity of cheesecloth which Duncan somehow managed to produce, some said from the mouth, though there were others who believed it came from other bodily orifices. A few bold critics snatched snippets of the ectoplasm, and on later examination this indeed turned out as they predicted – to be cheesecloth.

Her arrest and trial for fraud (not for witchcraft) were widely reported at the time, and threw into opposition those people who believed in spiritualism, and those who dismissed it as hocus-pocus. The parade of witnesses produced by her defence counsel, himself a believer in spiritualism, consisted of those who swore that what they had seen was in reality a spiritual experience; her opponents declared that the séances were no more than trickery, and dismissed them as mere entertainment. A rather exasperated Winston Churchill, in one of his celebrated little memoranda, grumbled threateningly to his law officers about 'ancient tomfoolery' and wanted to know why the prosecution had been brought. Nevertheless she was convicted and served six months of a nine-month sentence before being released to a later life in which nearly everyone forgot all about her. However, in spite of occasional police harassment, she continued with her supernatural practices until her death in 1956.

The statute under which she was condemned was perhaps not so ancient as Churchill supposed. Indeed, it was actually quite an enlightened measure that repealed the old medieval laws against witchcraft. It did, however, contain a provision (Clause 5) which imposed penalties on those who 'pretended to conjure the spirits of the dead', and this was a clause which suited Helen Duncan's case very precisely. She certainly 'pretended to conjure spirits', and it was with this that she was charged. In fact this 1735 law was not repealed until 1951, after the end of the war.

What was the purpose of what Churchill called 'tomfoolery'? Although the matter was never mentioned at her trial, no one seemed able to deny that Duncan somehow possessed quite unusual extrasensory powers. She commented in a séance on the sinking of the battleship *Hood* before the tragedy had happened, and later declared that the *Barham* had been sunk in the Mediterranean before the Admiralty released information about it to the public. These matters were never mentioned in Duncan's rather tiresome trial, all of which revolved round whether her séances were genuine or not, and not around the question of how she knew what she knew. All the same she was singled out for extremely harsh treatment. Many contemporaries thought that the authorities wished to protect the recently-bereaved from being exploited by exhibitions of such vulgar showmanship. Undoubtedly there were others who thought of the security dangers: Duncan lived and worked in Portsmouth, and military security might well be threatened if she said anything useful to the enemy about the invasion preparations that were going on so furiously in the area at the time. If a Nazi agent got to know of her clairvoyancy, and went to one of her meetings, he might pick up some useful tips about Allied invasion plans. So the authorities 'framed' her (though the principal prosecution witness, in 1998 living in New Zealand, to the end of his days denied that he took part in any conspiracy) and put her inside for six months until the invasion of Europe had safely taken place.

What was the secret of Slapton Sands?

One of the best-kept secrets of the war involved an elaborate subterfuge which remained unchallenged until 1984, when the deception eventually came to light as the result of a television company's investigation. The episode illustrates how scandalous conspiracies to conceal important information from the public can be maintained even in a modern democracy.

The events in question took place in April 1944 during elaborate rehearsals by American servicemen of the procedures for the D-Day landings in northern France. Slapton Sands, on the south coast of Devonshire near Dartmouth, was the location selected for these exercises. The whole operation, known as Operation Tiger, involved the removal of hundreds of civilians from the area, and the participation of thousands of troops and over 200 ships of various kinds, organized in the form of Convoy T-4. All this was supported by air attacks, the laying and the clearing of mines and the use of live ammunition during the staged fighting. During the hours of darkness before the operation began, nine German E-boats came upon this Allied fleet quite by chance. The E-boats (the English phrase is an abbreviation of 'enemy boat', but they were actually called by the Germans *Schnellboote,* or fast boats) were used for operations in the Channel and were lightly but sufficiently armed craft using rapid-fire deck guns and torpedoes. They were the pride of the seamen who manned them. These E-boats torpedoed three Allied landing craft and shot up others, causing an estimated 750 US casualties largely from drowning and hypothermia as they abandoned ship.

The casualties were buried in a mass grave, and the wounded cared for in a number of hospitals and, together with the survivors, threatened with court martials if they talked. The US commander of the exercise, Rear Admiral D.P. Moon, later committed suicide over the affair. American families at home received telegrams informing them that individuals had been 'killed in action', but with no further explanation. Oddly, the US 4th Infantry Division received fewer casualties at the Normandy landings on Utah beach than it had at its rehearsal at Slapton Sands. The extent of the debacle remained a closely guarded secret, and very few civilians in the area ever got to know about it. Information was only divulged forty years after the event.

It seems likely that considerations of military security and of public morale originally lay behind the elaborate secrecy, and that the Admiralty and the War Department were extremely anxious to preserve their reputations, so that it seems natural that the affair should not be publicized at a particularly delicate moment in the war. What is more difficult to understand is why it was thought necessary to hush up the affair for such a long time, when other and equally damaging admissions were being made about the conduct of the war. It now seems scandalous that the British and American governments did not reveal the truth about the fate of such large numbers of casualties, if only to the relatives of the deceased.

Were the Nuremberg Trials an international scandal?

The actions carried out by the Nazis in the Second World War led the Allied powers as early as 1943 to promise to bring war criminals to justice. These trials were held in Nuremberg between November 1945 and August 1946. The Allies set up an international Military Tribunal to judge the accused, the bench comprising four judges, with a deputy for each in case of illness, representing the four main Allied powers: Britain, France, the USA and the USSR. 199 were accused at Nuremberg, but thousands of others were tried elsewhere: in Allied military courts, by their own countrymen after the Allied withdrawal, and in former occupied countries. Important questions about the motives lying behind the trials and their legality were raised even at the time, and continue to be asked by those who think they were inspired more by vengeance than by justice.

At Nuremberg, the prisoners were tried on four counts: crimes against peace – preparing and carrying out acts of aggression; war crimes – the ill-treatment of prisoners of war and civilian populations; extremes of brutality against individuals or groups; and conspiracy – participation in plans to commit the other three offences. A number of the accused persons, including Hitler, Goebbels and Himmler, were already dead. Another, Robert Ley, former Head of the Nazi Labour front, hanged himself before the trial started; another, Hermann Goering, swallowed cyanide when it was over in order to avoid the gallows. Another, Gustav Krupp, was senile and did not understand the charges; quite remarkably his son Alfred was later tried and sentenced in his place. Of the twenty-four who were brought to trial, only three were acquitted. Three among the convicted, including Hitler's deputy, Rudolf Hess, received life imprisonment. Two got twenty years, one fifteen and Doenitz, who had made the final surrender to the Allies, was rewarded with ten years imprisonment. Twelve were hanged on 16 October 1946. A number of the accused, including Adolf Eichmann (responsible for administering the 'Final Solution' for the Jews) and Franz Stangl (the former Commandant of the camps at Treblinka and Sobibor), were later found abroad, brought to trial and convicted.

Week after week, the evidence had mounted up during the trial, evidence at the same time chilling and overwhelming. One of the accused, Hess, gave every sign of mental derangement; only Goering maintained his quick-witted awareness to the end. The others were broken men. One, Hans Frank, whose thirty-eight volume diary gave irrefutable evidence of his involvement in murder, starvation and extermination, despaired completely and summed up what many of them felt when he said: 'A thousand years will pass, and this guilt of Germany will not pass away!'.

But how justified was this trial and its outcome? Few disputed the moral justification for it. The crimes involved were so dreadful and so overwhelming that no one imagined there was no redress; everyone supposed that the legal basis for the trial lay in The Hague and Geneva Conventions. Though this supposition was extremely doubtful, the general reaction to the verdicts was that they went some way towards atoning for unprecedented atrocities.

Yet there remain disturbing features. *How* could aggression be illegal if there was no legislative agreement under which it could be punished? It was highly unusual for any state or any individual ruler to be punished for the offence of *breaking a treaty*, though a number of such trials have been held since Nuremberg. To spare the Soviet Union's embarrassment – for the USSR had also been guilty of exactly the same offences against Poland and against Finland – the charge was confined to aggression by *the Axis powers alone*. Thus the offence seemed to be specially designed to fit the crime and was applied only selectively. No Italians were ever charged. Italy had changed sides, and *to indict an ally* would have opened the door to a similar indictment against the USSR.

The accused were also condemned for crimes that were not crimes in international law *at the time they were committed*. If extreme crimes against humanity, or conspiracy to commit such crimes, had now become offences against international law, the same charges could have been brought against Churchill for his complicity in the bombing of Dresden, if the Germans had been victorious instead of defeated.

Furthermore, the accused were *not allowed to say*: 'But I was only obeying my orders.' To expect an individual subordinate to be able to distinguish between a legal order and a criminal one was quite extraordinary. The Allies themselves, throughout the war, considered men bound by superior orders, and not legally liable for them. But now the Allies were saying that obedience to orders was not a defence, but only a mitigation. This would have certainly been bad news to the bombardier aboard *Enola Gay* who was ordered to drop the first atom bomb on Hiroshima.

But the *most fundamental criticism* was the simplest. For punishment to have at least the appearance of justice, the prosecutor must not also be the judge. The judges at Nuremberg represented the nations that were parties to the action, and therefore could not be said to be impartial. It would have been better that the judges should have been empanelled from amongst neutral nations such as Sweden or Switzerland, for this would have given a greater impression of impartiality. The obvious partiality of the bench gave ammunition to those who maintained that the trials were merely acts of vengeance carried out by the victor against the vanquished. As Goering himself shrewdly observed at the trial: 'The victors will always be the judge, the vanquished the accused.' Such a criticism will always weaken the moral justification of the Nuremberg Trials and lead to the suggestion that such behaviour is a scandalous abuse of the rights of the defeated, though neither of them will lessen the frightfulness of the crimes that brought the trials about.

Bearing these points in mind, it would seem inadvisable in similar situations in future for the same, or a similar, device to be adopted. Before an international trial can enjoy the respect of the world, or even the respect of participating nations, the most glaring of the faults in the Nuremberg Trials must be rectified. These trials have set a regrettably bad precedent for the future.

Who was the 'unknown warrior'?

The Pentagon was embarrassed to discover in 1998 that the unknown Vietnam war hero buried in the tomb of the unknown warrior at Arlington Cemetery, Washington, was not in fact unknown at all.

The remains were those of Michael Blassie, an air force pilot whose jet was shot down in Vietnam in 1972. Five months later, a South Vietnamese Army patrol found his identity card, money and the shreds of his uniform along with his skeleton in the jungle. The money and card disappeared during the transfer of the remains, and in 1980 they were interred at Arlington as 'unknown'. President Reagan, speaking at the ceremony, said: 'Did he work beside his father on a farm in America's heartland? Did he marry? Did he have children?'. Now DNA tests on his remains have proved that the body was indeed that of Blassie, and that he did not do any of these things. He was twenty-four when he was shot down, single, athletic and a graduate of the Air Force Academy. His father was a butcher. After a long struggle against military bureaucracy, his family eventually secured his removal from the tomb to give him a family burial, so that he could have an identifiable grave of his own.

The idea for a special tomb for an unknown soldier dates from the First World War when a British army chaplain saw a simple cross on the head of a grave on the Western Front, dedicated to 'an unknown British soldier'. He put forward the idea of having a memorial to those buried in unmarked graves, and the idea was taken up, first in Whitehall, and later in other countries also. The Arlington tomb contains heroes from earlier wars, but advancing identification techniques made it unlikely that Vietnam would produce an unknown body for interment. Hence the body was seized upon as the most likely candidate, and the Pentagon seems to have connived at the suppression of evidence which suggested at the time that he was Blassie.

The episode shows that the US government was concerned that the Vietnam War should not pass without the due solemnification due to it at Arlington, and that it was perhaps over-hasty in providing for it a known body instead of an unknown one.

SCIENTIFIC SCANDALS

What was the truth behind the missing eleven days?

Astronomers had long known that the 365 days they had allotted for the passage of an earth year was only a rough approximation; the year was more precisely 365 days, 5 hours, 48 minutes and 49 seconds long. The Romans had known this, and as early as 46 BC Julius Caesar had introduced the idea of the leap year every fourth year in order to prevent the calendar and the seasons from gradually getting out of step. This was known as the Julian Calendar and remained in use until the sixteenth century. The two, however, did not keep perfectly in step, since the Julian calendar rather over-compensated for the difference: every four years there was now an interval of four times 11 minutes, 11 seconds (44 minutes, 44 seconds, of nearly three-quarters of an hour) when the human calendar crept ahead of the celestial one. By the sixteenth century a gap of over ten days had been created between the two. So in 1582 Pope Gregory XIII suppressed the ten days between the 5th and the 15th of October in order to bring back the Julian reckoning into line with the astronomical year. He also ordered that of the end-century (00) years, only the fourth should be a leap year. This was called the New Style or the Gregorian Calendar. It was still not a perfect alignment, since it left an interval of six hours per century between the two modes of reckoning (24 times three-quarters of an hour, or 18 hours from the 24 allowed by dropping one leap year). But it is the closest system of reckoning we have, and is still in use at the present time. Religious prejudice directed against the Papacy, however, prevented it from being implemented in Protestant Britain until 1752.

During the enlightened Pelham ministry in 1751, Philip Dormer Stanhope, fourth Earl of Chesterfield, introduced in Parliament a bill proposing a reform of the calendar. It was one of a number of reforming bills: one was for the naturalization of Jews and another for encouraging the national fisheries in the North Sea. Calendar reform was on the recommendation of James Bradley, astronomer-royal from 1742 to 1762, and his fellow astronomer Lord Macclesfield, who made the elaborate calculations involved. Parliament was convinced by their learned disquisitions and the bill passed both the Commons and the Lords without difficulty. In order to adjust the old calendar to bring it into line with the new one, the eleven days in September 1752 were abolished, so that the 3rd of the month became the 14th. But at the same time, New Year's Day, formerly 25 March, was to be advanced to 1 January. (In many old churchyards gravestones bearing odd dates in January, February or March may still be seen with inscriptions like *February 14, 1768/69*). The supposed loss of these eleven days produced an outcry in the whole country.

It was not only ignorant prejudice that persuaded people that a technical change in the method of reckoning the date amounted to a theft of a slice of their lives, those precious eleven days. The popular view was that almost a fortnight had been chopped out of their lifetime; time in which to earn money to feed their children, time to share with their families before they died. It was as if they had fallen asleep and woken up eleven days later. They felt they could not afford to lose such a portion of their lives; it was different, of course, for the lords and ladies who had more comfortable lives and might be expected to live longer.

But the change also had economic and financial repercussions. In the countryside, rents were paid either annually or quarterly, and tenants had strong objections to paying a full rent for a year or for a quarter that was eleven days short. This was a view especially voiced by those whose quarterly rent fell due on Michaelmas Day (25 September). Their ability to pay, of course, depended on the state of the harvest rather than on the vagaries of the calendar. If Michaelmas Day was now going to arrive eleven days *before* it was 'due', and tenants had to find their quarterly rent within 11 days instead of 22, they would suffer hardship. Those receiving the rent, of course, would get it eleven days *sooner*. It is easy to see why those on whom this burden fell should regard the change as something like a 'landlord's ramp'.

This misgiving was not shared by everybody. If you were paid weekly, it did not make any difference. If you received an annual salary, you might actually be better off, receiving the full sum even though the year was eleven days short. Businesses would be less affected – it all depended on the balance between their outgoings and their income. Those using the quarterly almanac would calculate they were in profit if more clients were due to pay them on quarter day than they were due to pay others at that time; they would suffer if the reverse was the case.

However, even for farmers, things were not going to be so grave as they were pretending; the change was made in the season of the harvest at a time when most farmers were solvent, though on Lady Day (25 March) or Midsummer Day (25 June) the story might have been a different one. So in practice the financial effects of the change were going to be small, though financial fears loomed much bigger and seemed very disturbing.

In any case, the farmers' fears in fact were quite misplaced. Those expressing these fears had simply *not read the text of the act.* Parliament had recognized that problems would occur as a result of the cancellation of these eleven days. In Clause VI of the statute it declared that no rents, interest or wages would be paid in respect of the lost days; but it also said that those close to achieving their majority (i.e. their twenty-first birthday) should gain their majority only when the *real* (not the *statutory*) time had elapsed. The same thing applied to the payment of rents: all rents were to become due only on the *real* day, i.e. *on the day they were due before the passing of the act.* All the same, many did not understand this: they had either failed to read the act, or, if they had read it, they had misunderstood it. They did not accept what they imagined to be their loss, and protests and riots occurred.

Even the bankers of London profited from the confusion – or perhaps they read the act more carefully. They refused to pay taxes on the usual date of 25 March 1753, but instead put back the date until 5 April. It is said that it was this shift which led to the end of the tax year being so dated: even today, each new tax year begins on 6 April.

As the result of this 'revolution' the malcontents poured angrily on to the streets, shouting: 'Give us back our eleven days!'. The authorities were completely astonished. They simply had not foreseen this violent and, to their way of thinking, unreasonable reaction.

In such a dilemma, the state might normally have expected the support of the Church for their decisions. But the Church's support was not forthcoming. Perhaps the clergy were only marginally less ignorant than the common populace; they were certainly equally vociferous.

Churchmen took the view that religious festivals were fixed by God and could not be adjusted by the temporal authorities to suit their own convenience. They too clung to the old calendar; anything was better, they argued rather illogically, than follow a lead given by the Pope (it was obvious to them that the Pope was the very last person to have a 'hot line' to God). So the Church curried a little popular favour and gave its unquestioning backing to the people's resistance to the new calendar.

The state authorities were completely dismayed by this resistance to what seemed to well-informed people to be no more than a technical adjustment. There was no popular movement that they could proscribe, no popular leader they could arrest and make an example of. No one had actually broken any law. Dissatisfaction and criminal conspiracy were two quite different things. There was only one thing the government could do to deal with the situation: they sat tight until the outrage burned itself out, and waited for the eleven days to be forgotten. And this is what eventually happened.

Dr Heinrich Schliemann: pioneer or poseur?

One of the most notorious scientific hoaxes of the nineteenth century was the widely-reported dig for the remains of the city of Troy by the distinguished German archaeologist Heinrich Schliemann in 1883. His discoveries in this city (called Ilium by Homer in his epic poem the Iliad) were widely accepted and admired, becoming an acknowledged part of the canon of historical fact, widely reported even in school history books. Only in the 1970s was it revealed that he was a fraud and a pathological liar, and that his supposed finds in the remains of Troy were an imposture of the most scandalous kind.

Schliemann had an odd and unhappy background. He was born in 1822 not far from Rostock in Mecklenburg, at a place called Neu-Buckow, where his father was minister. From his early youth he was interested in history. When he was only seven he received a book on ancient history at Christmas, in which he saw an illustration of Troy in flames. This caught his imagination, and gave him the idea which he never forgot, that perhaps something of the city still remained, even if only the massive ancient walls. But Schliemann's life was not an easy one. There were seven children altogether in the family, and on his mother's early death his father caused something of a local scandal, firstly by taking a local servant girl as mistress, and then by embezzling church funds, an offence for which he was dismissed from his post. At the age of fourteen the young Schliemann became a grocer's assistant, then he went to sea as a cabin boy, only to be shipwrecked on his first voyage. He finished up in Amsterdam, becoming a clerk and learning several languages. He built up a fortune selling saltpetre, indigo and sugar to the Russians during the Crimean War. Before that war, he became something of an adventurer, visiting the USA in 1850. In Washington he attended a reception for over 600 people, and met and conversed with the President, Zachary Taylor. He also went to see his brother in California, going on to Sacramento, where he claimed he made a fortune of some hundreds of thousands of dollars by trading in gold dust at the time of the Californian Gold Rush. He wrote in his diary that he was present in the city of San Francisco at the time of the Great Fire of 1851. Returning to Europe he developed his connections with Russia and married a beautiful Russian girl, but she did not share his interests, did not wish to travel, and the couple were soon divorced. He finally visited Greece in 1859 and realized the ambition of a lifetime by becoming an archaeologist. He studied the subject in Paris in the 1860s, travelling widely in the Mediterranean area. Finally he took his doctorate back in the University of Rostock where, according to his autobiography, he wrote his thesis in Classical Greek. Finally, an old friend, Archbishop Vimbos of Athens, helped him find Sophia Engastrominos, a sixteen-year-old schoolgirl, whose parents accepted him as an older suitor so that she became his wife and helper for the rest of his life.

It remained Schliemann's conviction that Troy was not just a legend, as many thought. He disagreed with the many scholars who thought it was to be found in the mountains well inland. He accepted Homer's statement in the *Iliad* that Greek heroes had ridden between Troy and the Black Sea coast several times a day, and so identified it at a place called Hissarlik, an hour from the sea. Obtaining permission from the Turkish government for his project, he engaged eighty workmen and set about his dig in 1871. As an archaeologist, however, Schliemann was careless if not completely incompetent. Finding several sets of remains on the site and convinced that ancient Troy must be the earliest, he ordered his men to dig a deep trench down to the lowest remains in order to study them. Little did he realize that Homer's Troy was not in fact the earliest; King Priam ruled a much later city. Without realizing it, he had dug through Homerian Troy in the late Bronze Age and reached the early Bronze Age. Hence in his enthusiasm he unwittingly destroyed much of the city he was seeking for, though he did locate what he thought was the royal palace, the city walls and the ramp leading to the Scaean Gate.

Homer, however, had spoken in his writings of a treasure in gold, and of this he could find no sign. By 1883, he was ready to give up his quest, when one day he caught a glimpse of something metal behind a wall, and, anxious that his workers should not uncover it and steal it, he waited until they were at a meal, and then with the help of Sophia, loosened the blocks of stone and, at considerable risk to his personal safety from falling masonry, brought out a hoard of marvellous gold treasure – drinking cups, bowls and jewellery – and moved them to safety. Afterwards he photographed his wife in ancient Greek finery, and a month later took his find back to Athens. It made him world-famous. In later years he went on to excavate the tombs at ancient Mycenae, where his guess about their location was proved correct. Schliemann died in 1890 at the age of sixty-eight; Sophia lived for a further forty years.

But how much of this was in fact true? When in 1972 Professor William Calder at the University of Colorado on the 150th anniversary of Schliemann's birth came to give close attention to his work, he was surprised to find how much of it depended on Schliemann's own sources, and how little could be corroborated independently. He found that his doctoral thesis was written in German (apart from five painfully inaccurate lines in Greek), and this prompted wider enquiry into his reliability. Closer examination showed that the reception for 600 people in Washington never took place, nor did his meeting with President Taylor. The fortune in dollars he got from gold dust dealings was found somewhat more modest, and to have been accumulated through a systematic defrauding of prospectors by giving them short weight. He was not in the Great Fire of San Francisco, which he misdated by a month as being on 4 June instead of 4 May 1851, but derived his knowledge of it second-hand from newspaper reports. Even the story that he saw a picture of the burning of Troy in a book he was given for Christmas when he was still a boy was untrue. Calder came to the conclusion that Schliemann was an incurable liar who craved attention for his achievements.

Even his account of his excavations at Troy and his finds there were riddled with inconsistencies and falsifications. Entries in his diaries had been altered and crossed out. His catalogue of finds of supposed treasure was entirely fictitious. It is true that he gave a detailed description of one gold cup to his publisher when he sent in his manuscript, and this in fact did not come from the treasure at all. The 'treasure' was confined to a number of terracotta pots and bronze dishes. Furthermore, Sophia was not present with him at the time of the supposed find; she was in Athens in mourning for her father, who had recently died. The exciting story about the discovery of the treasure was a fiction: the find had been made by Schliemann himself and a trusted overseer and, according to William Borlase, an English antiquarian who happened to be present at the time, did not consist of gold or jewellery, but only of a quantity of earthenware and bronze objects found in an enclosure outside the city wall.

No one can be absolutely sure why Schliemann set about spinning such a web of exaggeration and deceit about his work. Perhaps the best guess is that he felt undervalued, and invented his treasure trove to crown his life's achievements, and so set himself apart from ordinary archaeologists. The odd thing is that he had no need to do this: though he was lacking in the traditional archaeological skills, and vandalized the sites he excavated, he had a strange kind of intuitive skill in knowing *where* to dig, both at Troy and at Mycenae. Rogue and crook he may have been, but he was still 'the father of Classical Greek archaeology'.

Did Annie Besant merit her disgrace?

Birth control was one of the many taboo sexual subjects in Victorian times, and the ground over which most people trod with extreme delicacy. In 1877, when Mrs Annie Besant, together with her friend and colleague Charles Bradlaugh, published a book on birth control, there was a storm of protest. Victorian people were shocked and disgusted, and the guilty pair were universally condemned for their atrocious want of taste and decency.

Annie Besant was born Annie Wood in London in 1847 of a well-to-do Irish family. Her father died when she was only five, and she was brought up in rather reduced circumstances by an Evangelical aunt who was perhaps guilty of over-protecting her. Annie grew up a girl combining naivety and religiosity in almost equal parts, and when she was eighteen she married a clergyman, the Reverend Frank Besant. After living with him for seven years, she lost her religious conviction and refused to attend communion. The couple parted in 1873, when she became a freethinker. In 1877 she published her new book, *The Gospel of Atheism,* in which she set out her new philosophy. She also joined the newly-formed gradualist socialist group known as the Fabian Society.[1] Associated with her in her new life were Edward Aveling, who lived

1 The Fabians believed that socialism would come about, not through revolution, as most socialists thought, but by small steps, and was achievable by parliamentary means. The name was taken from that of the classical Roman general, Fabius Cunctator (the 'Delayer') who won his campaigns by avoiding pitched battles and gradually wearing the enemy down.

with her as her partner for a time, George Bernard Shaw, who said he regarded her as 'the greatest orator in England', and Charles Bradlaugh, also an atheist, who was elected as MP for Northampton. She joined the latter's National Secular Society, becoming its vice president and editor of its journal *The National Reformer*.

Charles Bradlaugh, born in 1833, was perhaps the leading republican and secularist of his generation. Elected in 1880 as a Liberal, though a radical and republican one, and hardly the sort of man whom Gladstone, the Prime Minister, would have invited to tea. He paraded his atheism by refusing to take the oath of allegiance on the grounds that it was a Christian oath and he was an atheist, and so was not allowed to take his seat. He was thrice returned to Parliament before being admitted (in 1886, after a period in which the electors of Northampton had in effect been denied representation in the House) by a Prime Minister whose Liberal opinions were clearly in conflict with his Anglican principles. Both Charles Bradlaugh and Mrs Besant were concerned with the many contemporary economic and social questions arising out of rapid industrialization, and saw birth control as the relevant key to them, as well as to female emancipation.

High food prices and low wages in the nineteenth century did not seem to be any bar to rapid population growth. Indeed, for many rural or urban labourers, large families seemed to appear in the light of a solution to their needs, since in the absence of restrictions on child labour, big families brought relatively big earnings at least in the short term. Nevertheless, economists such as Thomas Malthus issued grim warnings: he showed that there was a tendency for the production of raw materials and food supplies to increase in arithmetical progression, whereas population, if not controlled, would increase geometrically. He therefore pointed to the dangers of an uncontrolled population growth, suggesting that wars, epidemics, famines or other natural disasters were bound in the long run to await those societies lacking in the foresight necessary to counter this danger. Though he is supposed by his pessimistic outlook to have earned for economics the name of the 'dismal science', there is evidence that many people at the time did take him seriously. Whilst medical or mechanical methods of birth control were hardly ever employed, it was not uncommon to find in Victorian times later ages of marriage (particularly for girls), and sexual abstinence or *coitus interruptus* practised by couples already married who did not wish to produce more children.

All the same the rapid rise of the population in most western countries, and the failure of living standards to improve, brought renewed attention to the problem as the nineteenth century continued. The other features of this problem were dangerous overcrowding in the city slums, dirt, epidemic diseases, drunkenness, lack of medical or educational facilities, and the continuing abuse of women and young children in their family situation. To Mrs Besant and to Bradlaugh these problems seemed all of a piece: if men were paid more, women and children better protected by society, and if the state behaved in a more broad-minded, generous and humane fashion, the problem would solve itself. Hence they became ardent advocates of socialist teachings, keen trade union supporters, educational reformers, and champions of women's rights; they also believed in propagating the ideas of family planning.

All these elements combined to make them extremely unpopular. To the great majority, socialism was egalitarian claptrap, trade unions were full of work-shy saboteurs aiming at disrupting industrial effort, and supporters of health and educational reforms were meddlesome busybodies who ought to mind their own business. Perhaps the shrillest condemnation was reserved for the 'shrieking sisterhood' who advocated women's rights. They were reckoned to hail from the pampered villas of Hampstead and Bloomsbury, and to have nothing better to do with their time than tell working people how they ought to conduct their lives. 'Women's Rights are Men's Wrongs' was the conventional way in which they expressed their disapproval. As for family planning or birth control, this was nasty, dirty talk that ought to be punished with all the rigour of the law.

Annie Besant's offence was that, with Bradlaugh, she reprinted in 1877 a forty-year-old pamphlet explaining Malthus's views on over-population and detailing in a very cautious and circumspect fashion the methods of birth control. This modest little book caused a furore. It struck Victorian England in its most sensitive spot – its prudish disapproval of any mention of sex (remarkable in a society whose pornography was the grossest and most revolting of the world). The two culprits were charged with, and convicted of, obscenity, and were jailed for six months and fined £200. It is true that the conviction was quashed on appeal, but as a result of it Mrs Besant lost custody of her daughter. She remained however quite unrepentant; indeed shortly afterwards she published her own book on the subject, *The Laws of Population,* which sold well over 100,000 copies during the next decade. She also became an enthusiastic supporter of trade union militancy, supporting the Bryant and May's workers in the London match girls' strike in 1888, and Ben Tillett and Tom Mann in the London Dock Strike in 1889 for the famous 'Docker's Tanner'. She also became a prime mover at about the same time in the London School Board, where she successfully persuaded the guardians to waive school fees for the children of indigent families and even to provide them with free school meals. Later, however, she lost sight of her original purpose, taking up theosophy and becoming interested in meditative Eastern philosophy. She moved to India, where she died in 1933.

The scandal which she and her writings caused in later Victorian England shows how deliberately blinkered and unreceptive English society had become to even moderate and well-intentioned criticism, especially on delicate subjects. The country would rather suffer the continuance of unchecked evils than allow its prejudices to be flouted.

Why was Joseph Crabtree so underrated?

Joseph Crabtree, British poet and polymath of the eighteenth and nineteenth centuries, in his own day was never fully recognized. Indeed, most people had never even heard of him. It was only the assiduous research of over 200 academics connected with University College, London, which towards the end of the twentieth century revealed his true importance to the scientific world.

Born in 1754 in Chipping Sodbury, it was Crabtree who suggested and developed the first international system of decimalization. He went on to invent soda water and also to invent a device known as the Siamese marine engine. In his Italian period he sketched designs for the velocipede – an early form of bicycle – only to find his drawings afterwards attributed to Leonardo da Vinci. He counted Wordsworth, Goethe and Sir Walter Scott amongst his wide circle of acquaintances. He was said to have been involved in 1791 in an unsuccessful plot to poison Mozart. He lived to be 100, and was buried at Haworth with the Brontës.

How could such a formidable combination of talents ever be overlooked? How could a man so prominent in so many different fields of human endeavour ever have been denied his rightful fame by later generations?

The answer is a simple one. It is, in fact, that Joseph Crabtree never existed. He was the product of the minds of the academics of the London University College, who invented both him, and also the Crabtree Foundation, which had supposedly been created to honour his memory. They did this in the course of various scholarly but always extremely alcoholic social gatherings from 1954 to 1994 – an invention which, in the words of one of them, was 'the longest running academic joke, a lot of professors behaving badly.'

Further Reading

Readers may also like to consult the following texts, some of which have been used in the compilation of this book:

Blyth, Henry, *Skittles, the Last Victorian Courtesan,* (Rupert Hart-Davis, 1960)

Blythe, Ronald, *The Age of Illusion: England in the Twenties and Thirties, 1919–1940,* (Hamish Hamilton, 1963)

Brooke, J., *King George III,* (London, 1972)

Cullen, Tom, *The Prostitutes' Padre: the Story of the Notorious Rector of Stiffkey,* (Bodley Head, 1975)

Dening, Penelope & Bentley, Iris, *Let Him Have Justice,* (Sidgwick & Jackson, 1995)

Doig, Alan, *Corruption and Misconduct in Contemporary British Politics,* (Penguin, 1984)

Donaldson, Frances, *The Marconi Scandal,* (Rupert Hart-Davis, 1962)

Fraser, Antonia, *Marie Antoinette,* (Weidenfeld & Nicolson, 2002)

Fraser, Antonia, *Mary, Queen of Scots,* (Weidenfeld & Nicolson, 1969)

Keeler, Christine, *Scandal!,* (Xanadu, 1989)

Langford, Paul, *England, 1727–83,* (OUP, 1989)

Lewis, Chester, *Jeremy Thorpe, A Secret Life,* (Fontana, 1979)

Lewis, Michael, *The History of the British Navy,* (Penguin, 1957)

Mander, Charles, *The Reverend Price and His Abode of Love,* (Wakefield, EP Publishing, 1976)

Parris, Matthew, *Great Parliamentary Scandals,* (Robson, 1997)

Rudé, George, *Wilkes and Liberty,* (OUP, 1962)

Sanders, John, *Tony Martin and the Bleak House Tragedy,* (Forum Press, 2001)

Schwieso, Joshua, *Deluded Inmates, Frantic Ravers and Communists, a Sociological Study of the Agapemone,* (University of Reading PhD Unpublished Thesis, 1990)

Somerset, Anne, *Elizabeth I,* (Phoenix Press, 1991)

Tillyard, Stella, *Aristocrats,* (Chatto & Windus, 1994)

Waller, Maureen, *Ungrateful Daughters: The Stuart Princesses Who Stole their Father's Crown,* (Hodder & Stoughton, 2002)

Index

Entries highlighted in **bold** refer to topics which have a separate listing in the table of contents.